CROSS-CULTURAL
WORK GROUPS

The Claremont Symposium on Applied Social Psychology

This series of volumes highlights important new developments on the leading edge of applied social psychology. Each volume concentrates on one area in which social psychological knowledge is being applied to the resolution of social problems. Within that area, a distinguished group of authorities present chapters summarizing recent theoretical views and empirical findings, including the results of their own research and applied activities. An introductory chapter integrates this material, pointing out common themes and varied areas of practical applications. Thus each volume brings together trenchant new social psychological ideas, research results, and fruitful applications bearing on an area of current social interest. The volumes will be of value not only to practitioners and researchers but also to students and lay people interested in this vital and expanding area of psychology.

Books in the Series

Interpersonal Processes, *Stuart Oskamp and Shirlynn Spacapan, Editors*

The Social Psychology of Health, *Shirlynn Spacapan and Stuart Oskamp, Editors*

The Social Psychology of Aging, *Shirlynn Spacapan and Stuart Oskamp, Editors*

People's Reactions to Technology, *Stuart Oskamp and Shirlynn Spacapan, Editors*

Helping and Being Helped, *Shirlynn Spacapan and Stuart Oskamp, Editors*

Gender Issues in Contemporary Society, *Stuart Oskamp and Mark Costanzo, Editors*

Violence and the Law, *Mark Costanzo and Stuart Oskamp, Editors*

Diversity in Organizations, *Martin M. Chemers, Stuart Oskamp, and Mark Constanzo, Editors*

Understanding and Preventing HIV Risk Behavior, *Stuart Oskamp and Suzanne C. Thompson, Editors*

Cross-Cultural Work Groups, *Cherlyn Skromme Granrose and Stuart Oskamp, Editors*

CROSS-CULTURAL WORK GROUPS

CHERLYN SKROMME GRANROSE
STUART OSKAMP
editors

The Claremont Symposium on
Applied Social Psychology

SAGE Publications
International Educational and Professional Publisher
Thousand Oaks   London   New Delhi

For information address:

SAGE Publications, Inc.
2455 Teller Road
Thousand Oaks, California 91320
E-mail: order@sagepub.com

SAGE Publications Ltd.
6 Bonhill Street
London EC2A 4PU
United Kingdom

SAGE Publications India Pvt. Ltd.
M-32 Market
Greater Kailash I
New Delhi 110 048 India

Printed in the United States of America

Library of Congress Cataloging-in-Publication Data

Main entry under title:
Cross-cultural work groups/[edited by] Cherlyn Skromme Granrose
  and Stuart Oskamp
    p.   cm.
    "Claremont Symposium on Applied Social Psychology, vol. 10"—Prelim. p.
    Includes bibliographical references (p.   ) and index.
    ISBN 0-7619-0972-9 (cloth: acid-free paper).—ISBN 0-7619-0973-7
(pbk.: acid-free paper)
    1. Diversity in the workplace—Congresses. 2. Work groups—Congresses.
I. Granrose, Cherlyn Skromme. II. Oskamp, Stuart. III. Claremont Symposium
on Applied Social Psychology (13th: 1996: Claremont, Calif.)
HF5549.5.M5C76   1997
658.4'02—dc21   96-51222

97 98 99 00 01 02 03 10 9 8 7 6 5 4 3 2 1

Acquiring Editor:	Jim Nageotte
Editorial Assistant:	Kathleen Derby
Production Editor:	Astrid Virding
Production Assistant:	Denise Santoyo
Typesetter/Designer:	Marion Warren
Cover Designer:	Ravi Balasuriya
Print Buyer:	Anna Chin

Contents

1

Cross-Cultural
Work Groups
An Overview

CHERLYN SKROMME GRANROSE
STUART OSKAMP

Cross-cultural work groups are a reality in most contemporary organizations, yet social science research has separated this reality into several distinct domains: the study of *intergroup* interactions between members of different cultures within or between societies, the study of *intragroup* dynamics in work and nonwork settings, and the study of *management* of cultural diversity in organizations. Because this research is often done by scholars of different disciplines (most commonly sociology, social psychology, anthropology, and management), it is difficult to get a clear picture of what we know about cross-cultural work groups.

Understanding cross-cultural work groups is important for several reasons. First, they are becoming more common. Increasingly, many domestic U.S. work settings include cross-cultural work groups because the society itself is culturally plural, and because organizations are using more teams to accomplish organizational tasks. Although there has been separation of individuals of different cultural backgrounds into different levels or functions of an organization in the past, when the work is reorganized, reengineered, restructured, or downsized, people of different levels and functions find themselves on common work teams.

1

In addition to domestic diversity, more organizations are operating in multiple nations, including U.S. organizations doing business abroad, as well as non-U.S. multinational organizations operating within the United States. When an organization begins to do business in more than one nation, people of different cultures necessarily begin to work together and both temporary and permanent cross-cultural work groups are formed.

A second reason why it is important to examine cross-cultural work groups is that much of the previous research on intragroup dynamics either used homogeneous experimental groups to avoid the confounding effects of ethnicity, or had some cultural diversity in the groups being studied but failed to assess the effects of cultural differences on the group interaction. One unfortunate effect of a social science concerned with elegant experiments is that real groups, which are more complex than those created for laboratory experiments, may display phenomena not captured by the laboratory experimental design. Another unfortunate reality is that U.S. social science, conducted primarily by investigators of European descent, suffers from ethnocentrism when it assumes that what is true for homogeneous European American college student groups would be true of all groups, or that cultural background is unimportant to measure. In the recent past, studies of gender or race effects on group processes have become more common, but these studies frequently fail to address the complexity of individuals of multiple cultural backgrounds interacting in a single group—a more common occurrence today. Because recent research exists for gender differences and African American-European American differences in U.S. work settings, these aspects of cultural differences in work groups are not emphasized in this book. Rather, the emphasis is on cross-national cultural differences and on intranational cultural differences, which include multiple different cultural groups.

A third reason that the study of cross-cultural work groups is important is the persistent reality that, when these groups are expected to function in ways identical to homogeneous groups, organizations and group members are surprised, or more often disappointed, at the group process and outcome (Punnett & Shenkar, 1995). In some cases the process and the outcomes are deemed more creative and beneficial, but in many other cases the benefits are unrealized or the outcomes destructively conflicted. Organizations often anticipate that creating cross-cultural work groups will generate more creative ideas and a wider variety of problem solutions in decision-making groups. These outcomes can occur if groupthink norms are not operating, but then the decisions take longer—a source of frequent disappointment in today's short-term, deadline-oriented, U.S. business climate. In international business, or in businesses sensitive to their plural domestic society, organizations anticipate gaining the perspective of the nonmajority groups so that business may be more responsive to these groups' needs. If minorities perceive that expression of different points of view will be ignored or punished, however, they reduce their advocacy of new ideas and thus diminish these hoped-for gains.

Another socially conscious benefit that organizations may expect from creating cross-cultural work groups is the promotion of equal opportunity, social justice, or economic development by incorporating members of traditionally deprived groups into majority-dominated organizations and work groups. Although these are laudatory goals, disappointment often results when placement of people in groups of diverse composition fails to achieve equality or justice either inside or outside the work group itself.

Many of these disappointments arise from basic intergroup dynamics—such as the apparent universal tendency to view one's own group as superior and more trustworthy than other groups (Brewer, 1986). When the distinction of ingroup and outgroup membership is based on cultural group (ethnocentrism), rather than the work group, then prejudice and individual or institutional discrimination against members of different cultures within a work group interfere with effective functioning and positive human relationships.

Even in organizations in which blatant prejudice and discrimination are socially unacceptable, other reactions to cultural differences may exist in milder or more indirect forms that also interfere with positive work group interactions. *Intergroup anxiety* is the worry and arousal present when people interact with outgroup members. This may lead to avoidance or to excessive politeness, which is detrimental to optimal work group functioning (Stephan, 1994). *Modern racism,* often expressed in beliefs that intergroup problems have been solved, or that the outgroup has more than it deserves (McConahay, 1986), *symbolic racism* or emphasizing ingroup values to justify unequal treatment of the outgroup (Kinder & Sears, 1981), and *benevolent sexism or racism,* resulting in protective paternalism (Glick & Fiske, 1994), also may lead to unequal treatment of, or unequal opportunities for, group members not belonging to the most powerful cultural ingroup.

Because most of these mechanisms are functioning in work groups as well as in larger organizational contexts, it becomes easier to understand why members of cultural groups, who feel like outgroup members compared to the most dominant ingroup in a work group or an organization, fail to contribute "new ideas." Identifying ways of neutralizing overt and covert prejudice and discrimination and promoting the most beneficial outcomes of cross-cultural work groups constitutes the final and most important reason for creating this book.

The goal of this book is to begin a dialogue between disciplines, to start to synthesize what we know now, and to identify important questions yet to be answered about how we can make cross-cultural work group settings more effective for group members and organizations. To achieve this goal, we have asked a varied group of scholars to apply the knowledge of their disciplines and their own scholarship to the issue of understanding cross-cultural work groups in organizational settings. We specifically sought diversity in the cultural populations that scholars studied and in the methodologies they used, to gain a broad range of perspectives on this issue. Although this diversity of perspectives may challenge the reader to shift from one point of view to another between chapters, we hope that these mental leaps will provide insight into this complex phenomenon.

The broad questions we address in this dialogue include: What are the important dimensions of culture that influence work group dynamics? How do cultural intergroup relationships in the society at large affect intragroup and intergroup relationships inside organizations? What actually happens when members of different cultural groups interact in a common work group? What aspects of organizational dynamics and management practices facilitate effective cross-cultural work groups? Although we cannot provide complete answers, this volume provides one array of responses to these important questions; we hope it will stimulate more questions in readers, and more research to answer these questions about cross-cultural work groups.

Emerging Themes

Looking across the contributions in this volume, several themes emerge. First, many authors emphasize the pervasiveness of cross-cultural contacts, which occur at the national, regional, organizational, and individual level. All current societies contain multiple cultural groups (see the chapters by Berry, Goto), and most societies' workforces are also becoming more diverse (Moghaddam). This is evident in multinational companies (Dorfman and Howell, Granrose, Tung), but it is also true in other executive teams (Maznevski and Peterson) as well as blue-collar work groups. It is produced, not only by the globalization and restructuring of businesses, but also by the recent revolutionary changes in communication technology (Tung). In addition to these internal organizational changes, interactions of various cultural groups take place in business contacts with outside groups, such as selling products to customers from many cultures (Murphy and Ensher).

Difficulties caused by intercultural contacts occur on many levels. They may involve threats to a person's social and self-identity, or "face" (Earley and Randel), or problems in understanding and communicating with others (Orasanu, Fischer, and Davison; Tung). They may arise particularly in leadership activities (Dorfman and Howell) or in mentoring relationships (Murphy and Ensher), where power differentials may amplify cultural misunderstandings (Goto). They may lead to workers' diminished commitment to the organization and poor overall organizational performance (Granrose), or intercultural contacts can also lead to successful accommodation (Berry).

When different cultural groups interact, there are several possible models that specify changes in the groups' cultural patterns (Berry, Granrose). A number of authors have emphasized the importance of a particular acculturation strategy, equally valuing characteristics of each culture involved in the group, if cross-cultural work groups are to succeed. Berry defines this strategy as *integration,* and identifies predictors and outcomes that make this type of interaction more likely. Evidence for the necessity of adopting this strategy as an organizational policy appears in the chapters by Tung, Granrose, and Murphy and Ensher.

Moghaddam, however, points out the difficulty of changing organizational or cultural practices, because informal social norms often perpetuate stable interaction patterns despite strenuous official attempts to change them.

There are a number of broad cultural orientations that influence how individuals from different cultures will interpret events around them—such dimensions as their time orientation, beliefs about humans' relationship to nature, individualistic versus collectivistic societal patterns, and expectations about the proper "power distance" between high- and low-status persons (Dorfman and Howell, Maznevski and Peterson).

These orientations largely determine what events people notice, how they interpret them, how possible response alternatives are evaluated, and how they ultimately respond. Goto presents another useful model of the many variables that affect the results of intercultural contact, and Earley and Randel describe a model of factors affecting cross-cultural interaction within organizations.

Other authors identify culture-specific aspects of interpersonal interactions that have a significant impact on the way cross-cultural work groups function. A common theme is the need to recognize that interactions involve individuals, each of whom has a different perspective, instead of assuming all group members are perceiving the world in similar ways. Meznevski and Peterson identify differences in cultural beliefs, Goto emphasizes differences in attitudes toward interpersonal interactions, Earley and Randel note differences in judgments of self and others, and Orasanu looks at language differences as sources of different individual perspectives.

The organizational mechanisms to facilitate cross-cultural work groups—whether training (Tung), mentoring (Murphy and Ensher), socialization (Granrose), or leadership (Dorfman and Howell)—need to be modified if this form of work organization is to succeed. The common theme is that all formal and informal organizational processes, not just official policies, need to be revised to take into account multiple perspectives and equality of all cultural groups, if effective functioning of cross-cultural groups is to be achieved (Berry, Moghaddam). Elimination of covert and unintended prejudice and discrimination depends on evaluating everything from the perspective of each cultural group, because each of their perspectives is different—a formidable task many organizations avoid or try to shortcut.

Tung's chapter discusses the skills and competencies needed to deal effectively with diverse work groups, and it proposes a variety of methods that can help to develop these skills. Granrose focuses specifically on how workers from differing cultural backgrounds can be socialized into effective organizational groups. In discussing the inevitable tension between differentiated treatment of employees and integrating them into a stable and consistent organizational culture, she emphasizes the importance of individual-organizational "fit" in producing organizational commitment and effective performance. Murphy and Ensher describe aspects of training that can help to improve the mentoring process and thus help to reduce the barriers to the advancement of women and ethnic minorities. Finally, Dorfman and Howell examine differences in leadership processes that are most appropriate for various cultures.

If we think about each of these themes, the most striking conclusion is that those who assume that cross-cultural work groups function like mono-cultural work groups underestimate their complexity. The societal environment, the organizational context, the actual cultural groups represented in the work group, as well as the task and the individual differences of work group members, contribute to this complexity. The danger is that organizations, scholars, and employees will throw up their hands in despair in the face of this complexity and either pretend cross-cultural work groups are simpler than they are, or try to use only homogeneous work groups (as if such groups really exist), or declare a victory (that they are working as effectively as they can) and go home. In contrast, the scholars contributing to this volume have chosen to address this complexity with the skills and tools of social science.

Overview of the Volume

The chapters in Part I, Cultural Group Interactions in Organizations, address broad issues about the context of cross-cultural work groups. They look at the relationships between multiple groups in plural societies, and at how cultural differences and relationships are expressed in the organizational context within which cross-cultural work groups are embedded. A common claim in organizations is that individuals bring the larger society to work with them, and it is unrealistic to expect that positive or negative intergroup relationships within or between nations or ethnic groups will be excluded from cross-cultural work group settings.

In Chapter 2, John W. Berry describes acculturation strategies that occur when two different cultural groups encounter each other through migration, war, or colonization. He presents a model of plural societies and identifies specific predictors of group interaction strategies. The strategies he identifies are Assimilation (adopting the majority culture, with frequent contact), Integration (maintaining both cultures as valuable, with frequent contact), Separation (maintaining one's own culture while rejecting contact with the other), and Marginalization (maintaining neither one's own culture nor contact with the other).

Berry reminds us that these strategies may be adopted at different levels of analysis: by societies through social policy, by organizations through organizational policies and practices, and by individuals in their choices of daily interactions. He uses a Canadian university as a case study of a work setting in a plural society to demonstrate one specific attempt at adopting and implementing an official national government and university institutional policy of integration. He reports moderate success, with substantial change in several aspects of the organization. Some members of the university community still express reservations, however, and advocate assimilation strategies in defense of "scholarship standards" and "proper conduct," rather than adopting the university policy of an integration acculturation strategy. Berry concludes with a call for social scientists to continue to study these issues as the only ethically acceptable and practical response to cultural pluralism.

In the Chapter 3, Fathali M. Moghaddam takes a somewhat pessimistic stance toward organizational change to adapt to multiple cultural group members. He provides one explanation for why intergroup relations, such as those described by Berry, are so difficult to change in organizational settings. He maintains that organizations are characterized primarily by stability, largely because change agents, when viewing behavior through a positivist causal lens, often change only the formal systems of organizations, and fail to understand the primacy of the informal system of normative behavior. Moghaddam supports his thesis using examples of organizational change strategies such as implementing TQM, reengineering organizational processes, and developing a specific corporate culture supporting diversity. He presents *reducton theory* as a way of explaining adherence to informal norms regarding interactions. A *reducton* is a bit of social behavior created by socialization to specific group norms. Because informal behavior is culturally prescribed—that is, it is groups and streams of reductons—it is very resistant to change by official actions such as changes in organizational policies. When this viewpoint is applied to developing cross-cultural work groups, Moghaddam suggests that the important fulcrum for changing difficult intergroup and intragroup relations into effective interaction is to examine informal social processes.

Part II, Interpersonal Interactions Within Cross-Cultural Groups, responds to the call of Moghaddam to examine informal interactions by considering those that may occur in cross-cultural work group settings.

These chapters describe both influences on the nature of the interactions as well as some spectacular consequences of failed interactions.

Chapter 4, by Martha Maznevski and Mark F. Peterson, carefully examines how specific cultural dimensions influence interpersonal behavior in a work group setting. This chapter uses the concept of *event management*—the ways in which individuals notice, interpret, and use events—to describe how cultural dimensions create differences in behavior and perceptions of group tasks, processes, and outcomes. The authors examine five key cultural dimensions—relationship to nature, time orientation, concept of human nature, relationships between people, and preferred mode of activity. They stress how cultural differences are more frequently expressed in weak organizational settings, where the demand for a single response is less prevalent, and how cultural differences are less often expressed in strong organizational settings, where only one particular response would be tolerated or considered effective. They recommend decentering, taking the perspective of the other, and recentering, identifying a common view of the situation and common norms, as mechanisms that cross-cultural work groups can use to maximize the benefits from having members with different perspectives, while minimizing conflicts that might arise from the differences among group members.

In Chapter 5, Sharon C. Goto describes an empirical test of a portion of the Triandis model of interpersonal interactions across cultural group boundaries. In particular, Goto examines relationships between African Americans and European Americans by developing separate models of predictors of the outcomes of intergroup interactions for each group. In general, interpersonal interaction variables were found to be stronger predictors of interaction attitudes and intentions than were cultural variables.

As examples of more specific findings, for both groups, *positive attitudes toward the other group* were predicted by satisfaction with past interactions. For European Americans, however, past opportunity to interact with the other group was negatively related to a positive attitude toward African Americans, whereas for African Americans, past interactions were positively related to positive attitudes toward European Americans. Common predictors of *satisfaction with intergroup interactions* included past opportunities for interaction, perceived similarity, and less perceived cultural distance; but there were also differences in predictors for each group.

Although the data Goto used were from secondary schools rather than from employment settings, when examined in the light of other research in work settings, her results indicate there are differences in perspectives on intergroup relationships, depending on group membership. These results suggest that differences of perspectives are one source of group difficulties that deserve more attention in attempts to facilitate cross-cultural work group interactions.

Another aspect often ignored when examining interactions in cross-cultural work groups is the concept of "face"—a person's self-identity and social identity, based on the judgments made by oneself and by others. In Chapter 6, P. Christopher Earley and Amy E. Randel explore the role that "face" plays in interactions within a work group. They identify two dimensions of "face" in the Chinese tradition—*lian,* or moral character, and *mianzi,* or reputational status—and they present a model of "face" in the organizational context. Using these definitions and the model, they analyze Japanese group decision making, and United States, Scandinavian, Israeli, and Japanese participative work groups. Their discussion suggests cultural differences in the degree of emphasis on *lian* or *mianzi,* which may be important to understanding the dynamics of groups in each culture, but may also be useful if members of these cultures encounter each other in cross-cultural work groups.

In Chapter 7, Judith Orasanu, Ute Fischer, and Jeannie Davison describe the practical communication difficulties encountered when a specific type of cross-cultural work group, namely airplane cockpit crews, tries to work together. They outline different categories of problems in the communication process and how each can lead to difficulty, and even disaster, when members of a crew who come from different cultural backgrounds do not understand each other or do not understand an air traffic controller from another culture.

Part III, Management of Cross-Cultural Groups, addresses the practical issues of implementing effective cross-cultural work groups in a variety of organizational settings. Socialization, training, mentoring, and leadership processes are necessary to resolve the difficulties that occur, and to bring out the benefits that may accrue in cross-cultural working relationships. Chapters in this part of the book explore how these processes themselves are transformed when performed in a cross-cultural context.

In Chapter 8, Rosalie L. Tung identifies social and business trends that are creating similarities in managing intranational and international cultural diversity. Based on these similarities, Tung identifies three core competencies needed by 21st-century managers: the ability to balance conflicting demands of global integration versus local responsiveness, the ability to work with people from diverse functional and industry backgrounds, and the ability to work with people from diverse ethnic heritages. She then describes six mechanisms to develop these managerial skills: international assignments, multicultural communication training, specific language training, negotiation training, consciousness raising, and revisions in business education. Tung presents two case studies, the International Officers Program of the Hong Kong Bank and the women's advancement program of the Bank of Montreal, as illustrations of functioning programs designed to develop these needed skills.

In Chapter 9, Cherlyn Skromme Granrose explores socialization of employees from different cultural backgrounds into a common organizational culture. Addressing the dilemma of integration versus differentiation of organizational practices on one hand, and a strong organizational culture versus a culturally diverse workforce on the other, she uses findings from research on culture and identity, organizational socialization, and intergroup contact to propose a model of socialization to enhance perceptions of individual-organizational fit among members of different cultural groups.

Granrose uses data from managers from Hong Kong, Taiwan, Singapore, Thailand, and Japan working for U.S. multinational firms, to test the model. Results indicate that formality of socialization procedures and practices of affirming employees are positively related to individual-organizational fit, but that aspects of national culture also contribute to behavioral and affective commitment to the firm. Compared to men, the Asian women managers were less likely to believe they fit and less likely to intend to remain with the U.S. organizations. Compared to U.S. employees, Japanese and Chinese (but not Thai) employees were less likely to intend to remain with the organizations.

Granrose makes several suggestions for effective socialization of employees into cross-cultural organizational settings. These include implementing formal, and ethnic culture-affirming, socialization practices; promoting an organizational culture that affirms equal status of all cultural groups and emphasizes attainment of organizational goals rather than attainment of uniform practices; attending to Asian concepts of attachment to a firm; and training U.S. employees in aspects of Asian culture. Implementation of these recommendations could increase individual-organizational fit as well as affective and behavioral commitment.

In Chapter 10, Susan E. Murphy and Ellen A. Ensher discuss mentoring in a cross-cultural work environment. After describing the positive effects of culturally diverse mentoring and showing the similarity between mentoring and leadership, the authors present a model of mentoring relationship development. The phases of the model include attraction, contracting, growth, maturation, and transition. The authors explore the cultural components of their model using illustrations based on research findings concerning the cultural characteristics of Asian Americans, Latinos, and African Americans.

Murphy and Ensher conclude with suggestions for improving cross-cultural mentoring relationships. Their recommendations emphasize training in cultural differences, training in communication skills, and clarification of ground rules for mentoring.

The final chapter, Chapter 11, by Peter W. Dorfman and Jon P. Howell, presents a detailed examination of cultural differences in leadership between Mexican and U.S. managers. After reviewing issues in cross-cultural leadership and important relevant characteristics of Mexican and U.S. cultures, the authors summarize five studies in a long-standing program of research. Study 1 used broad interviews to look at leadership in maquiladoras, finding that authoritarian and paternalistic, but not punitive or autocratic, leadership was common and effective in these settings. Study 2 was a decade-long investigation of the functional equivalence of leadership behaviors of maquiladora managers and U.S. managers. Supportive, contingent reward, and charismatic leadership behaviors were linked to positive, but sometimes different, outcomes in the two cultures. Participative leadership and contingent punishment had positive outcomes in the United States, whereas directive leadership had positive outcomes in Mexico. In Study 3, focus groups and intensive interviews explored the conceptual equivalence, or differences and similarities in the meaning of leadership, in the United States and Mexico. Effective leadership in Mexico focused on maintaining good interpersonal relationships, including maintaining employee dignity, recognizing employees' family context and cultural roots, and demonstrating both empathy and persona. Study 4 examined measurement equivalence of scales in the two nations, and identified etic and emic items in leadership scales. In a brief overview of Study 5, the chapter authors summarize their current participation in GLOBE, a 60-nation cross-cultural study of leadership.

Summary and future directions. These chapters point to many con-
clusions that should be helpful in creating better-functioning cross-cultural work groups. For instance, factors that influence the course of
intergroup contact include its voluntariness, and permanence, and the
possibilities for mobility in the relationship (Berry). Berry also
proposes that, in changing institutional patterns, it is crucial to consider
not only the characteristics of the personnel involved, but also the nature
of the institutional practices, and the surrounding organizational and
societal context. Granrose reminds us that institutional conditions
favoring success in cross-cultural intergroup contact include the
presence of a superordinate goal, cooperative activity, equal-status
positions, and rewarding outcomes. Moghaddam emphasizes that organizational change is often unpredictable and difficult to create, in
large part because informal norms may persist and oppose official
efforts toward new practices. Maznevski and Peterson point out that the
influences of culture and informal norms are most potent in "weak
situations" where the cues for behavior are uncertain or ambiguous, and
Granrose similarly stresses the importance of formal socialization of
workers into an organizational culture that is explicitly multicultural.
Goto's findings are hopeful in showing that people's personal satisfaction in groups and their intentions to interact with members of other
cultures may be influenced less by cultural differences than by interpersonal experiences.

At the same time, these chapters point to several key questions that
need additional attention from researchers and practitioners. What are
the most important barriers to cross-cultural groups avoiding conflict
and moving toward patterns of mutual accommodation? Are there additional problems posed by international cross-cultural groups beyond
those typical of such groups within a single nation? For instance, how
must leadership patterns be adapted to be effective in collectivistic
cultures (Dorfman and Howell)? Are questions of preserving "face" and
of achieving a bottom-up consensus more important in cross-cultural
work groups with members from some Asian cultures (Earley and
Randel)? How much do cultural differences add to language problems
in communication (Orasanu)? How can managers of multinational organizations build an effective general organizational culture and simultaneously allow flexibility and responsiveness to local cultural patterns
(Granrose, Tung)? How can mentoring and leadership training create
greater understanding of cross-cultural differences and provide ways to
overcome their divisive effects (Murphy and Ensher)? These questions

have just begun to be studied, and their answers are crucial to developing more effective cross-cultural work groups.

Acknowledgments

Finally, we wish to acknowledge the assistance of those who made the symposium and this volume possible. We are grateful for financial support of this year's session of the Claremont Symposium on Applied Social Psychology from Claremont Graduate School, the Kravis Leadership Institute at Claremont McKenna College, and the other four Claremont Colleges. We are indebted to the many people who helped make the conference a success, especially the authors of chapters in this volume and Susan Murphy of CMC, who chaired the afternoon session. The help we received from the office staff of Jane Gray, Gloria Leffer, B. J. Reich, and Pamela Hawkes was crucial, and the efforts of the CGS students who assisted on the day of the conference were much appreciated. We hope that readers will benefit as much as we have from the combined efforts of all these contributors.

References

Brewer, M. B. (1986). The role of ethnocentrism in intergroup conflict. In S. Worchel & W. G. Austin (Eds.), *Psychology of intergroup relations* (2nd ed., pp. 88-102). Chicago: Nelson-Hall.

Glick, P., & Fiske, S. T. (1994). *The ambivalent sexism inventory: Differentiating hostile and benevolent sexism.* Unpublished manuscript, Lawrence University, Appleton, WI.

Kinder, D. R., & Sears, D. O. (1981). Prejudice and politics: Symbolic racism versus racial threats to the good life. *Journal of Personality and Social Psychology, 40,* 414-431.

McConahay, J. B. (1986). Modern racism, ambivalence, and the modern racism scale. In J. F. Dovidio & S. L. Gaertner (Eds.), *Prejudice, discrimination, and racism* (pp. 91-125). Orlando, FL: Harcourt Brace Jovanovich.

Punnett, B. J., & Shenkar, O. (Eds.). (1995). *Handbook for international management research.* Cambridge, MA: Blackwell.

Stephan, W. G. (1994, October). *Intergroup anxiety.* Paper presented at the meeting of the Society of Experimental Social Psychology, Lake Tahoe, CA.

PART I

CULTURAL GROUP INTERACTIONS IN ORGANIZATIONS

2

Individual and Group Relations in Plural Societies

JOHN W. BERRY

All contemporary societies are now culturally plural. There are no longer any societies that can claim to be homogeneous with respect to objective cultural markers (such as ethnic origin, language, religion), or subjective indicators (such as one's ethnic identity or personal expressions of one's culture).

Such diversity elicits a variety of responses at a number of levels: national societies, institutions, and individuals can celebrate or deny it; they can share it or isolate it; they can accommodate it or attempt to squash it. Whatever the attitude or course of action, however, both history and contemporary experience provide compelling evidence that cultural pluralism is durable, even if its forms and expression evolve over time. Such continuing diversity challenges the conceptualization and functioning of work groups (Chemers, Oskamp, & Costanzo, 1995). A long-established consensus about how to work together may no longer be widely shared, because so much of human behavior is demonstrably rooted in culture.

This chapter portrays a set of ideas, some empirical findings, and a few practical implications for working together in plural settings. It is rooted in my experience as both a cross-cultural psychologist and a social psychologist (Berry, Poortinga, Segall, & Dasen, 1992) concerned with understanding and managing intercultural relations internationally and in one particular plural society: Canada. Although my own cultural filters may differ from yours, this perspective (and the implicit comparison) may serve to enlighten all of us, whatever our personal backgrounds and sociopolitical orientations.

Plural Societies

For many reasons (colonization, migration, enslavement) all contemporary societies have become culturally plural (Goodenough, 1976; Triandis, 1976). That is, people of many cultural backgrounds have come to live together in a diverse society. In many cases they form cultural groups that are not equal in numerical, economic, or political power. These power differences have given rise to popular and social science terms such as "mainstream," "minority," "ethnic group," and so on. In this chapter, although recognizing these unequal influences, I employ the term *cultural group* to refer to all groups in the plural society, and preface it with the terms *dominant* and *nondominant* to refer to their relative power, where such a difference exists and is relevant to the discussion. This is an attempt to avoid a host of political and social assumptions that have distorted much of the work on psychological acculturation and intercultural relations—in particular the assumption that "minorities" are inevitably, or should be in the process of, becoming part of the "mainstream" culture (Berry, 1990a). Although this does occur in many plural societies, it does not always occur, and in some cases it is resisted by either or both the dominant and nondominant cultural groups, resulting in continuing cultural diversity (Berry, 1984a; Kymlicka, 1995; UNESCO, 1985).

There are two contrasting, usually implicit, models of cultural group relations in plural societies (see Figure 2.1). In the mainstream-minority view, there is (or should be) one dominant society, on the margins of which are various minority groups; these groups typically remain there, unless they are "gently polished and reclaimed for humanity" (as Montaigne phrased French colonial policy) and incorporated as indistinguishable components into the mainstream. In the multicultural view, there is a national social framework of institutions that accommodates

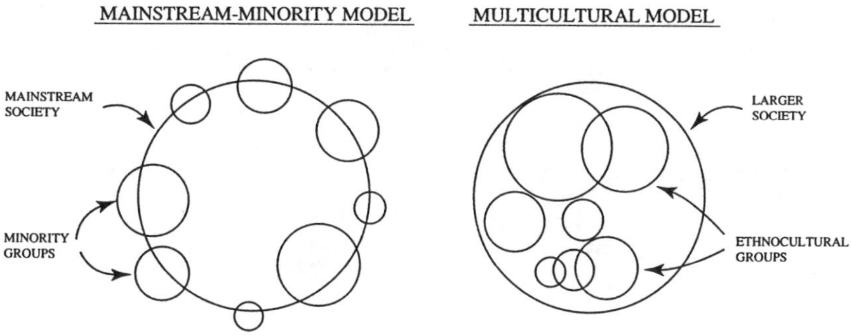

MAINSTREAM-MINORITY MODEL   MULTICULTURAL MODEL

Figure 2.1. Two Implicit Models of Plural Societies

the interests and needs of the numerous cultural groups, which are fully incorporated as cultural groups into this national framework. Both implicit models refer to possible arrangements in plural societies: The mainstream-minority view is that cultural pluralism is a problem and should be reduced, even eliminated; the multicultural view is that cultural pluralism is a resource, and inclusiveness should be nurtured with supportive policies and programs.

Psychological research in culturally plural societies traditionally has been divided into two domains: acculturation and ethnic relations (see Figure 2.2). The first has come to us from anthropology, and considers the issue of how groups and individuals may change as a result of continuous intercultural contact (Berry, 1990a). As I shall argue, the outcomes of such contact are highly variable, depending on a number of social, political, and psychological factors that are present in the two groups in contact. Some of the psychological factors and outcomes are listed at the left of Figure 2.2; these are elaborated elsewhere (Berry, 1990b).

The second area (ethnic relations) has been more central to social psychology, but has clear links with sociology and political science. The concepts (for both psychological phenomena and outcomes) are probably more familiar, with the possible exception of Multicultural Ideology; which is explained next.

As is evident from Figure 2.2, in both of these domains of research, pluralism can lead to a state of affairs that ranges from conflict and stress to mutual accommodation and adaptation. Where cultural group

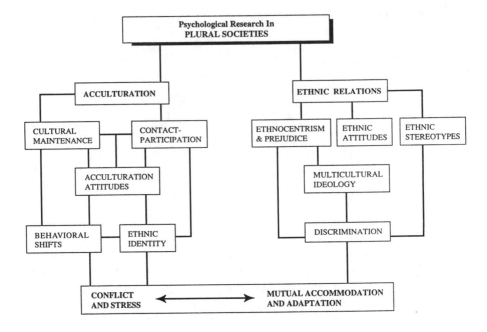

Figure 2.2. Psychological Research in Plural Societies

relations fall on this dimension is a function, at least in part, of the individual psychological phenomena identified in Figure 2.2. Thus the study, analysis, and interpretation of these phenomena are essential if we are to contribute to more positive cultural group relations in plural societies.

Many kinds of cultural groups may exist in plural societies, and their variety is primarily due to three factors: voluntariness, mobility, and permanence (see Figure 2.3). Some groups have come to live together voluntarily (e.g., immigrants) whereas others are in each other's company without having sought it out (e.g., refugees, slaves, indigenous peoples). Some groups are in contact because they have migrated to a new location (e.g., immigrants and refugees), whereas others have had the new culture brought to them (e.g., indigenous peoples and national minorities). And among those who have migrated, some are relatively permanently settled into their new society (e.g., immigrants and ethnocultural groups), whereas for others the situation is a temporary one

MOBILITY	VOLUNTARINESS OF CONTACT	
	VOLUNTARY	**INVOLUNTARY**
SEDENTARY	ETHNOCULTURAL GROUPS	INDIGENOUS PEOPLES
MIGRANT permanent temporary	IMMIGRANTS SOJOURNERS	REFUGEES ASYLUM SEEKERS

Figure 2.3. Three-Dimensional Classification of Constituent Groups in Plural Societies

(e.g., sojourners such as international students and guest workers, or asylum seekers who may eventually be deported).

Despite variations in factors leading to the establishment of plural societies, the basic processes of intercultural relations and psychological adaptation appear to be common to all these groups (Berry & Sam, 1996). What varies is the course, the level of difficulty, and to some extent the eventual outcome of their contact; the three factors of voluntariness, mobility, and permanence, as well as other factors, all contribute to this variation.

Varieties of Cultural Group Relations

In all plural societies, dominant and nondominant cultural groups and their individual members must deal with two primary issues of how to relate to each other in their daily encounters. These issues are: *cultural maintenance* (to what extent are one's cultural identity and characteristics important to maintain), and *contact and participation* (to what extent should one become involved with other cultural groups, vs. remaining primarily among one's group members).

When these two underlying issues are considered simultaneously, a conceptual framework is generated (Figure 2.4), which posits four strategies of acculturation and intercultural relations. These two issues can be responded to on attitudinal dimensions, represented by bipolar arrows. For purposes of presentation, generally positive or negative ("yes" or "no") responses to these issues are illustrated, and they intersect to define four strategies. These strategies have different names, depending on which group (the dominant or nondominant) is being considered. From the point of view of nondominant groups, when individuals do not wish to maintain their cultural identity and seek daily interaction with other cultures, the Assimilation strategy is defined. In contrast, when individuals place a value on holding onto their original culture, and at the same time wish to avoid interaction with others, then the Separation alternative is defined. When there is an interest in both maintaining one's original culture, and being in daily interactions with other groups, Integration is the strategy; here, one maintains some degree of cultural integrity while at the same time seeking to participate as an integral part of the larger social network. Finally, when there is little possibility of or interest in cultural maintenance (often for reasons of enforced cultural loss), and little interest in having relations with others (often for reasons of exclusion or discrimination), then Marginalization is defined.

This presentation is based on the assumption that nondominant cultural groups and their individual members have the freedom to choose their intercultural relations strategies. This, of course, is not always (or even usually) the case (Berry, 1974). When the dominant group enforces certain forms of relationships, or constrains the choices of nondominant groups or individuals, then other terms need to be used. Most clearly, although people may sometimes choose the Separation option, when it is required of them by the dominant society, the situation is one of Segregation. Similarly, when people choose to Assimilate, the notion of the Melting Pot may be appropriate; but when forced to do so, the metaphor is a Pressure Cooker. Regarding Marginalization, people rarely choose such an option; rather, they usually become marginalized as a result of attempts at forced assimilation (Pressure Cooker) combined with forced exclusion (Segregation); thus no other term seems to be required beyond the single notion of Marginalization.

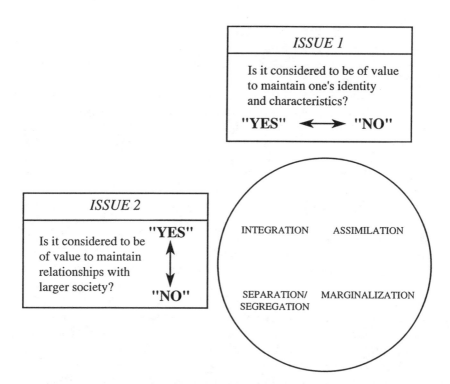

Figure 2.4. Four Orientations to Cultural Group Relations Based on Two Basic Issues

The view of acculturation and group relations illustrated in Figure 2.4 is clearly a bidimensional one. This conceptualization was introduced (Berry, 1970; Sommerlad & Berry, 1970) to challenge the unidimensional assumption that individuals can be viewed (and assessed) as being in a sort of "transition" between some "traditional" (or "minority") and some "modern" (or "mainstream") cultural situation. Ethnographic work among members of cultural communities generally reveals that there are *two* issues (cultural maintenance, and contact/ participation), and that they are independent of each other. When the two dimensions are kept separate (both conceptually and empirically), the many varieties of acculturation become evident (Berry, 1980). Intercultural contact can lead to cultural homogeneity, to mixing or balancing, to rejection, or to being rejected. The common bias is to assume that the "others" both want to, and will eventually, become like "us." Parallel conceptualization and research on cultural identity (Berry, 1970; Ferdman, 1995; Kalin & Berry, 1995; Phinney, 1990; Phinney, DuPont, Esinosa, Revill, & Sanders, 1994) has shown that individuals often are comfortable with a bicultural identity; it is not necessary to choose one or the other in an inclusive, pluralistic society.

It is essential to note that the term integration as used here is not a euphemism for assimilation. Figure 2.4 clearly links Integration to a substantial degree of cultural maintenance (rather than to cultural loss or homogenization as in Assimilation). Just as important, it is evident that integration can only be "freely" chosen and successfully pursued by nondominant groups when the dominant society is open and inclusive in its orientation toward cultural diversity (Berry, 1991). Thus, a mutual accommodation is required for integration to be attained, involving the acceptance by everyone of the right of all groups to live together as culturally different peoples. This strategy requires nondominant groups to *adopt* the basic values of the larger society, while at the same time the dominant group must be prepared to *adapt* national institutions (e.g., education, health, labor) to better meet the needs of all groups living together in the plural society.

Obviously, the integration strategy can only be pursued in societies that are explicitly multicultural (as described earlier), in which certain psychological preconditions are established (Berry & Kalin, 1995). These preconditions include the following: widespread acceptance of the value to a society of cultural diversity (i.e., the presence of a positive "multicultural ideology"), relatively low levels of prejudice (i.e., minimal ethnocentrism, racism, and discrimination), positive mutual attitudes among cultural groups (i.e., no specific intergroup hatreds), and a sense of attachment to, or identification with, the larger society by all groups (see also Kalin & Berry, 1995).

Just as obviously, integration (and of course separation) can only be pursued when other members of one's ethnocultural group share in the wish to maintain the group's cultural heritage. In this sense, these two strategies are "collective," while assimilation is more "individualistic" (Lalonde & Cameron, 1993; Moghaddam, 1988).

Other terms than those used here have been proposed by researchers. In particular, the term *bicultural* has been employed to refer to acculturation that involves an individual participating simultaneously in two cultures that are in contact (Cameron & Lalonde, 1994; LaFromboise, Coleman, & Gerton, 1993; Szapocznik & Kurtines, 1993); this concept corresponds closely to the integration strategy as defined here. Similarly, Gordon (1964) refers to two forms of incorporation: cultural assimilation and structural assimilation. In my terms, when both forms occur, complete assimilation is likely to result; however, when structural assimilation is present (a high degree of contact and participation) combined with a low degree of cultural assimilation (a high degree of cultural maintenance), then an outcome similar to integration is likely.

In measuring these strategies, a number of domains of daily behavior (e.g., language, food, dress, club membership) are selected in which cultural choices can be made. For each domain, a statement is drafted for each of the four strategies; respondents indicate their preferences (usually on a 5-point scale) for each strategy. Despite diverse domains, usually an overall coherent preference for one particular strategy emerges (as evidenced by Cronbach alpha coefficients in the .70 to .80 range; see Berry, Kim, Power, Young, & Bujaki, 1989).

There can, however, be variation in relative preferences. First, variation can occur according to one's location: In more private spheres or domains (such as the home, the extended family, the cultural community) more cultural maintenance may be sought than in more public spheres (such as the workplace, or in politics); and, less intergroup contact may be sought in private spheres than in the more public ones. Second, the broader national context may affect acculturation strategies, such that in explicitly multicultural societies individuals may seek to match such a policy with a personal preference for integration; or in assimilationist societies, acculturation may be eased by adopting an assimilation strategy for oneself (Krishnan & Berry, 1992). That is, individuals may well be constrained in their choice of strategy, even to the point where there is a very limited role for personal preference. Indeed, when personal preferences are in conflict with national policies, stress may result (Horenczyk, in press). Third, there is evidence that during the course of development, and over the time period of major acculturation, individuals explore various strategies, eventually settling on one that is more useful and satisfying than the others (Kim, 1988). As far as is known, however, there is no set sequence with which different strategies are used (Ho, 1995), nor specific ages at which one strategy is more likely to be used.

Levels of Analysis

Both individuals and groups may exhibit various orientations toward their intercultural relations. These orientations consist of both preferences (attitudes) and actions (behaviors). Together, these attitudes and behaviors comprise what we have called acculturation strategies (Berry, 1990a). Attitudes toward these four alternatives have been measured in numerous studies (reviewed in Berry, Kim, Power, Young, & Bujaki, 1989). National policies and programs also may be analyzed in terms of these four approaches: Some societies seek assimilation, expecting all ethnocultural groups to become like those in the dominant society; others seek integration, being willing (even pleased) to accept and incorporate all groups to a large extent on their own cultural terms; yet others have pursued segregation policies; and others have sought the marginalization of unwanted groups. Thus the framework in Figure 2.4 can be used to analyze and categorize orientations toward cultural group relations of both individuals and groups, in both the dominant and nondominant sections of society, and at three levels. These are illustrated in Figure 2.5.

As noted previously, at the national level, it is not difficult to identify what kinds of intercultural relations the dominant and nondominant groups are seeking, and to discern whether they are compatible or in conflict. In the case of Canada, the national multiculturalism policy was a long time in the making. Although numerous historical attempts were made to assimilate Canada's diverse population to British cultural norms, by 1956 the federal government's view was that assimilation had not worked anywhere in the contemporary world, and that it was impracticable as a general policy. In 1971, the prime minister announced a policy of multiculturalism, the key elements of which were designed to achieve harmonious intercultural relations by promoting simultaneously cultural maintenance, and intergroup contact and participation in the larger society:

> National unity, if it is to mean anything in the deeply personal sense, must be founded on confidence in one's own individual identity; out of this can grow respect for that of others and a willingness to share ideas, attitudes, and assumptions. A vigorous policy of multiculturalism will help create this initial confidence. It can form the base of a society which is based on fair play for all. . . . The government will support and encourage the

LEVELS	DOMINANT	NON-DOMINANT
	• Mainstream	• Minority Group
	• Larger Society	• Cultural Group
NATIONAL	National Policies	Group Goals
INDIVIDUAL	Multicultural Ideology	Acculturation Strategies
INSTITUTIONAL	Uniform or Plural	Diversity and Equity

Figure 2.5. Levels of Analysis and Use of Four Orientations

various cultures and ethnic groups that give structure and vitality to our society. They will be encouraged to share their cultural expression and values with other Canadians and so contribute to a richer life for all. (Government of Canada, 1971, pp. 3-4)

This is clearly an integration policy, in the terms used in this chapter (see Berry, 1984b; Berry & Laponce, 1994, for a more detailed description and analysis of the policy).

For most cultural groups in Canada, their articulated goals express some version of this integrationist policy. For example, Aboriginal Canadians generally seek cultural self-determination within the larger Canadian society, and most French Canadians (particularly those outside Québec) generally espouse the same goal. More recent immigrant-derived cultural group organizations all express this preference for some degree of cultural maintenance, combined with full rights to participation in the larger society.

At the individual level, the views of acculturating individuals in nondominant groups have been assessed in hundreds of studies (reviewed by Berry et al., 1989; Berry & Sam, 1996; Ward, 1996). In most studies, the clear preference is for integration, with least desire for marginalization. Depending on the group, either assimilation or separation fall in second or third place in the preference hierarchy.

Although less commonly studied, the views of individuals in the larger society are known in Canada (Berry & Kalin, 1995; Berry, Kalin, & Taylor, 1977) and in the United States (Lambert & Taylor, 1988). A scale of multicultural ideology has been used in national surveys in Canada. This scale assesses support for having a culturally diverse society in Canada, in which ethnocultural groups maintain and share their cultures with others. There are 10 items, with 5 in a negative direction (hence it is a balanced scale). Of these negative 5 items, 2 advocate assimilation ideology, one advocates segregation, and 2 claim that diversity "weakens unity." Two examples are supporting or opposing the view that "Recognizing that cultural and racial diversity is a fundamental characteristic of Canadian society," and agreeing or disagreeing that "The unity of this country is weakened by Canadians of different ethnic and cultural backgrounds sticking to their old ways." Figure 2.6 shows how mean scores vary by ethnic origin of respondents and region of residence.

Generally, there is moderate support for multiculturalism in the Canadian population: The ratio of those supporting to not supporting it is 69% to 27%, respectively, and this has been gradually increasing since 1974. The mean score in the total population (4.6 on a 7-point scale) is one half a *SD* above the theoretical midpoint, and varies only slightly according to ethnic origin and region of residence of respondents. Most support is among British origin and Other origin Canadians living in Québec, and French origin Canadians living outside Québec; least support is evidenced among French origin Canadians inside Québec. The interpretation of this pattern (Berry & Kalin, 1995) is that the policy can help a cultural group to feel secure in their identity when they are in a nondominant situation, but that French origin Canadians feel threatened by multiculturalism inside Québec, their cultural home and bastion.

In addition to these two levels (the national and the individual illustrated in Figure 2.5) there is a third area in which much of the contemporary debate about pluralism is being carried out. At the institutional level, competing visions rooted in these alternative intercultural strategies confront and even conflict with each other daily. Most frequently, nondominant cultural groups seek the joint goals of diversity and equity. This involves, first, the recognition of the group's cultural uniqueness and specific needs, and second, having their group be met

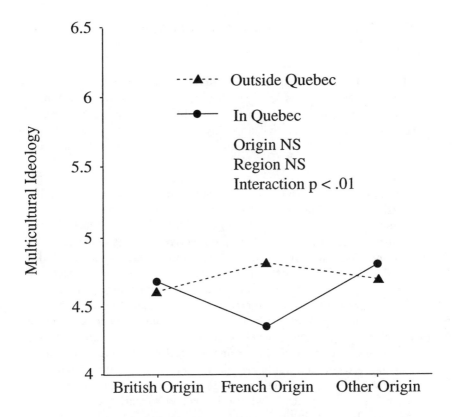

Figure 2.6. Multicultural Ideology in Canada by Ethnic Origin and Region

with the same level of understanding and support as those of the dominant group(s). The dominant society, however, may often prefer more uniform programs and standards (based on their own cultural needs) in such core institutions as education, health, justice, and defense.

The goals of diversity and equity correspond closely to the integration strategy (combining cultural maintenance with inclusive participation), whereas the push for uniformity resembles the assimilation approach. Largely absent from the contemporary debate are advocates of segregation/separation or of marginalization. How to achieve institutional change to create appropriate institutions for plural societies is considered in the next section.

Achieving Institutional Change

Most institutions in culturally plural societies were established at a time when pluralism was less a reality, either because it was actually less or because it was less important in political discourse. As a result of increased pluralism, there is now a dysfunction between most institutions and the needs of the cultural groups they attempt to serve (Martin, 1993).

A common approach to the analysis of these dysfunctions is through a consideration of human rights. Whereas most codes have traditionally emphasized individual rights, recent national and international initiatives have promoted the need also to consider collective rights. Sometimes the acceptability of promoting collective rights is questioned on the grounds that they would conflict with individual rights. Kymlicka (1995, p. 7) makes a distinction, however, between two aspects of collective rights: internal restrictions and external protections. In the former, groups may limit the liberty of their members; this undoubtedly conflicts with individual rights. In the latter, groups may seek to "limit the economic or political power exercised by the larger society over the group, to ensure that the resources and institutions on which the minority depends are not vulnerable to majority decisions." In this latter case, individual rights are not restricted, and may even be promoted. The following discussion deals with this second meaning of collective rights, as well as with individual rights. The issue of how cultural groups interact within themselves is beyond the scope of this chapter.

To exemplify the issues of intergroup relationships, I have chosen to consider change in educational institutions; other work settings, such as health institutions (Beiser et al., 1988) or defense institutions (Landis, Dansby, & Faley, 1993) could serve equally well. Although I draw from my experience at Canadian universities that are in the process of achieving institutional change (Berry et al., 1991, 1993), it is clear that these issues are common to all work settings in contemporary plural societies.

The first step is to analyze the components and structure of a university: see Figure 2.7 (Berry et al., 1991).

The first component (at top) is the body of students attending a university, with specifiable cultural-origin and cultural-needs profiles. Social psychological techniques (interviews, observations, surveys) can

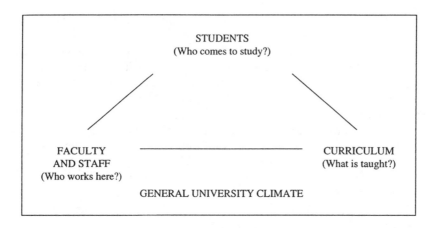

STUDENTS
(Who comes to study?)

FACULTY
AND STAFF
(Who works here?)

CURRICULUM
(What is taught?)

GENERAL UNIVERSITY CLIMATE

Figure 2.7. Diversity and Equity in Educational Institutions

provide information on both their present situation, and the changes that are desired. Our initial examination of one university showed a substantial difference between the composition of the student body and the general population, and an intense dissatisfaction among minimally represented groups with the education they were receiving. As the university was rooted in Scots Presbyterianism, there was a need to tear down what is called locally "the tartan curtain," to open up the admissions process and curriculum to greater diversity.

Second, the faculty and staff component was examined as part of meeting the requirements of the national policy of Employment Equity. This policy requires all institutions and corporations in Canada who do business with the federal government to carry out a series of steps, and to submit reports. First, institutions must conduct a self-identification survey of all employees, with four categories (gender, disability, Aboriginal, visible minority). Second, they must select and justify a comparison group in the Canadian population (national, regional, or local), which the workforce ideally should eventually resemble. Third, they must propose a plan and schedule of action to move the present profile toward that of the selected comparison group. In the absence of this plan, or success in implementing it, federal funding is cut off. Our university survey showed a substantial shortfall in all categories and at most occupational levels, and a plan of change was produced.

Third, the institution must examine what gets taught and researched at a university, including curricular supports such as the library. Analysis of courses, texts, and library holdings, and of students' views about these, revealed cultural biases that were incompatible with a plural population and with multicultural policies. As a result, new courses have been added, and others have been modified or renamed to reflect their content.

Finally, the whole university climate (which is the broad context for the first three) was examined, including support services (health, counseling, housing, food), information (publications, promotional material), cultural policy (art, concerts, lecture invitations), honorary degrees, and religious observances.

It is essential to note that these four components are functionally interrelated, such that one of them cannot be changed successfully without also simultaneously changing the others. It is useless to hire new faculty to represent a particular cultural group, without creating a relevant course and providing them with interested students and a welcoming climate. It is equally useless to recruit a new array of students if they cannot find themselves in the curriculum or if they feel unwelcome.

These institutional changes are being pursued under the banner of "diversity and equity." The policy goal is integration, in the sense used in this chapter: Diversity involves both enhanced cultural group representation, and institutional and personal acceptance of this diversity. The alternatives are generally rejected by those at the university (although sporadic rear guard activity continues). No voices are heard promoting assimilation to the old Scots norms, nor are segregation or marginalization advocated for those who are not of the "right background." The usual advocacy of maintaining "standards of scholarship" and "proper conduct," however, are still heard. In response, a widening of the meaning of "scholarship" has been proposed to include other ways of knowing and understanding; and, prohibitions on "racism" and "harassment" have been added to the code of conduct. The key novel position is to advocate that "excellence" in institutions can only be achieved by pursuing such changes, based on the argument that in a culturally plural society, a culturally diverse institution is superior to one that is not as diverse as the society it serves.

It is not possible to generalize this analysis of one university, in one country, at one point in time, to other institutions and organizations. Broadly similar issues, however, confront others in contemporary Western societies. Most fundamentally, the "climate for diversity" is one feature that is undergoing challenge and change across many forms of work and service organizations. Increasingly, climates that are "chilly," exclusionary, derogating, and marginalizing are under attack by those seeking to participate on their own terms; they are also being defended by those who prefer established patterns of cultural group relations, which are often to their own benefit.

Beyond the educational setting, parallel analyses and proposals for change are being advanced. Customers demand products and services that meet their (partly) culturally based needs; employees demand work environments and structures that allow them to observe schedules and social obligations that derive from their cultural identities; and, governments demand hiring and promotion practices that meet the standards of social justice.

Conclusion

This widespread social movement toward diversity and equity deserves our attention as social scientists. In my view, analyses, research, and programmatic applications of the type outlined here are the only ethically acceptable, and practical, responses to pluralism. Diversity is a fact of contemporary life and is here to stay. Our role is to understand it, and to suggest ways in which we can all learn to accommodate it. The negative consequences of doing otherwise are well documented, including stress (Berry, 1992; Berry, Kim, Minde, & Mok, 1987) and social conflict. I believe that our responsibility is not only to promote the pluralist option, but to challenge the alternatives, while using our conceptual and empirical training to defuse the tension in public debate.

References

Beiser, M., Barwick, C., Berry, J. W., da Costa, G., Fantino, A., Ganesan, S., Lee, C., Milne, N., Naidoo, J., Prince, R., Vela, E., & Wood, M. (1988). *After the door has been opened: Mental health issues affecting immigrants and refugees.* Ottawa: Health and Welfare Canada.

Berry, J. W. (1970). Marginality, stress, and ethnic identity in an acculturated Aboriginal community. *Journal of Cross-Cultural Psychology, 1,* 239-252.

Berry, J. W. (1974). Psychological aspects of cultural pluralism: Unity and identity reconsidered. *Topics in Culture Learning, 2,* 17-22.

Berry, J. W. (1980). Acculturation as varieties of adaptation. In A. Padilla (Ed.), *Acculturation: Theory, models, and findings* (pp. 9-25). Boulder, CO: Westview.

Berry, J. W. (1984a). Cultural relations in plural societies: Alternatives to segregation, and their sociopsychological implications. In M. Brewer & N. Miller (Eds.), *Groups in contact* (pp. 11-27). New York: Academic Press.

Berry, J. W. (1984b). Multicultural policy in Canada: A social psychological analysis. *Canadian Journal of Behavioural Science, 16,* 353-370.

Berry, J. W. (1990a). Psychology of acculturation. In J. Berman (Ed.), *Cross-cultural perspectives: Nebraska symposium on motivation* (pp. 201-234). Lincoln: University of Nebraska Press.

Berry, J. W. (1990b). The role of psychology in ethnic studies. *Canadian Ethnic Studies, 22,* 8-21.

Berry, J. W. (1991). Understanding and managing multiculturalism. *Journal of Psychology and Developing Societies, 3,* 17-49.

Berry, J. W., et al. (1991). Toward diversity and equity at Queen's: A strategy for change. *Queen's Gazette, 23*(Special Suppl.).

Berry, J. W. (1992). Acculturation and adaptation in a new society. *International Migration, 30,* 69-85.

Berry, J. W., et al. (Eds.). (1993). *Institutional strategies for change in race and ethnic relations at Canadian universities.* Kingston, Ontario: Queen's University.

Berry, J. W., & Kalin, R. (1995). Multicultural and ethnic attitudes in Canada. *Canadian Journal of Behavioural Science, 27,* 301-320.

Berry, J. W., Kalin, R., & Taylor, D. (1977). *Multiculturalism and ethnic attitudes in Canada.* Ottawa, Canada: Supply & Services.

Berry, J. W., Kim, U., Minde, T., & Mok, D. (1987). Comparative studies of acculturative stress. *International Migration Review, 21,* 491-511.

Berry, J. W., Kim, U., Power, S., Young, M., & Bujaki, M. (1989). Acculturation attitudes in plural societies. *Applied Psychology: An International Review, 38,* 185-206.

Berry, J. W., & Laponce, J. (Eds.). (1994). *Ethnicity and culture in Canada: The research landscape.* Toronto: University of Toronto Press.

Berry, J. W., Poortinga, Y. H., Segall, M. H., & Dasen, P. R. (1992). *Cross-cultural psychology: Research and applications.* New York: Cambridge University Press.

Berry, J. W., & Sam, D. (1996). Acculturation and adaptation. In J. W. Berry, M. H. Segall, & C. Kagitcibasi (Eds.), *Handbook of cross-cultural psychology. Vol. 3, Social behavior and applications* (pp. 291-326). Boston: Allyn & Bacon.

Cameron, J., & Lalonde, R. (1994). Self, ethnicity, and social group memberships in two generations of Italian Canadians. *Personality and Social Psychology Bulletin, 20,* 514-520.

Chemers, M., Oskamp, S., & Costanzo, M. (Eds.). (1995). *Diversity in organizations: New perspectives for a changing workplace.* Thousand Oaks, CA: Sage.

Ferdman, B. (1995). Cultural identity and diversity in organizations: Bridging the gap between group differences and individual uniqueness. In M. Chemers, S. Oskamp, & M. Costanzo (Eds.), *Diversity in organizations* (pp. 37-61). Thousand Oaks, CA: Sage.

Goodenough, W. H. (1976). Multiculturalism as the normal human experience. *Anthropology and Education Quarterly, 7,* 4-7.

Gordon, M. M. (1964). *Assimilation in American life.* New York: Oxford University Press.

Government of Canada. (1971). *Debates* (verbal record of debates in parliament, October 8).

Ho, E. (1995). *The challenge of culture change: The cross-cultural adaptation of Hong Kong Chinese adolescent immigrants in New Zealand.* Unpublished doctoral dissertation, University of Waikato, New Zealand.

Horenczyk, G. (in press). Migrant identities in conflict: Acculturation attitudes and perceived acculturation strategies. In G. Breakwell & E. Lyons (Eds.), *Changing European identities.* London, UK: Pergamon.

Kalin, R., & Berry, J. W. (1995). Ethnic and civic self-identity in Canada. *Canadian Ethnic Studies, 27,* 1-15

Kim, U. (1988). *Acculturation of Korean-immigrants to Canada.* Unpublished doctoral dissertation, Queen's University, Canada.

Krishnan, A., & Berry, J. W. (1992). Acculturative stress and acculturation attitudes among Indian immigrants to the United States. *Psychology and Developing Societies, 4,* 187-212.

Kymlicka, W. (1995). *Multicultural citizenship.* Oxford, UK: Clarendon.

LaFromboise, T., Coleman, H., & Gerton, J. (1993). Psychological impact of biculturalism: Evidence and theory. *Psychological Bulletin, 114,* 395-412.

Lalonde, R., & Cameron, J. (1993). An intergroup perspective on immigrant acculturation with a focus on collective strategies. *International Journal of Psychology, 28,* 57-74.

Lambert, W. E., & Taylor, D. M. (1988). Assimilation versus multiculturalism: The views of urban Americans. *Sociological Forum, 3,* 72-88.

Landis, D., Dansby, M., & Faley, R. (1993). The Military Equal Opportunity Climate Survey. In P. Rosenfield, J. E. Edwards, & M. D. Thomas (Eds.), *Improving organizational surveys* (pp. 122-142). Newbury Park, CA: Sage.

Martin, J. (1993). Inequality, distributive justice, and organizational legitimacy. In J. K. Murnighan (Ed.), *Social psychology in organizations* (pp. 296-321). Englewood Cliffs, NJ: Prentice Hall.

Moghaddam, F. M. (1988). Individualistic and collective integration strategies among immigrants. In J. W. Berry & R. C. Annis (Eds.), *Ethnic psychology* (pp. 69-79). Amsterdam: Swets & Zeitlinger.

Phinney, J. (1990). Ethnic identity in adolescents and adults: A review of research. *Psychological Bulletin, 108,* 499-514.

Phinney, J., DuPont, E., Esinosa, C., Revill, J., & Sanders, K. (1994). Ethnic identity and American identification among ethnic minority youth. In A. M. Bouvy, F. Van de Vijver, P. Boski, & P. Schmitz (Eds.), *Journeys into cross-cultural psychology* (pp. 167-183). Lisse, The Netherlands: Swets & Zeitlinger.

Sommerlad, E., & Berry, J. W. (1970). The role of ethnic identification in distinguishing between attitudes toward assimilation and integration. *Human Relations, 23,* 23-29.

Szapocznik, J., & Kurtines, W. (1993). Family psychology and cultural diversity. *American Psychologist, 48,* 400-407.

Triandis, H. C. (1976). The future of pluralism. *Journal of Social Issues, 32,* 179-208.

UNESCO. (1985). *Cultural pluralism and cultural identity.* Paris: Author.

Ward, C. (1996). Acculturation. In D. Landis & R. S. Bhagat (Eds.), *Handbook of intercultural training* (2nd ed., pp. 124-147). Thousand Oaks, CA: Sage.

3

Change and Continuity
in Organizations
Assessing Intergroup Relations

FATHALI M. MOGHADDAM

> They called me up at the factory and asked me if he was one of my men. They weren't satisfied with me just telling them on the phone, they still wanted me to go down there in person. So I went and got the coal. Both of us were agents from the same factory, but they only wanted to do business with me, whom they *know....* So in China, supply and marketing work relies on your factory's good planning and allocation from above, and also on human relations.

This quotation, from the head of a supply and marketing department of a factory in Beijing, was presented by Yang (1994, p. 105) as part of her highly insightful and detailed analysis of *guanxixue,* a central feature of social relations in China. Yang (1994) demonstrated how *guanxixue,* the art of creating a network of obligations and responsibilities by doing favors for others, has continued to be central to social relationships over time and across political upheavals. There are two particular themes in Yang's (1994) analysis that serve as the point of departure for the present discussion.

First, throughout her investigation of *guanxixue,* Yang (1994) high-lights the important distinction between formal and informal aspects of social relationships. Formal aspects are defined and manufactured by authority figures (e.g., an important government official, a head of a factory) who enjoy high status and influence in political, economic, and other spheres. They establish the norms and rules for how things are officially supposed to be done: how to order goods for a factory, how to decide on organizational goals, how to select people for jobs, how to distribute resources among employees, and so on.

But parallel to formal and explicit social relationships there exist informal ones, which evolve inevitably within the context of an infor-mal and implicit normative system. The informal normative system, immanent in everyday social practices, prescribes how things should actually be done according to peoples' everyday understandings, rather than according to "officialdom." For example, how factory orders are actually put in ("they still wanted me to go down there in person") rather than how they are officially supposed to be made (e.g., agents from the same factory officially have the same authority to put in factory orders).

There is always tension between the formal and the informal norma-tive systems, between how things are officially supposed to be done and how they are actually done, between the way life is supposed to run "according to the books" and how it actually runs. People are aware of this tension, and they know that the informal very often proves more powerful than the formal. Frequently the informal system involves matters of personal honor and prestige, and is part of the expressive order of society (Harré, 1993).

A second theme in Yang's (1994) analysis that serves to launch the present discussion is the continuous and resilient nature of the informal normative system. On the surface, social relations in China seem to have undergone dramatic changes during the 20th century, particularly through the impact of Maoism. For example, the traditional binary authority relationships (emperor/subject, father/son, husband/wife, and so on) were apparently set aside, and egalitarianism prevailed. Also, self-interest was dismissed, and the collective interest became primary. More generally, things now were done through official channels, and gaining concessions through "gifts, favors, and banquets," *guanxixue,* was officially abandoned.

But at a deeper level, there was stability rather than change in many ways. Far from changing leader/follower traditions, Mao, the most important of the "New Emperors" (Salisbury, 1992), seems to have followed in the footsteps of the other Chinese emperors.

With respect to self-interest, during the Cultural Revolution it became routine to chant,

> "Do nothing to benefit yourself;
> devote yourself to benefiting others."

But behind this chant was a different reality (Yang, 1994, p. 57), which became public again in the "liberal" post-Mao era and is reflected in the popular slogan,

> "When people do not look out for themselves,
> heaven will expel and earth will destroy them."

More generally, although *guanxixue* was heartily condemned by communist authorities ("It is the remnants of traditional China's feudal and clan systems' way of thinking . . . a product of the intermingling of [feudal thought] with radical bourgeois individualism and selfishness," Yang, 1994, p. 58), this informal system of social relations proved extremely resilient. Indeed, it is through *guanxixue* that a lot of things, perhaps the most important things in every life, continue to get done.

Reflecting Back on Ourselves

Cross-cultural research provides an invaluable service by holding up a mirror before us, so that we may reflect back on our own society and critically assess social life from a new perspective, one that is instructive in novel ways. It may seem that communist China is far removed from the capitalist West, and the United States in particular. I shall argue, however, that the two themes that emerge from Yang's analysis of China, the primacy of the informal over the formal and the continuous nature of important aspects of the informal, also are central to social relations in capitalist societies, including the United States. Just as factory agents in communist China rely primarily on the informal system to get their work done, so do employees in U.S. organizations.

Similarly, just as the informal normative system is resilient to change in Chinese organizations, so it is in U.S. organizations.

I shall begin this chapter by focusing on the issue of change in organizations, and more specifically on the puzzle of stability. My thesis is that in the domain of intergroup relations, as in most other areas, despite all the legal and "official" changes, a great deal remains the same.

In the second part of this chapter, I shall briefly review traditional approaches to changing organizations, and this will include discussions of total quality management (TQM), reengineering, and corporate culture. My first critical theme is that these traditional approaches do not give adequate attention to the continuous informal system. This informal system consists of rules and norms that prescribe correct behavior and constitute a normative guideline for individuals. The informal system is an integral part of culture, and acquired through socialization processes. This is how we learn to behave correctly as employees, managers, colleagues, as well as citizens, men, women, parents, children, and so on. There is considerable cross-cultural variation as regards the correct behavior prescribed by different cultures (Moghaddam, Taylor, & Wright, 1993). We shall consider some possible consequences of this variation.

A second criticism is that, following traditional psychology, these approaches adopt a causal rather than normative model of behavior. This is a complex issue, related to the influence of a positivist philosophy of science, and leading to mechanistic and overly simplistic models of human behavior.

In the third section of the chapter I assess change and stability in organizations by applying ideas from social reducton theory, a recent contribution to the field (Moghaddam & Crystal, in press; Moghaddam & Harré, 1995). The major proposition of social reducton theory was summarized by the intellectual historian Daniel Robinson (personal communication, October 1994) in the statement, "culture will always triumph over politics." That is, long-established normative systems and their associated patterns of everyday social interactions will not be quickly changed by "officialdom." Indeed, in many cases political and corporate authorities fail to manage change in the direction they desire. It is the informal system, the "culture" Robinson refers to, that often has more influence on the course of events. In so far as this "culture" reflects expressive activities we could also say "the expressive will always triumph over the political."

Change and Continuity in Organizations

The issue of change is seen to be central to modern organizations (McWhinney, 1992), as well as a key factor in many elements of organizational life, such as leadership (Hunt, 1991). A first assumption underlying many discussions of modern organizations is that change is continually taking place, often in dramatic and rapid ways. Cascio (1995) began his seminal discussion of the future direction of organizational psychology by stating that, "As citizens of the 20th century, we have witnessed more change in our daily existence and in our environment than anyone else who ever walked the planet. But if you think the pace of change was fast in this century, expect it to accelerate in the next one" (p. 928). Given the extraordinary transformation of English life in the first 30 years of the Industrial Revolution, however, or the vast changes various indigenous people in Africa and Asia experienced when they were "discovered" by Western colonialists (or the multitudes of other examples of rapid change taking place outside 20th century North America), Cascio's statement is, to say the least, controversial. The same assumption, however, concerning "unprecedented rapid change" underlies research in organizational behavior.

The traditional approach in organizational behavior has been to draw on the research foundations of the social sciences, particularly psychology, to better understand, predict, and control change in organizations (for examples, see Hersey & Blanchard, 1993; Newstrom & Davis, 1993). In essence, the priority and focus of those concerned with organizations has been the management of change (for a broader discussion of change and psychology, see Moghaddam, 1990). The "innovations" in organizational thinking have revolved around new ways of managing change, the "how to" approaches of reengineering, TQM, and the like.

In contrast to the attention lavished on change, the issues of continuity and stability are given scant consideration. I argue that fundamentally important aspects of social and organizational life are characterized by continuity rather than change. This continuity becomes more apparent when we look carefully at studies that evaluate "change creation" projects. For example, a comprehensive study involving interviews with 350 executives from 14 industries revealed that as many as 70% to 80% of change initiatives had failed (Arthur D. Little, Inc.,

1994, cited in Cascio, 1995). A number of more detailed case studies of change initiatives in specific organizations reveal the same picture (Mowdy & Sutton, 1993). For example, Stevenson and Gilly (1991) studied the efforts of hospital management to change the procedures for handling patient complaints. A new procedure was formalized and a number of hospital personnel were identified as having specific responsibility for channeling and responding to complaints. The study revealed that after the change initiative, however, hospital personnel continued to use the informal communications network more than the new formal network, despite their knowledge of the formal procedures.

The stubborn continuity of established "ways of doing things" are all too apparent to students of national development, and those attempting to foster and accelerate change in intergroup and intragroup relationships and development in Third World societies (see Moghaddam, 1990). Even countries that have the material resources, such as oil-rich Arab States, find that building the physical infrastructure, setting up an organizational chart, putting employees in place, teaching managers and others the formal rule system, and taking other similar steps involving material and formal changes, are only the first, and usually the least difficult, steps toward creating an efficient organization. Constructing a new factory building in a Third World country is often far quicker and easier than training the personnel. Obvious as this may seem, it is a point that has not been understood well enough, in part because of a blind spot that social scientists continue to have regarding causal sequences in human behavior.

It is sometimes useful to turn our assumptions about causal sequences upside down. For example, the economist Albert Hirschman (1984) made the following point in a discussion of change and national development:

> I continue to collect inverted, "wrong-way-around" or "cart-before-the-horse" development sequences for a simple reason: The finding that such sequences exist "in nature" expands the range of development possibilities. They demonstrate how certain forward moves, widely thought to be indispensably required as first steps in some development sequence, can instead be taken as second or third steps. From prerequisites and keys to any further progress, these moves are thus downgraded to *effects,* induced by other moves that, so it turns out, can start things going. Perhaps these other moves will be within easier reach of certain . . . cultures than the dethroned prerequisites. (p. 1)

Intergroup Relations in Organizations

One of the ways in which organizations have been changing since the 1960s is in terms of increased workforce diversity (Chemers, Oskamp, & Costanzo, 1995). There are now more women and ethnic minorities in organizations, and increasingly they are breaking through to management positions. This change is very evident in the United States and Canada, where the ethnic makeup of immigrants and residential settlement patterns have been changing (Moghaddam et al., 1993). Between 600,000 and 1,000,000 immigrants arrive in North America annually, and the percentage of newcomers who are from outside of Western Europe has been growing steadily.

But it is not just in the United States that the workforce has become more diverse. This trend also is evident in Europe, as shown by the presence of millions of South Asians in the United Kingdom, North Africans in France, Turks in Germany, and East Europeans, Asians, and other minorities in the rest of Western Europe. Indeed, a review of research findings reported in journals such as *International Migration Review* and *International Journal of Intercultural Relations* reveals that large-scale movement of populations is by no means exclusive to Western societies, but is a worldwide phenomenon likely to persist and even increase as communications systems in the "global village" further improve.

Increased workforce diversity has been seen as another example of dramatic change, another indication that things "do not remain the same" in global transformations (see Harris & Moran, 1991). Inevitably, researchers in the business sciences have developed a number of proposals for how to understand, predict, and control this change, so that "the promise of diversity" is realized (Cox, 1993; Cross, Katz, Miller, & Seashore, 1994; Thomas, 1991). As in most other cases of "change management," however, these schemes are characterized by a number of invalid assumptions, some of which I discuss in the next section.

Rethinking Change and Stability in Organizations

The focus on change in organizations has been misguided in a number of ways. First, there have been incorrect assumptions about the nature of the changes taking place. Second, the issue of continuity has been neglected.

Cascio's (1995) statement about the fast pace of change during the 20th century reminds me of a lecture I heard a few years ago by a senior psychologist at one of the eminent U.S. universities. He started his lecture by declaring that psychologists should remember that much of "great" psychology has an ancient history, which goes as far back as the 1950s!

I do not deny that some types of change have taken place at a furious pace during the 20th century. I would contend, however, that by far the most important source of change has been technological innovations, rather than managerial policies. For example, the motorcar has brought about far more change than could ever be achieved by way of managerial "restructuring." Second, such changes have not been predicted or controlled. As anyone who has taken part in the development of a 5-year plan or any kind of forecasting model knows, it is impossible to predict and control change over a period of more than a few months, and sometimes weeks or days! The only way to keep 5-year plans or long-term forecasting models on the same path as actual events is to revise the plans/models every few months, to make them fit with the real events. This critical point is raised by the economist Paul Ormerod (1994) in his attack on the traditional "understanding, prediction, and control" approach to planning,

> The proprietors of the models interfere with their output before it is allowed to see the light of day. These "judgment adjustments" can be, and often are, extensive. Every model builder and model operator knows about the process of altering the output of a model, but this remains something of a twilight world, and is not well documented in the literature. One of the few academics to take an interest is Mike Artis of Manchester University, a former forecaster himself, and his study carried out for the Bank of England in 1982 showed definitely that the forecasting record of models, without such human intervention, would have been distinctly worse than it has been with the help of the adjustments, a finding that has been confirmed by subsequent studies. (pp. 103-104)

Of course, this does not mean that we should abandon planning for new technological innovations. By investing in some types of research and development (R&D) projects rather than others, for example, it is possible to have some influence on the domains in which new technological breakthroughs will be made. In such a broad sense, we can "manage technology" (see Betz, 1987). It is not possible to predict, however, which particular R&D projects will be successful; nor is it possible to predict and control the consequences of an innovation once it is launched into the market.

In the specific domain of intergroup relations in organizations, the complex set of forces leading to greater diversity in organizations has not been predictable or controllable. Greater diversity and the increased representation of minorities in managerial positions have been part of collective mobilization among minority groups generally (Powell, 1993). A number of theories are available for those aspiring to understand changes in intergroup relations (see Taylor & Moghaddam, 1994), but most social science research in the domain of intergroup relations is better at "predicting" backwards rather than forwards in time. For example, after the Berlin Wall was brought down, a lot of theorists were able to "predict" the collapse of the Eastern communist hegemony.

A second critical comment I believe should be made about the literature on "organizations and change" is that the issue of continuity has been neglected. Change has taken place at a fast pace during the 20th century, but in some fundamental respect "things have remained the same." For example, although the formal structure of organizations has changed over the 20th century, and despite all the various discussions about "bottom-up," "transformational," and other styles of leadership (e.g., Bass, 1985), most organizations continue to have a hierarchical structure with the power to make the most important decisions concentrated in the hands of a few leaders at the top. In short, authority relations in organizations have remained essentially stable.

In adopting this position, I am aware that I am at loggerheads with the orientation of at least some writers in organizational psychology. For example, in discussing the new work conditions, Cascio (1995) has stated:

> Although by no means universal, much of the work that results in a product, service, or decision is now done in teams—intact, identifiable social systems (even if small or temporary) whose members have the authority to manage their own task and interpersonal processes as they carry out their work. Such teams go by a variety of names—autonomous work groups, process teams, and self-managing work teams. All of this implies a radical reorientation from the traditional view of a manager's work. In this kind of environment, workers are acting more like managers, and managers more like workers. (p. 930)

It seems to me that when one looks at the larger picture, the statement "workers are acting more like managers, and managers more like workers" is simply wrong. The so-called "self-managed" work team has some influence in the way it goes about carrying out a limited set of designated tasks, but this has not diminished the power or changed the role of upper-level management. Managers have not become workers! Indeed, in the 1990s era of restructuring and downsizing, when corporations such as AT&T cut 40,000 or more jobs in just one step, the system has become more autocratic rather than less. As Thomas Moore (1996) has pointed out, the workforce has become more "disposable" and more unstable.

So-called "joint governance" in the workplace has been discussed, and some insightful ways of improving the influence of employees have been considered (see the collection of papers in Kaufman & Kleiner, 1993). This has done very little, however, to increase the actual power and influence of employees. As Verma and Cutcher-Gershenfeld (1993) point out,

> In practice most worker participation programs and union-management cooperation initiatives in North America are limited in scope. They are primarily advisory mechanisms in which final decision-making authority still resides with management. (p. 197)

It may be argued that, in this age of "downsizing," workers may not feel like managers, but managers often feel like workers! This viewpoint overlooks the hierarchical power structure that continues to exist when managers and workers find new jobs in alternative organizations. Also, increasing specialization may lead us to assume that employees with specialized knowledge hold more power. We should not confuse the very limited power of specialists and work groups at the level of projects, however, with the power of top managers to make decisions that are consequential for entire organizations. Increased specialization means that top managers are unable to fathom the details of specialized research. Consequently, in many cases, even technically competent managers have to rely on specialized experts to inform them about particular projects. The actual power of experts is very limited, however, because experts are confined to their own narrow domains. This very narrowness ensures that those with expertise remain locked in a subordinate position in relation to the traditionally powerful individuals (for a broader discussion of the consequences of increasing specialization, see Moghaddam, 1997).

Increased diversity in organizations has had little impact on authority relations. The few minority group members, whether women or ethnic minority members, who have moved up the corporate hierarchy, have done so as individuals, and have helped to strengthen the existing status quo (see Taylor & Moghaddam, 1994, Chapter 7). That is, having made it up the corporate ladder, they have legitimized the system and "validated" its openness (also see "circulation of elites" in Taylor & Moghaddam, 1987, Chapter 7). This would suggest that increased diversity has not had any significant impact on the hierarchical structures of organizations.

Thus, despite the claim about changes in leadership style and the evolution of "flat" organizations, the power to make important decisions that have an impact on the entire organization is concentrated in the hands of top managers. More broadly, I would contend that authority relations have remained stable, and in practice are very difficult to change. Within the work teams themselves, there tend to emerge hierarchies that mirror the hierarchy found in the larger traditional organization.

The explanation for stability is to be found in micro-level social practices that form the bedrock of human societies. To unravel such social practices, we must focus on the informal rather than the formal organization, take note of stability as well as change, and highlight how things actually get done rather than how they are supposed to be carried out according to "MBA manuals." In the next section, I briefly consider traditional approaches to understanding and changing organizations, and point out their shortcomings.

Traditional Approaches to Managing Organizational Change

A contradiction characterizes the most influential traditional approaches to understanding and managing change in organizations, particularly TQM and reengineering. On one hand they emphasize the importance of conceptualizing the organization as a whole, but on the other hand they tend to neglect the informal organization.

The Total Quality Management (TQM) Approach

The principal focus of a TQM organization is to provide goods, services, or both that meet or preferably exceed the external (or final) customer's expectations in terms of functional requirements, value, and cost. (Thomas, 1995, p. 185)

Total quality management (TQM) is an approach to managing the whole organization, with specific focus on customer requirements (see Bowles & Hammond, 1991; Crosby, 1996; George & Weimerskirch, 1994; Hradesky, 1995; Juran & Gryna, 1988; McInerney & White, 1995). The most important elements that contribute to the quality of the end product are specified by the Malcolm Baldrige National Quality Award, established in 1987; these elements include leadership, information and analysis, strategic quality planning, human resources development and management, management of process quality, quality and operational results, and customer focus and satisfaction.

TQM sees each employee in the production process as both a producer and a customer. Thus, each employee has to satisfy the requirements of other employees who are his or her immediate customers, in a sequence of activities that have the requirements of the "final" customer as an end point.

The TQM approach requires that changes be brought about within the formal structure of the present organization; it is a matter of taking what is already available and incrementally improving quality. Mechanisms for bringing about change tend to vary, but typically they include greater employee participation, improved communication between departments, reorganized and increased specialization, and changes in process engineering.

The main focus of TQM so far has been on the formal organization: how things are supposed to be done according to the formal rules. In monitoring change, emphasis is placed on statistical methods, process flow charts, and procedures designed to maximize quantification. Implicit in all of this is the assumption that formal, rational, explicit organizational procedures are the most important in determining how well customer requirements are met.

The TQM approach has not given much attention to the informal organization, and the "alternative" or "shadow" culture that often exists in organizations side-by-side with the formal culture. A few writers have discussed "irrationality" (e.g., Thomas, 1995, Part II) and "nonconformity" (e.g., Bounds, Yorks, Adams, & Ranney, 1994, pp. 121-124), but this has not amounted to a serious endeavor to incorporate the informal organization in TQM.

Cross-cultural work groups and TQM. What kinds of work groups would most likely be created by TQM procedures in organizations composed of individuals with different cultural backgrounds and with different normative systems? The answer seems to be that multicultural work groups would be focused on developing formal procedures and building relationships toward improving customer satisfaction. The exclusive focus on formal systems and formal outcome would be maintained unless customer satisfaction declined to unacceptable levels. If this happened, then a fine-grained search for remedies might indirectly identify cross-cultural differences as worthy of attention.

Because TQM focuses exclusively on the formal organization, cross-cultural variations and the informal organization would only receive attention indirectly, and only when they act as a source of inefficiencies. Consequently, possible benefits of cultural diversity would remain untapped, and culturally diverse work groups would be characterized by greater inefficiencies when cultural differences in informal systems are ignored. Ironically, then, the TQM approach, which takes customer satisfaction to be the central goal, is likely to create cross-cultural work groups with limited possibilities of maximizing customer satisfaction. This is an important shortcoming, because as cultural diversity is increasing, so is the importance of the informal organization.

Cross-cultural differences in social behavior, which exist in a variety of social domains (Moghaddam et al., 1993), are manifested in the informal organization. Consider the example of cross-cultural differences in manager-employee relations, in such things as the degree of direction employees expect to receive from a manager in either a group or individual setting. A manager socialized to adopt a "democratic" style of leadership and employees used to a more directive and strict leadership will experience misunderstandings and perhaps even conflicts. But these experiences will be rooted in, and probably remain part of, the informal system.

Ironically, the importance of the "informal system" of how things actually get done, as opposed to how they are supposed to be done, is very clear from the activities of organizations themselves. For example, consider the issue of marketing and customer requirements. A critical assessment of marketing strategies for products such as cars would suggest that customers require cars that make them feel good—advertisements for cars tell customers almost nothing about engineering features, but instead appeal at the emotional level to try to get customers to feel good about the product. In the terminology of social cognition research, the attempt at persuasion is through the peripheral rather than central route, through affect rather than logical reasoning (see Fiske & Taylor, 1991). Although TQM groups composed of members from multiple cultures might have important information to contribute to effective marketing, formal systems and conformity might suppress this information.

This emphasis on the "feel good" approach to automobile advertising underlines another aspect of "customer requirements," an aspect that often remains implicit and is seldom part of the formal system. "Customer requirements" are not fixed; they are flexible and are constantly being reconstructed through marketing and other means. Thus, the "final" customer requirements that act as an end point for TQM are a moving target, and this means that a TQM exercise can be made more or less successful through manipulating the end point, the "customer requirements" adopted as a final target.

Reengineering

Reengineering isn't another idea imported from Japan. . . . It isn't a new trick that promises to boost the quality of a company's product or service or shave a percentage off costs. . . . Business reengineering isn't about *fixing* anything. Business reengineering means starting all over, starting from scratch. (Hammer & Champy, 1993, p. 2)

As these authors point out in the previous quote from the introduction to a "radical" manifesto *Reengineering the Corporation,* reengineering is very different from TQM and other approaches attempting "incremental improvement" in the organization. Reengineering proposes nothing less than dismantling the entire organization and rebuilding from scratch. Inevitably, the proposal extends to "reengineering" (in more traditional terms "retraining" or at least "reorienting") management (see Champy, 1995).

The need for a complete change arises, according to advocates of reengineering, from what they refer to as the fragmented and rigid nature of modern organizations. The divisions of labor and hierarchical structures of contemporary organizations must be set aside, to make room for a more flexible system, with less specialization and more open communications channels. These changes must particularly come about in four areas: business process, jobs and structures, management and measurement systems, and values and beliefs.

As part of the "revolution," the terminology for conceptualizing organizations is changed. The term "reengineering" suggests precision, as well as action on a scientific basis. Managers become "coaches" rather than supervisors, and executives become leaders rather than "scorekeepers."

Cross-cultural work groups and reengineering. What kinds of cross-cultural work groups would most likely be created by reengineering procedures? In addressing this question, we need to keep in mind two limitations of reengineering. First, reengineering shares with TQM the assumption that one only needs to be concerned with the formal organization to bring about change. The focus of reengineering, as with TQM, is the formal system. It is assumed that if the formal organization is changed, this will bring about a change in the structure of the organization, ignoring the dominant role of the informal system. Although the "reengineered" organization will have the same employees, they will now behave differently because the reengineered organization will cause them to do so. Reengineering processes will not necessarily create a larger or smaller number of work groups with members of different cultural backgrounds, however, employees may be asked to work with a new group of coworkers with cultural backgrounds different from their former peers. If cultural differences in informal social interactions are ignored in these three groups, expected benefits will not occur.

A second limitation is that reengineering is not flexible on the issue of authority relations. Despite changes in terminology (managers will be coaches not scorekeepers), reengineering will be led by top (reengineered) managers (Champy, 1995).

These limitations mean that the cross-cultural work groups created through reengineering would have major shortcomings. This is because the fundamentally important role of the informal organization is neglected. Consider, for example, the case of sexual harassment at Mitsubishi Motor Manufacturing of America plant in Normal, Illinois. When one considers the formal system—what was "on the books"— then it is difficult to explain why so many women employees were abused for so long. But an analysis of the informal system reveals that among some groups of male employees it had become normative to sexually harass women employees at the plant. That is, the "correct" thing to do was to harass women and be supportive of others who did so. One male employee who decided to go against this norm and prevent one of his male colleagues from harassing a female employee soon found himself ostracized and pressured. Referring to the woman he tried to protect, this male employee said, "I stood up for her, and I pretty much made a lot of enemies for it" (Grimsley, 1996). If similar norms regarding treatment of individuals different from the majority persist in work groups composed of members from different cultural groups, dysfunctional consequences should be expected.

Corporate Culture and
the Causal Model

The term *corporate culture* (synonymous with organizational culture) became popular in the management literature in the 1970s, as social scientists began the systematic study of different organizations as cultural units (rather like anthropologists studying different tribes). Although the literature on corporate culture is not as extensive as that of TQM, it has a more academic flavor (see Deal & Kennedy, 1982; Frost & Moore, 1991; Ott, 1989), particularly in the case of Schein's (1985, 1992) analyses. The concept of corporate culture does not enjoy the same level of influence and status as TQM, however, or even reengineering, in the practical world of business management.

Corporate culture is typically defined as the norms, values, roles, and so on, of people in an organization. Schein (1992) places particular emphasis on the role of leaders in shaping organizational culture. His distinction between primary and secondary mechanisms by which leaders influence change is useful; the first concerns the style or manner in which leaders do their work, and the second embodies procedures and rules. The focus on "style" and other less tangible aspects of corporate life indicates that the corporate culture approach does give attention to the informal organization.

Cross-cultural work groups and corporate culture. The corporate culture approach could lead to more efficient and successful cross-cultural work groups. This is because the corporate culture approach does a far better job than TQM and reengineering of incorporating both informal and formal aspects of the organization. More specifically, Schein (1992) and other leaders of the corporate culture approach guide managers to give attention to the particular cultural characteristics of the corporation, and implicitly the variations in informal culture within organizations. For example, in one organization I found that an important project group ran into difficulties because the group leader, a Middle Easterner, was seen by group members as a time waster. "All he does is get us to socialize," was a typical comment from group members. But the group leader's explanation was rational, from his cultural perspective: "I believe we must first get to know and trust one another, then we can succeed as professional colleagues. How can I work with people I do not know personally?" By attending to such culturally shaped variations in behavior, the corporate culture approach can create more dynamic and effective cross-cultural work groups.

This "advantage" has not led to much progress, however, in large part because corporate culture is still hampered by a causal model of behavior that underlies all three traditional orientations (TQM, reengineering, and corporate culture). The causal model, arising out of a positivist philosophy of science, assumes that human behavior is causally determined (see Moghaddam & Harré, 1995, for a discussion in psychology, and Ormerod's [1994] chapter on "mechanistic modeling" for a discussion in economics). The terminology of traditional research methodology, such as independent variable (assumed cause) and dependent variable (assumed effect), is based on this assumption. Followed to its logical conclusion, this approach leaves very little or no room at all for human agency. Behavior is assumed to be caused mechanistically by "factors."

A causal explanation of human behavior matches neither the research evidence nor our own everyday experiences (Harré, 1993; Moghaddam & Harré, 1995). The essential feature of human life is the ability of individuals to choose between different possible courses of action. Such choices are to a large extent patterned according to normative systems (rules, norms, and so on) that prescribe correct behavior in each culture. Individuals are not condemned, however, to follow normative ways of behaving; they can generate and make influential new normative systems, and reject existing ones. Such innovations are not mechanistically determined by "factors," nor are they inevitable.

The traditional approaches to managing change in organizations, particularly TQM, have tended to focus on the formal and ignore the informal aspects of the organization. Second, they have assumed that changes in the formal organization will causally determine the behavior of employees, and ultimately the performance of the entire organization.

Change and Stability in
Intergroup Relations

The themes common to traditional approaches to managing change in organizations, generally, are also characteristic of more specific approaches to managing change in minority-majority relations in organizations (e.g., Thomas, 1991). The emphasis has been on the formal structure and on the assumption that changes in this will cause predictable changes in the entire pattern of behavior.

The formal structure for achieving justice in intergroup relations has been in place for some time. The Civil Rights Act of 1964 prohibited discrimination in employment on the basis of race, color, religion, sex, or national origin; the Age Discrimination in Employment Act of 1967 prohibited age discrimination for individuals 40 years or older; and the Americans with Disabilities Act of 1991 prohibited discrimination against individuals who are disabled but qualified to perform job tasks with reasonable accommodation. These are examples of Equal Employment Opportunity (EEO) laws. In addition, some organizations also have on paper affirmative action programs intended to foster, develop, and promote minorities in their workforce.

In practice, however, we find that things do not get done in the way they are supposed to according to "the book." The informal system persists, so that, for example, women still find themselves hitting a "glass ceiling." Discrimination continues to influence hiring, retention, and promotion practices, despite the "formal" ban on discriminatory practices.

We are reminded here of the case of *guanxixue* in Chinese society, the persistence of micro-level practices in social relations, despite attempts to bring about fundamental change through "reengineering" Chinese society. How can we account for this situation? How can we explain the persistence of discrimination, when the formal structure of organizations explicitly rejects such practices?

The Puzzle of Stability in
Organizations: Social Reducton Theory

Reengineering and TQM focus on change and propose methods for achieving change, but they fail to explain what I have been emphasizing as the most important feature of organizational life: continuity. In most organizations continuity persists in many everyday social practices, in "how things get done around here" at the very basic level—despite leadership changes, employee turnover, "restructuring," "take-overs," and even downsizing. More specifically, discrimination against women and other minorities often proves to be highly resilient. One reason for this, according to social reducton theory, is because of continuity in social practices at the very micro level. Such micro-level practices are often implicit, and are carried out by people without conscious effort— rather like a skill, such as how one sits to dine at a table without consciously attending to all the things one has to do to "behave correctly" at the table.

A *reducton* is an elementary piece of social behavior, requiring social skills to carry out, but not requiring conscious attention after it has been acquired through socialization in a culture. For example, children initially need to be conscious of the norms and rules that prescribe "correct behavior at the table." But after a child has become skilled at eating "like an adult," then she can dine with adults and "behave correctly" without much conscious effort.

Social reductons are sustained by *carriers,* which are formalized sets of social activity that embody very specific rules about correct behavior. For example, in two related studies, a group of us at Georgetown and Oxford are studying "ballet" as a carrier of reductons. Our interviews show that parents choose to send their daughters to ballet classes (but not "tap" or "jazz" dancing) because this will lead to their girls acquiring the "poise," "grace," "discipline," and so on that "young ladies should have." That is, a whole set of reductons (micro-social practices concerned with how young ladies should sit, walk, talk, and so on) are embodied and sustained by the "carrier" of ballet training. In another field study, we have investigated the flag of the State of Georgia as a carrier. Those opposed to the flag see it as embodying "the lifestyle of the Old South, and the racism associated with it," whereas those who defend the flag see it as representing the "good Old South" and the gentility, civility, and hospitality of that world.

Social reducton theory leads us to look carefully at the details of social relationships, at how things actually are, rather than at the formal and the large scale. This is in line with recent research on the "new" racism and sexism, which is implicit rather than explicit, and camouflaged in politically correct rhetoric (for examples, see Sears, 1988). In this 21st-century era, most people know it is "wrong" to discriminate against minorities, but discrimination can manifest itself in many subtle ways.

Research by Sonnert and Holton (1995) on female scientists provides a detailed demonstration of the power of micro-level practices in maintaining continuity in discrimination despite the politically correct nature of the formal organization. There were two phases to this research. The first involved administering questionnaires to 191 women and 508 men, all of them recipients of NRC and NSC fellowships from the years 1952-1985. All of the women and over 97% of the men were white. The second phase of the study involved face-to-face interviews with 108 women and 92 men. Attempts were made to match the males and females in the study on key characteristics, including age, professional qualifications, and the like. The most interesting results from the point of view of our present discussion are the many subtle ways in which discrimination against women can come into being. For example, an essential part of "becoming a scientist" involves developing networks and gaining acceptance as part of a network. It was found that women were more often left out of conversations with visiting scientists, conversations that tend to take place "by accident" in corridors, in elevators, and in other informal settings. Women were less likely to become part of the informal network of science, which provides opportunities for making progress in the formal hierarchy.

The results of this research also show, however, that women have had a lot more success in biology, perhaps because they have been involved in this field a lot longer and now represent more than half of the biological scientists. By implication, the much smaller group of ethnic minorities in science may be facing even greater challenges then those confronting women scientists. This may in part explain why there continue to be such low representation of ethnic minorities in key positions in research institutes and universities.

Conclusions and Implications

A main thrust of my argument in this chapter has been that in attempting to bring about change in organizations, two of the traditional approaches, TQM and "reengineering," have focused too much on the formal and too little on the informal aspects of the organization. Consequently, they are likely to create cross-cultural work groups that are less effective. This is because in such work groups, attention will only be given to cross-cultural differences when they act as a source of inefficiencies that are detected in the functioning of the formal system. Because TQM and reengineering do not attend to the informal system, they will not capitalize on potential benefits to be gained from having cultural diversity in work groups (such as finding alternative approaches to tackling problems, technical or otherwise). Second, all three major traditional approaches have adopted a causal model of behavior, which in practice proves to be simplistic and wrong. Third, I have argued that more attention needs to be given to everyday social practices that act as "barriers" to change and thus preserve continuities in organizational behavior. Social reducton theory was introduced as one approach to understanding the nature of such everyday social practices.

I believe my arguments have certain implications for the management and socialization of culturally diverse work groups (see Granrose, this volume). The most profound and powerful impact of cultural diversity in organizations is manifested in an informal rather than in a formal manner. It is not in the formal organizational chart and the written procedures of the organization, but in the informal normative system, that cultural differences are revealed. Also, it is in the details of everyday social interactions, rather than the grand formal plans or stated financial policies, that cultural nuances show themselves. Thus, those intending to improve the effectiveness of culturally diverse work groups should attend more closely to the informal normative systems that pattern everyday social interactions. It is these informal aspects of the organization that can stubbornly foster continuities, even when the entire formal structure is intentionally mobilized for change.

References

Arthur D. Little, Inc. (1994). *Managing organizational change: How leading organizations are meeting the challenge*. Cambridge, MA: Author.

Bass, B. M. (1985). *Leadership and performance beyond expectations*. New York: Free Press.

Betz, F. (1987). *Managing technology: Competing through new ventures, innovation, and corporate research*. Englewood Cliffs, NJ: Prentice Hall.

Bounds, G., Yorks, L., Adams, M., & Ranney, G. (1994). *Beyond total quality management: Toward the emerging paradigm*. New York: McGraw-Hill.

Bowles, J., & Hammond, J. (1991). *Beyond quality: New standards of total performance that can change the future of corporate America*. New York: Berkeley.

Cascio, W. F. (1995). Whither industrial and organizational psychology in a changing world of work? *American Psychologist, 50,* 928-939.

Champy, J. (1995). *Reengineering management*. New York: Harper.

Chemers, M. M., Oskamp, S., & Costanzo, M. A. (Eds.). (1995). *Diversity in organizations*. Thousand Oaks, CA: Sage.

Cox, T. (1993). *Cultural diversity in organizations: Theory, research, and practice*. San Francisco, CA: Berret-Koehler.

Crosby, P. B. (1996). *Quality is still free*. New York: McGraw-Hill.

Cross, E., Katz, J., Miller, F., & Seashore, E. (Eds.). (1994). *The promise of diversity*. New York: Irwin.

Deal, T. E., & Kennedy, A. A. (1982). *Corporate culture: The rites and rituals of corporate life*. Reading, MA: Addison-Wesley.

Fiske, S., & Taylor, S. (1991). *Social cognition* (2nd ed.). New York: McGraw-Hill.

Frost, P. J., & Moore, L. (Eds.). (1991). *Reframing organizational culture*. Newbury Park, CA: Sage.

George, S., & Weimerskirch, A. (1994). *Total quality management: Techniques proven at today's most successful companies*. New York: John Wiley.

Grimsley, K. D. (1996, May 26). Why men stay silent: Fear of retaliation fostered abusive atmosphere, Mitsubishi workers say. *Washington Post,* pp. H1, H7.

Hammer, M., & Champy, J. (1993). *Reengineering the corporation*. New York: Harper Business.

Harré, R. (1993). *Social being* (2nd ed.). Oxford, UK: Blackwell.

Harris, P. R., & Moran, R. T. (1991). *Managing cultural differences*. Houston, TX: Gulph.

Hersey, P., & Blanchard, K. H. (1993). *Management of organizational behavior* (6th ed.). Englewood Cliffs, NJ: Prentice Hall.

Hirschman, A. O. (1984). *Getting ahead collectively: Grassroots experiences in Latin America*. New York: Pergamon.

Hradesky, J. L. (1995). *Total quality management handbook*. New York: McGraw-Hill.

Hunt, J. G. (1991). *Leadership: A new synthesis*. Newbury Park, CA: Sage.

Juran, J. M., & Gryna, F. M. (Eds.). (1988). *Juran's quality control handbook* (4th ed.). New York: McGraw-Hill.

Kaufman, B. E., & Kleiner, M. M. (Eds.). (1993). *Employee representation: Alternatives and future directions*. Madison, WI: Industrial Relations Research Association.

McInerney, F., & White, S. (1995). *The total quality corporation: How 10 major companies turned quality and environmental challenges to competitive advantage in the 1990s*. New York: Truman.

McWhinney, W. (1992). *Paths of change: Strategic choices for organizations and society.* Newbury Park, CA: Sage.

Moghaddam, F. M. (1990). Modulative and generative orientations in psychology: Implications for psychology in the Three Worlds. *Journal of Social Issues, 46*(3), 21-41.

Moghaddam, F. M. (1997). *The specialized society: The plight of the individual in an age of individualism.* New York: Praeger.

Moghaddam, F. M., & Crystal, D. (in press). Revolutions, Samurai, and reductons: Change and continuity in Iran and Japan. *Journal of Political Psychology.*

Moghaddam, F. M., & Harré, R. (1995, September). *Psychological limitations to political revolutions: An application of social reducton theory.* Paper presented at the International Congress on the Occasion of the 225th Birthday of F. Hegel, Hegel Institute, Berlin.

Moghaddam, F. M., Taylor, D. M., & Wright, D. M. (1993). *Social psychology in cross-cultural perspective.* New York: Praeger.

Moore, T. S. (1996). *The disposable workforce: Worker displacement and employee instability in America.* New York: de Gruyter & Walter.

Mowdy, R. T., & Sutton, R. I. (1993). Organizational behavior: Linking individuals and groups to organizational contexts. *Annual Review of Psychology, 44,* 195-229.

Newstrom, J. W., & Davis, K. (1993). *Organizational behavior: Human behavior and work* (9th ed.). New York: McGraw-Hill.

Ormerod, P. (1994). *The death of economics.* London, UK: Faber & Faber.

Ott, J. S. (1989). *The organizational culture perspective.* Pacific Grove, CA: Brooks/Cole.

Powell, G. N. (1993). *Women and men in management* (2nd ed.). Newbury Park, CA: Sage.

Salisbury, H. E. (1992). *The new emperors: China in the era of Mao and Deng.* New York: Avon.

Schein, E. H. (1985). *Organizational culture and leadership.* San Francisco: Jossey-Bass.

Schein, E. H. (1992). *Organizational culture and leadership* (2nd ed.). San Francisco: Jossey-Bass.

Sears, D. O. (1988). Symbolic racism. In P. A. Katz & D. A. Taylor (Eds.), *Eliminating racism: Profiles in controversy* (pp. 53-84). New York: Plenum.

Sonnert, G., & Holton, G. (1995). *Gender differences in science careers: The project access study.* New Brunswick, NJ: Rutgers University Press.

Stevenson, W. B., & Gilly, M. C. (1991). Information processing and problem solving: The migration of problems through formal positions and networks of ties. *Academy of Management Journal, 34,* 918-928.

Taylor, D. M., & Moghaddam, F. M. (1987). *Theories of intergroup relations: International social psychological perspectives.* New York: Praeger.

Taylor, D. M., & Moghaddam, F. M. (1994). *Theories of intergroup relations: International social psychological perspectives* (2nd ed.). New York: Praeger.

Thomas, B. (1995). *The human dimension of quality.* New York: McGraw-Hill.

Thomas, R. R. (1991). *Beyond race and gender: Unleashing the power of your total workforce by managing diversity.* New York: AMACOM.

Verma, A., & Cutcher-Gershenfeld, J. (1993). Joint governance in the workplace: Beyond union-management cooperation and worker participation. In B. E. Kaufman & M. M. Kleiner (Eds.), *Employee representation: Alternatives and future directions* (pp. 197-234). Madison, WI: Industrial Relations Research Association.

Yang, M. M. (1994). *Gifts, favors, and banquets: The art of social relationships in China.* Ithaca, NY: Cornell University Press.

PART II

INTERPERSONAL INTERACTIONS WITHIN CROSS-CULTURAL GROUPS

4

Societal Values, Social Interpretation, and Multinational Teams

MARTHA MAZNEVSKI
MARK F. PETERSON

Multinational executive teams are coming of age. The days are passing when major multinational corporations (MNCs) such as General Electric or Matsushita, could operate complex, dynamic industries from the unambiguous cultural base of a home country. The traditional practice of organizations such as Philips or Unilever, of simplifying multinational relations by radically separating national organizations from one another, is becoming quite limiting. Resources are likely to flow toward MNCs that know when and how to use multicultural teams as business conditions require them (Bartlett & Ghoshal, 1995).

Multinational executive groups present an especially important paradox for managers. Multinational teams offer the potential for more innovative and higher-quality solutions to global business problems than do monocultural teams. They bring together people having information about different pieces of a multinational corporation's world. They also provide different frames of reference for projecting potential future scenarios for an MNC. The dynamism of multicultural group processes also forces an immediate awareness of different viewpoints. Multicultural teams give immediacy to the need to reconcile otherwise latent differences in viewpoint and values that ultimately need to be addressed in any MNC.

Paradoxically, multinational executive teams also present challenges to effective group interaction that can vitiate their potential advantages. The same cultural differences that offer potential for high performance also create different expectations for group processes (Maznevski, 1995). Members from different cultures will notice different pieces of the global picture and interpret them differently, leading to disagreements about what the MNC's world is "really" like. The ability of managers who have varied backgrounds to project different scenarios onto an unknown future means that alternative managerial choices can be evaluated in radically conflicting ways. Lack of the needed consensus to move from analysis to action can extend analysis to the point where no action is taken. More often than not, multicultural teams do not achieve their potential due to these difficulties in integration.

To improve effective interaction in multicultural groups, members and managers need to answer two questions. First, when does culture influence the group? And second, how should cultural differences be managed when they do affect the group? The two questions are closely intertwined. To achieve high performance, members need a knowledge base to anticipate likely differences and similarities among themselves. They need to use the similarities to bridge the differences. They need to learn from the available multiple perspectives.

This chapter explores these two questions in an attempt to provide assistance to multicultural teams. We will begin by casting team interactions as a process of making sense of events that members notice, interpret, and respond to. Next, we will outline how the elements of a situation systematically evoke predictable interpretations and responses from work group members in ways influenced by culture. Finally, we will outline how this information can be used to understand and improve interactions in multicultural work groups.

Team Processes as Event Management

What is the purpose of a multinational team? What is its job? To most managers, and, indeed, management researchers, the answer seems simple and unambiguous—enough so that our tendency is to jump to the matter of how to achieve the team's purpose rather than to examine what the team is about in the first place. Even the definition and approach to understanding a team in an organization differ, however, from one culture to another. The United States and Canada use a rhetoric consistent with a "mastery" orientation (Lane, DiStefano, & Maznevski, 1997). Managers from these countries are accustomed to a language of "decision making." Their ideal is to be clear, firm, and concise. Key events are noted. Problems are formulated. Situations are assessed. Alternatives are generated. Decisions are made. Actions are taken. But, the reality they experience does not correspond fully to this decisive rhetoric. The rhetoric of managerial choice serves as a mask over uncertainty to provide confidence in the legitimacy of managers' actions. The reality they experience is the struggle to determine what to notice and how to make sense of what is noticed.

In other parts of the world, the rhetoric of social process can be quite different from that typical of North America. The centrality of "decision" and "choice" is replaced in the Arab world and in much of Latin America by a language of relationships and trust. In these cultures, a team's goal may be to develop trusting relationships among members, so that action can be taken later that is unquestioned and to which everyone is committed. In Japan, a team serves to develop and reinforce understanding among members. Trust is assumed by virtue of membership in the same group, and decisions are reached indirectly in interactions that go far beyond the team itself. Consequently, reaching a point where a choice can be announced, or where a new level of trust is established, or where better understanding is achieved, are three different resolutions of a multicultural team process that differ in importance by culture.

A basic point of departure for analyzing multicultural teams, therefore, cannot be one that is overly determined by the culturally rooted rhetoric typical of a single part of the world. We must develop a foundation that can be used to treat these three alternative resolutions, and others as well, as special cases. To do so, we propose that a universal quality of human beings in social situations is that they seek to make sense of a myriad of events by linking them to their prior experiences.

Hence, our first step in analyzing multicultural executive teams is to abandon the position that they are fundamentally decision-making groups. Instead, we will treat them as groups that seek to make sense of various work-related events. The event management approach we are taking (Smith & Peterson, 1988) links closely to analyses of sense making and behavior in organizations (Weick, 1995).

An event can be defined as "a partially abstracted bit of social reality that serves as a unit of information processing, interpretation, or meaning constructed by a social actor in interaction with other social actors" (Peterson, 1993, p. 7). Managers notice events and attach meaning to them, then respond to events based on their interpretation. Always and everywhere, managers notice some of what is happening around them and try to make sense of it. Sometimes, and in some places, managers announce decisions or the sense they are making by taking some kind of clear-cut action.

The processes of noticing, interpreting, and responding to events are all influenced by an individual's past experiences as well as by elements of the situation itself. Past experiences are categorized and encoded into cognitive structures within the individual; these structures can be referred to as "schemas." Codified responses to schemas are referred to as "scripts" (Sims & Gioia, 1986).

For example, a Scandinavian member of a multinational executive team may have had experiences at an earlier career stage in "self-managed teams" in which all members were of equal status and made decisions by consensus. If the group was effective, then the member is likely to have a schema relating to "effective work group" that includes elements of equal status and consensus decision making. Events that conform to or contradict this schema are likely to be noticed and interpreted as good in the former case and bad in the latter. One day, our hypothetical Scandinavian may notice the event of all group members sitting together at a table. This event might be initially identified as a "group meeting," because it conforms with group meetings the individual has experienced in the past. Its interpretation may evoke a set of scripts, including a norm to promote equal time talking for each member, calling for a vote to determine the level of consensus, or pointing out when one member seems to be assuming a higher status than others. On the other hand, if this same member notices two members of the work group chatting in the corridor, the event is unlikely to be placed in the category of "group meeting" and the related scripts will not be elicited.

The concept of organization team implies a bounded set of people working together to contribute something to other parties in the organization. This concept implies that teams must carry out two kinds of functions (Cartwright & Zander, 1968). In organizational teams, members must not only make sense of, and respond to, events in ways that promote progress in the task they are undertaking on behalf of outside parties. They must also notice, interpret, and respond to events as they have implications for the group's own internal processes. If a team's mandate is to plan and implement a reorganization of a business unit, members are likely to take note of events that happen within the unit, such as work processes that seem to be especially effective or ineffective. But they may also shift focus from the implications their actions have for accomplishing their task to the level of consensus and conflict among members of their own team.

Once these events are noticed, members must interpret them, or give meaning to them. They may turn to a broad array of sources to gain this meaning, including their own experiences, other team members, manuals and procedures, historical precedent, common belief, external reference sources, superiors, friends, and so on. The interpretation that is finally given to an event will influence how people respond to it, and whether it evokes a standardized script or a problem-solving process initiating a creatively new course of action.

The operation of schemas and scripts restricts the range of probable interpretations and behaviors a multinational team member will engage in, given a specific situation. Although this restriction may not result in optimal responses in all situations, it expedites the process of giving meaning to events. Given the costs of thorough analysis (March & Simon, 1958), it is not surprising that groups accept the same bounded rationality that individuals accept. It is also important to note the iterative and social nature of event management. When any person acts, that action changes the situation and presents a new situation for that person and others to notice, interpret, and respond to.

Clearly, predicting and explaining which events are noticed and how they are given meaning in work groups is important to understanding group processes and effectiveness in those groups. In the next section, we will show how culture systematically influences the process of noticing, interpreting, and responding to events.

Culture's Influence on Event Management

We use the word *culture* here to represent a set of assumptions and deep-level values concerning relationships among humans and between humans and their environment, shared by an identifiable group of people (Kluckhohn & Strodtbeck, 1961; Maznevski & DiStefano, 1995; Smith & Peterson, 1995). Cultural assumptions and values begin to be learned very early in life, as we are socialized into families and institutions within a particular society. Consequently, culture presents a very deep, usually subconscious, influence on individual values and social behaviors.

According to Kluckhohn and Strodtbeck (1961), there are five basic questions to which each society (group of people) must develop common answers to interact effectively. Each of these questions has a limited set of answers, and the configuration of answers developed by each society describes the main dimensions of its culture. Furthermore, although societies generally have a preference for one solution to each answer, all solutions exist in all cultures, and some may be equal to or almost as strong as the "primary" one. The five basic questions are the following:

1. What is our relation to nature?
2. What is our orientation to time?
3. What do we assume is the basic nature of humans?
4. What are the most essential relationships among people?
5. What is our preferred mode of activity?

These questions will be elaborated on next (see also Lane et al., 1997).

Culture is far from the only influence on behavior, and individual members of a culture certainly do not always reflect the norms of the culture, either in values or behavior. Culture is particularly relevant, however, to understanding effectiveness in multinational work groups for two reasons. First, given little or no other information about an individual's values and behavior, culture provides a good first interpretation of that person. In the absence of other information, one is likely to assume another group member is just like oneself. If the other group member is from another culture, though, this assumption is less likely to be true than if the person is from the same culture. Having an understanding of the other member's cultural background provides a set of more realistic expectations about what may be similar and different, and these expectations can guide interactions with the other member. Second, cultural assumptions and values describe the nature of relationships between people and their environment and among people themselves. Clearly the work performed by multinational teams requires interaction among members and with the environment. Whatever an individual's personality, then, culture's influence will be strongest in precisely the type of situations presented to multicultural executive teams.

Culture influences all aspects of the event management process. It affects what events are noticed and the initial schemas and scripts into which they are placed. Culture affects the processes of individual deliberation and social discussion through which events are more fully interpreted. It also affects preferences for responding and the criteria used to evaluate possible responses. In organizational team settings, members must make sense of and respond to events with a view toward their implications for both the group's task and the group's own internal processes. Not only does culture influence which events will be noticed, but it also influences whether members are prone to recognize an event's task-related implications, process-related implications, or both. The sources used to develop an interpretation of the event are also culturally influenced (Smith & Peterson, 1995), as are the types of task- and process-related responses that are developed and implemented (Smith & Peterson, 1988).

In the following sections we will outline the potential implications of each of Kluckhohn and Strodtbeck's value orientations for noticing, interpreting, and responding to events in multinational teams. We will also identify the different types of contributions members socialized within the different cultural orientations can be expected to make. This discussion is summarized in Table 4.1. A later section will address the problems posed by trying to integrate people with different perspectives into a single team.

Relation to Nature

Human societies prefer one of three basic relationships with nature: mastery, subjugation, or harmony. In a mastery-oriented culture, it is considered normal and even desirable for humans to control nature. Tool and technology development is a high priority, and technology is used to alter or control the environment. In a subjugation-oriented culture, people tend to accept a predestined overall plan, dictated either by nature itself or by some supernatural force. Individuals' challenge is to work with this greater plan to try and achieve the "will" of the plan.

(text continues on page 72)

Table 4.1
Cultural Orientations and Their Effects on the Event Management Process and Potential Contributions of Members in Multicultural Teams

				Event Management Process		
Orientation	*Variation*	*Assumption*	*What is Noticed*	*Sources for Interpretation*	*Preferred Response*	*Potential Contributions*
Relation to nature	Mastery	Control nature and environment	Events implying loss of control	Control procedures, problem-solving experts	Active interventions designed to increase control	Identify and implement potential interventions to improve
	Subjugation	Controlled by nature or supernatural	Unavoidable constraints	Cultural norms, supernatural	No attempt to change the unchangeable, "do one's best" to address the rest	Prevent wasted effort at attempting to change relatively fixed constraints
	Harmony	Balance relations among elements of environment, including self	Imbalances in organizational systems	Sources with holistic approaches	Restore and maintain harmony and balance	Identify and implement whole system, synergistic approaches

Time	Past	Respect for past and tradition	Discrepancies with past and tradition	Traditions, stories, records	Consistent with past practice	Identify similarities between past and current situations; learn from past
	Present	Today's needs most important, also short-term future	Failure to address immediate concerns	Current data, short-term projections	Address immediate criteria, little concern for past or future	Promote sense of urgency, address immediate threats and opportunities
	Future	Focus on long-term future	Potential long-term implications	Forecasts of trends into future	Sacrifice today for long-term future benefits	Draw attention to events with long-term implications, incorporate into current planning and action
Nature of humans[a]	Evil	Humans' basic nature is evil, harmful acts are normal and expected	Harmful and untrustworthy behavior, situations with potential for such behavior	Those harmed by an action, sources designed to prevent harm (e.g., legal and corporate control systems)	Little or no trust until relationship well established; continual monitoring	Monitor people and behavior, prevent team/company from being taken advantage of
	Good	Humans' basic nature is good, harmful acts are anomalies	Helpful and trustworthy behavior	For harmful events—external situational explanations	Trust, little monitoring	Encourage trusting environment within group; encourage information sharing, nonpersonal explanations

Table 4.1
Continued

					Event Management Process		
Orientation	Variation	Assumption	What is Noticed		Sources for Interpretation	Preferred Response	Potential Contributions
Relation-ships among people	Individualistic	Responsibility to and for self, immediate family	Will not notice those who do not make themselves noticed explicitly		Topic experts, regardless of group membership or status	Preserve own self-interests first	Expect self and others to contribute fully, uniquely, and in important ways
	Collective	Responsible to and for larger group, for example, extended family, peer group	Whether others respect lateral group relations		Sources that would not cause loss of face for anyone	Preserve interests of group, if necessary at expense of own self-interests	Maintain group relations, promote active listening
	Hierarchical	Unequal distribution of power and responsibility, those higher have power over and responsibility for those lower	Whether deference is offered to senior people, offered by junior people		Supervisors, senior team members, those with high status	Senior members to control group; junior members to obey others in group	Make good use of senior members', supervisors', and outside experts' knowledge and experience

Mode of activity					
Doing-achieving	Constantly strive to achieve goals and continually engage in productive work; live to work	Discrepancies between plan and actual	Anything that provides satisfactory, immediate meaning; may skip explicit interpretation	Immediate action to achieve goal as quickly as possible	Set goals; ensure goals are achieved
Being-feeling	Do what you want when you want; work to live	Feelings, intuitions at least as much as external events	Own and others' intuitions, feelings; trusted sources	Response that feels right, when time is right	Maintain group relations, draw attention to affective information
Thinking-reflecting	Rational, developmental approach; think through everything carefully	Evidence that plans have or have not been thought through carefully	Wide variety of sources rationally justified; extensive interpretation	Rational response, may be delayed due to interpretation	Ensure multiple analyses and explanations are considered

a. A third variation is "mixed," which assumes humans' nature is a mixture of good and evil. A fourth variation is "neutral," which assumes that humans' nature is neither good nor evil and behavioral tendencies are determined by the environment. Their implications can be seen as a combination of those outlined for "good" and "evil" here.

People accept the fact, however, that the plan may not always be understood and events may not progress as anticipated. In a harmony-oriented culture, people assume that humans are only one element of a much larger, interconnected system, and that it is humans' duty to work within and help maintain the balance of that system.

Group members' beliefs about society's relation to nature influences what events they notice and the schemas to which events are initially attached. For example, a mastery-oriented member may be quick to notice a slow-down in sales and take it as evidence that current procedures are not accomplishing their purpose of encouraging customers to buy the firm's products. A subjugation- oriented member may not notice this slow-down as an event at all, but may attend instead to the types of constraints preventing sales from happening. A member from a harmony-oriented culture may not notice the slow-down in itself, but may see imbalances in the economic and organizational system that could lead to difficulties for the firm. Interestingly, the initial classification of events as "threats" or "opportunities," which is central to much management decision theory (Cohen, March, & Olsen, 1972; Jackson & Dutton, 1988; Nutt, 1984) reflects the mastery-oriented culture of U.S. business at the point of initial noticing.

In a parallel way, relation to nature influences where events are initially linked to process-related schemas. Members from mastery-oriented cultures are likely to note whether or not members are taking control of processes and situations adequately, whereas members from harmony-oriented cultures will notice when the balance of forces and processes in the group is not being maintained. Members from subjugation-oriented cultures will tend to notice whether members are "tempting fate" by planning or attempting to control too much.

To more fully interpret, or draw meaning from, these events, members of different cultures will turn to different sources of information. Members from mastery-oriented cultures will give most credence to sources such as standard control procedures, and staff experts or MNC members (including themselves) with direct experience who are likely to contribute information and expertise to diagnosing the problem and proposing interventions to resolve it. Members from subjugation-oriented cultures will draw on cultural norms supported by stories having broad scope to indicate the indeterminacy of actions and the risks of wasting resources while trying to change the unchangeable. Members from harmony-oriented cultures are more likely to turn to those who specialize in understanding the connections among parts and how they come together to make a whole system, to develop an interpretation of a situation that has been noticed.

Finally, the types of criteria for evaluating action alternatives that are preferred by members of the three types of cultures will be different. Members of mastery cultures are likely to insist on active interventions to resolve the immediate problem, using the members as tools to fix it. Members of subjugation cultures, on the other hand, are more likely to identify elements of the situation that are fixed constraints or unpredictable, and will resist any attempt to change those elements. Members of harmony cultures will seek responses that maintain the balance or return a system to its balance. Contrary to a mastery-oriented approach, these responses are as likely to incorporate ceasing an intervention as they are to recommend introducing one, and any intervention introduced will be systemwide.

Each of these responses has the potential to contribute in different ways, both to promoting task accomplishment and to facilitating group process.

Members of each of the three cultures, then, can make contributions to the effectiveness of a multinational team. A member from a mastery culture can identify the potential of events to be threats or opportunities, and can help extend diagnosis until a constructive line of action is agreed on. The subjugation-oriented member can influence and focus the team's attention by separating events likely to be capable of influence from those best treated as fixed constraints, and can bring closure by ending expenditure of time and resources to analyze the unchangeable or unpredictable. A harmony-oriented team member will help the team to maintain a view of the larger picture and to identify inconsistencies in the group or the organization before they cause problems, and can also point to solutions that bring elements of the firm's system together in synergistic ways.

Orientation to Time

Kluckhohn and Strodtbeck (1961) suggest that societies tend to have one of three types of orientations toward time. Past-oriented societies look to tradition and precedent to give meaning to events. They notice whether things are the same or different from past years or generations, and use the past as a guide to anticipating the future unfolding of present events. Present-oriented societies are more concerned about the here-and-now, and perhaps the immediate future. Problems tend to be resolved in a short time, but with little regard for the long-term future implications. Future-oriented societies look to the distant future, and are willing to sacrifice benefits in the present for potential future gains.

A member's orientation to time affects what events that person notices and whether the noticed events are viewed as having task implications, process implications, or both. For example, suppose the crew on a production line reports that, according to records and manufacturers' recommendations, maintenance on a key machine is due to be conducted. A past-oriented member may take note of that report if, in the past, maintenance has been conducted according to a schedule. A present-oriented member may disregard the report, and may not notice the need for maintenance until the machine shows signs of breaking down. A future-oriented member may notice the report because of its potential implications for future performance of the machine.

Likewise, time orientation influences whether events having process-related implications are noticed. For example, if a new leader is assigned to the group, past-oriented members are likely to notice whether he or she uses procedures the group has used in the past. Present-oriented members may not notice if traditional procedures are used, but are likely to notice whether the agenda addresses immediate issues in a timely way. Future-oriented members, though, are more likely to notice whether discussion of future implications of issues is included in meetings.

In interpreting the meaning of events that have been noticed, members of the team with different time orientations will go to different sources of information. Past-oriented members will look toward traditions, stories, records, and codified procedures that have served the firm well in the past. Present-oriented members will examine current data on the group, the firm, and its environment, whereas future-oriented members are likely to examine historical trends and try to forecast these trends into the future. For example, in the maintenance example given previously, members with a past orientation may look to records and past practices that suggest maintenance should always be conducted at this time. Those with a future orientation may also see a need for maintenance, not because it is traditionally conducted at this point but because maintenance now will prevent future breakdowns. Members with a present orientation, scanning current production figures, are less likely to discern the immediate need for maintenance.

As suggested by the preceding paragraphs, time orientation will also affect how team members respond to events they notice and interpret. Again following the maintenance example, a past-oriented member will want to respond by conducting standard maintenance as it has been conducted in the past. A future-oriented member will also respond by conducting maintenance, but is more likely to examine the machine's current and expected performance and to advocate maintenance that will lead to continued or enhanced performance. A present-oriented member, though, may not respond at all until the machine shows signs of disrupting production schedules, and then will respond immediately.

Members with all orientations to time can contribute significantly to the work and process of a multinational team. The expected contribution of a member whose socialization has been within a past-oriented culture will be to influence the team by directing attention to similarity between the present situation and those experienced in the past, and to draw on cultural norms and traditions that provide an elaborated combination of tacit understanding and formal plans for interpreting and handling present situations. A member from a present-oriented culture will direct the team to address immediate threats and opportunities, draw selectively on multiple viewpoints, and instill in the group a sense of urgency to bring closure while handling the immediate implications of recent events. A member who has been socialized in a future- oriented culture can be expected to direct the team's attention toward aspects of their situation that pose no immediate threat, but that might be a prelude to longer-term threats or opportunities. He or she will suggest risk analysis designed to anticipate long-term developments of present situations, and will encourage the group to engage in thorough analysis to avoid potential long-term side effects of solutions to immediate problems.

Nature of Humans

Societies differ in their tendency to assume whether the basic nature of humans is good, evil, neutral, or mixed. In addition, the basic nature of humans may be seen as changeable or unchangeable—that is, even though people are born essentially bad, some cultures believe they can change to become essentially good (and vice versa), while other cultures do not. If humans are assumed to be basically good, then people are generally trusted, unless specific evidence suggests they should not be.

Acts that harm others, such as stealing, are seen as anomalies and elicited by the situation, not inherent in the person. If humans are assumed to be basically evil, then people tend not to trust each other unless they have specific evidence that another can be trusted (this evidence can take the form of common subgroup membership, such as being an immediate family member). In such cultures, it is assumed that humans have an inherent tendency to engage in harmful acts, such as corruption and stealing, although it is generally recognized that, if they are "socialized properly," people can overcome this tendency in their actual behavior, if not in their thoughts. Cultures that assume human nature is neutral see humans as being born with a "blank slate," and believe that the environment determines whether humans become good or evil in their nature. Finally, some cultures assume that some people are inherently good while others are inherently bad, or that all people have a mix of good and bad tendencies.

Multinational team members' assumptions about human nature influence what they notice, both in terms of the group's task and its internal processes. Members of cultures that assume human nature is evil tend to monitor others' behavior constantly so they can "catch" (i.e., notice) malicious acts as soon as possible. They also tend to monitor situations to ensure that there is little temptation or ability for others to engage in harmful acts. Members of cultures that assume human nature is essentially good, however, are less likely to monitor such situations closely. Members from the former cultures, therefore, will probably notice events that have the potential to harm the firm or team members before those from the latter cultures do. As an example, assume that two firms form a joint venture, one from a culture assuming human nature is good and the other from a culture assuming human nature is evil. If the joint venture managers assign someone to conduct a market analysis, and the analysis is not completed on time, managers from the first parent company may notice that market conditions changed during the assigned writing of the report (which would cause the analysis to take longer), whereas managers from the second parent company may notice that the marketing manager has been contacting someone from a strong competitor. In both cases, managers notice something about the "late analysis" situation, but what is salient to each is different. Furthermore, members from the culture assuming humans are essentially bad may notice the others' reluctance to attribute personal motives to the marketing analyst, and may begin to suspect ulterior motives on the part of the other managers.

Members from the two types of cultures will also draw on different sources to interpret what they notice, and will interpret the events differently. In both cases, team members are most likely to depend on information sources they expect will confirm their assumption. Members socialized in cultures assuming human nature is evil will go to those who have been harmed by the event and document their testimony, and will consult sources that can support the harmful intentions of those involved in the event. Members socialized in cultures assuming human nature is good, if they even notice the "harmful" event, are more likely to turn to situational sources and explanations.

Members' responses to the events will also vary depending on their assumptions about human nature. Those from cultures assuming human nature is evil will respond by increasing surveillance and control systems. In the example described previously, they may ask for more frequent updates from the truant marketing analyst or appoint trusted coworkers to work with—and monitor—the analyst. In future situations where an external person is hired to do work for the joint venture, they may insist on a detailed contract with expectations and penalties outlined explicitly. Managers from cultures assuming human nature is essentially good may not respond actively to the event of the late report at first. If they do respond, they will most likely ask the analyst what he or she needs to facilitate the report's completion. Within the group, those who are socialized to believe that humans are essentially bad are less likely to trust other members with confidential information or material until the group has worked together effectively for a period of time.

Members of both types of cultures can make important contributions to the externally oriented work and internal processes of a multinational team. Those who have been socialized in a nontrusting culture can be expected to monitor the motives of those important to the group's work and those within the group, and to withhold confidential information until trust is earned, preventing the team or the firm from being taken advantage of by those who may thwart its purposes. This focus on others' malicious motives, which can become unproductive to the team if taken to an extreme, can be tempered by members socialized in trusting cultures. The latter group of people can encourage and reinforce a trusting atmosphere within the team by making all personally held information and opinions available to all members, thus making full and effective use of sources of meaning, and by taking the contributions of all members at face value as reflecting an effort at problem solving rather than as politicking for personal payoffs. They can also be expected to look for situational and more complete explanations for negative events.

Relations Among People

Relationships among people can be described by three basic patterns. If a society's members view their primary responsibility as for and to themselves individually, with this responsibility perhaps including the nuclear family, then the relationships are described as individualistic. Societies that see their primary responsibility for and to a much larger group, such as an extended family or peer group, are called collective. Finally, in some societies, relationships among people are arranged in a hierarchical fashion, such that those higher in the hierarchy have responsibility for those below them, while those lower in the hierarchy have a duty to obey those above them. A hierarchical orientation can be found in combination with either an individualistic or collective one; the levels of power can be held by individuals or by groups.

The implications of this orientation tend to be greatest for processes within the team itself. For example, the team may discuss something of controversy among the group. Members socialized in individualistic cultures will expect each member to be responsible for putting forth his or her own ideas, and will not notice members who sit silently or avoid open conflict. Members from collective cultures tend to engage in "face-saving," or ensuring that others are not offended in group settings. Thus, they are more likely to notice when members are being offensive or confrontational to each other. People from hierarchical cultures will be sensitive to hierarchy within the group, and will notice whether proper deference is being offered to the senior members of the team.

These orientations also affect which relationship-oriented aspects of organizational tasks will be noticed by different members of multinational teams. For example, in assigning responsibility for a product design flaw, members of individualistic cultures will notice the skills and actions of the designers themselves. Members of collective cultures may notice the dynamics within the design group, and members of hierarchical cultures will take note of the design team's relationship with its senior members and supervising managers.

The relationship orientation clearly influences the sources drawn on by different team members when interpreting events. Members of hierarchical cultures are most likely to go to their supervisors or senior members of the team or organization when trying to understand events. Members of individualistic cultures will go to the person or source considered most expert in the situation, disregarding lines of hierarchy or group membership. Members of collective cultures will go to others for information only if it causes neither party to lose face. If asking a question implies either that the asker should have known the answer him- or herself, or that the responder should have given the information in the first place without being asked, then the question will not be asked directly. Instead, indirect means will be used or other sources will be referred to. In this way, no one is offended and group harmony is maintained.

Members of multinational teams also will respond to events in ways consistent with their relationship orientations. Returning to the example of the group discussion, members of individualistic cultures can be expected to respond to their understanding of the dynamics in a way that ensures that their own self-interests are preserved. They will continue to present their own arguments and directly counter those of others. Members of collective cultures will not volunteer information that might contradict the interests of other group members or of the group as a whole. Those from hierarchical cultures, if they perceive themselves as having a relatively low status within the group, will respond by waiting until their opinions have been asked for, and then will offer them only deferentially. If they perceive themselves as having high status within the group, they will try to control the meeting. Note that these patterns can be self-reinforcing. The individualistic members may openly present their views without being contradicted by collective members (who may be offended and hurt by the presentation) or by those of lower status among hierarchical members. This vicious circle can be overcome, however, if members are aware of these differences and manage them deliberately to ensure all contributions are heard.

Members from each of the different orientations to human relationships can make important contributions to a multinational team. A member whose socialization has been within an individualistic culture will make full use of his or her own background to give meaning to events, and will expect other members to fully use theirs. A member from a collectivist culture will tend to listen carefully to other group members, making full use of their contributions, and will expect other group members to seek one another's ideas. Both individualistic and collective members can ensure that contributions from lower-status team members and external information sources can be heard. Finally, a member whose socialization has been within a hierarchical culture will direct the group's attention to initiatives and contributions from senior organization members outside the group, and to those of any team member whose experience or background has resulted in appointment as team leader, and will personally make most use of any official mandates or informally communicated purposes of senior organization members outside the group, or of guidance from the team leader.

Mode of Activity

There are three basic modes of activity that are characteristic of different cultures. In a doing-achieving society, the basic mode of activity is incessant striving toward specific goals and accomplishments. It is assumed that human nature is to be engaged in productive work, and that life gains meaning from this work. In these societies, leisure activities are undertaken, but are either seen as necessary to make one more productive in the long run or as a means to accomplish goals in themselves. In a being-feeling culture, people generally see work as secondary to living. The approach to activity is to do what you want, when you want. This does not mean that work does not get accomplished; indeed, when the time is "right" to work, nothing else takes priority. Finally, in thinking-reflecting cultures, members prefer to take a more rational and developmental approach to activity. Everything is thought through as carefully as possible, and people resist jumping into activities the implications of which have not yet been considered.

In work groups, the mode-of-activity dimension relates most strongly to how people approach the group's processes and develop task strategies. First, members of each culture will notice the events most salient to their activity orientation. For example, suppose a multicultural team is responsible for overall profits of a group of subsidiaries, and the forecasts for the current time period suggest profits will be lower than expected by headquarters. Members from doing-achieving cultures will immediately notice the mismatch between what is forecast and what is expected, and will jump quickly to interpreting and responding to the event. Those from being-feeling cultures may not notice the event, but even if they do, they may not feel a need to understand and respond to it immediately. Team members from thinking-reflecting cultures may notice the event, then scan the environment to see if other events are also worthy of note, before moving to interpretation.

The interpretation phase will be approached very differently by members of the different types of cultures. Those from doing-achieving cultures will turn to close sources that can provide satisfactory (if not optimum) immediate interpretations, and will move rapidly to responding. They may even skip explicit interpreting, instead relying on well-rehearsed scripts for responding to categories of events. Members from being-feeling cultures are more likely to draw on sources they intuitively feel will help in the interpretation. These sources must be trusted at a deep level, and are at least as likely to relate to affective interpretations as they are to cognitive ones. Those from thinking-reflecting cultures will tend to engage in extensive interpretation, going to a wide variety of sources that can be rationally justified, and seeking many different types of explanations for the event. In fact, the interpretation process may continue indefinitely.

Likewise, responses from members of the three types of cultures will be different in predictable ways. Members of doing-achieving cultures will respond with immediate interventions to achieve specific goals, whereas those from being-feeling cultures will respond when "the time is right" in a way that "feels right," and those from thinking cultures will respond in a careful, measured manner and only after extensive interpretation. In the example of forecasted profits potentially not meeting expected profits, members from doing-achieving cultures can be expected to implement immediately cost-cutting measures, revenue-enhancing measures, or both. Team members from being-feeling cultures are more likely to look at the larger situation, and respond actively only if their intuition and experience suggest specific changes should be made. Finally, members from thinking-reflecting cultures will carefully examine all contributions to both revenue and costs, as well as the larger economic situation and past and expected changes in that situation, before deciding first whether or not to intervene, and second, what type of intervention would be best.

All of these perspectives are valuable to multinational organizations. Members socialized in doing-achieving cultures can be expected to ensure, quite simply, that the team gets things accomplished in a timely way. Those socialized in being-feeling cultures can often be counted on to promote the health of the group itself, for example, by cutting short discussion when it is no longer productive, or moving laterally to new topics and thus inducing creativity in the group. And members socialized in thinking-reflecting cultures will ensure that responses are not made without adequate interpretation, thus preventing the group from engaging in needless activity or jumping to solutions that will create more problems, in the long run, than they solve.

Culture's influence on event management is profound. Multicultural teams must somehow address the fact that different members will notice, interpret, and respond to events differently. In groups having high variability in event management, a broader range of information is likely to be noticed. Varied schemas will link this information within a larger number of alternative conditions. A wide spectrum of scripts will offer more potential future scenarios of implications and actions for innovation and creative responses. But the different responses, in themselves, are likely to create conflicts in the group because consensus on responses is difficult to achieve. Furthermore, team members may notice and interpret actions of other members themselves as events that pose hindrances to effectiveness. How is a multicultural team to sort out and manage these effects? It is to this question we now turn. The first part of the answer lies in understanding exactly when culture's influence is likely to be strongest, as addressed in the next section.

Culture's Influence Under Conditions of Uncertainty and Ambiguity

As noted earlier, we know that there are many causes of a person's behavior, both within the person behaving and in the situation itself. The field of comparative and multicultural management has been struggling with the recognition that, although culture is certainly an important influence on behavior, it is not the only influence. The previous discussion articulates culture's potential to influence the sense making and behavior of multinational team members. We now address the important question: *When* is culture most likely to influence behavior? In other words, what characteristics of events most lend themselves to be noticed, interpreted, and responded to using culture-related schemas and scripts, rather than person- or situation-related ones?

In the field of social psychology, Mischel and colleagues (Mischel, 1973; Shoda, Mischel, & Wright, 1993) have described "strong" and "weak" situations. Strong situations are those in which environmental and social cues to behavior are clear. They rely on a generic "follow me" script that all people are assumed to possess, and cues in the situation immediately evoke the script so that it is followed with little reflection. Weak situations do not present such unambiguous guides to behavior. A person must interpret the events in weak situations with a more deliberate series of judgments to structure his or her own actions. In examining the influence of personality versus situation on behavior, these researchers suggest that individual differences (personality) influence sense making and responses to events in weak situations, but that in strong situations, individual differences are minimized and the situation provides a greater influence (Mischel, 1973).

Because culture has its effects on individuals through a socialization process affecting scripts and schemas, a parallel argument can be made for the influence of culture. In strong situations, cultural schemas and scripts will not be as relevant as will the situation. In an organization, strong situations are those in which there are procedures, explicit rules, and policies to guide behavior, which are supported by norms and are actively followed. Weak situations are those in which frameworks for noticing, interpreting, and responding to events are not commonly held. Although a few situations faced by multicultural teams may be of a "pure" strong type, most of the kinds of situations we envision for multicultural teams at the outset are complex and ambiguous, and therefore are weak in at least some aspects. Furthermore, the weak situations faced by multinational teams are most likely to be those regarding relationships among people or between people and the environment—that is, precisely those types of situations for which cultures provide assumptions and guidelines. Hence, the multicultural team situation is exactly the kind in which culture's influence will be strongest.

A further element of complexity must be added here. Weak situations present uncertainty and ambiguity. But to people of different cultures, there are different sources of uncertainty and ambiguity. For example, imagine that a production line has produced a higher-than-ever number of defective products, and the workforce is of a different national background than the majority of members in the management group (e.g., a Japanese-owned plant in the United States, or a German-owned maquiladora in Mexico). Management has given a binational management team a mandate to decrease the number of defective products by a given date, has assigned a leader to the group, and has identified particular areas of relevant expertise in each member. In this way, management has explicitly prescribed the team's assumptions regarding mode of activity (a specific goal implies a doing-achieving assumption), time (the deadline and type of goal suggest a present orientation), and relationships among people (hierarchical with a given leader; individualistic with each member having unique and important expertise). The most salient sources of uncertainty in this case, then, relate to people's relationship to nature and the basic nature of humans. In other words, the situation is weak with respect to relationship-to-nature and nature-of-humans orientations, and strong with respect to the other elements of culture. In this situation, cultural differences among members on mode of activity, time, and relationships among people will not be likely to influence processes or effectiveness of the team. If there are cultural differences among members in their relationship-to-nature, nature-of-humans orientations, or both, the differences will become evident as members approach the task and may be a source of innovation as well as contention. Differences in these areas must be managed explicitly.

In another case, a self-managed, multinational team of engineers may be brought together in a research-and-development project initiated by a 50/50 joint venture between two high-technology companies. The parent and joint venture management may give the team a clear description of the finished product's specifications, and then ask the engineers to develop it within a given time frame. Given the mandate and the engineers' training and selection into product design, the situation is now relatively strong (low uncertainty and ambiguity) with respect to relation to nature and time. The engineers, however, are working in a highly competitive industry where confidentiality in development is critical, they have been asked to work as a self-managed team, and they may have different approaches to goal setting and achievement. The situation is thus weak (high uncertainty and ambiguity) with respect to three cultural orientations: nature of humans, relationships among people, and mode of activity. Cultural differences in these three elements may have a significant impact on this team's ability to function effectively, and therefore these differences must be managed by team members. Cultural differences on time and relation to nature, however, are less likely to require explicit attention.

To summarize the argument thus far, culture influences event management processes in work groups through its effect on how events are noticed, interpreted, and responded to. These effects are seen both in how group members approach their task, and in how they approach the group processes themselves. The influence of culture is particularly salient in culturally weak situations—that is, situations where there is uncertainty and ambiguity with respect to relationships among people or between people and the environment. Moreover, the nature of the uncertainty in a given situation will determine the element(s) of culture that become salient in the event management processes. What still remains to be described, then, is how work groups can use this information to improve their work processes.

Implications for Multicultural Teams

Effective multicultural teams develop synergistic approaches to their work by integrating and building on the different perspectives brought by members. Two critical processes for achieving this synergy are decentering and recentering (DiStefano & Maznevski, 1996; Maznevski, 1995). Decentering is taking the perspective of others and explaining problems with respect to the differences in perspective rather than blaming them on other group members. Recentering calls for identifying or building a common view of the situation and a common set of norms. Both the view and the norms must be acceptable to all work group members. The two processes are closely interrelated: Decentering provides information necessary for recentering, whereas recentering provides a core foundation to build on using the different perspectives.

The framework outlined in the previous section can aid work group members both in decentering and in recentering. Using this framework, members can identify the type of uncertainty presented in a situation, and can also predict in which types of situations they will tend to have fundamentally similar and different approaches to the group's work and processes. The differences that are likely to cause problems among group members are ones that are related to the elements of uncertainty in a situation. These areas of difference can be explained with respect to cultural orientations, and members can use these explanations to understand problems that the group encounters in its work, thus engaging in effective decentering. Areas of similarity, deriving either from the strong situational elements or from overlap in approaches, can serve as the foundation for recentering.

It may seem that one of the recommendations for managers and members of multicultural work groups should be to "create strong situations wherever possible." Strong situations can be dictated by management; for example, explicitly telling the group members that each member's idea will be heard before any of the ideas are evaluated. Strong situations can also arise implicitly. In an international firm, "home country" or "headquarters country" norms and perspectives may be the ones used and reinforced using subtle or obvious cues. Certainly, strong situations reduce the potential for friction in the group and facilitate smooth interaction by providing explicit, socially acceptable guidelines for behavior and approach.

When the potential implications of this recommendation are explored, however, it becomes clear that a strong situation should be suggested only in certain circumstances. Strong situations also suppress the potential for cultural differences to be combined in ways that potentially lead to unique, innovative approaches and can be translated into competitive advantages. Furthermore, group members who are forced by the situation to operate under norms with which they are not personally comfortable will not be as satisfied with the group. They will not be as committed to the group's decisions, will not offer their own contributions as consistently, and, in short, will perform suboptimally within the work group.

An important contingency factor here is the multinational team's task. If the team is expected to perform a routine task in a stable environment where consistency and speed of response are important, then the creation of a strong situation seems desirable. These task characteristics describe the management of standardized procedures within an organization, such as production, assembly, internal bookkeeping, records control, and so on. The creation of a strong situation may also be best when the team is facing a crisis that must be resolved immediately, even if the fastest solution is a satisfactory rather than a maximizing one (remembering, however, that members of different cultures define "crisis" and "immediately" and "satisfactory" differently).

If the team's mandate requires members to accomplish something nonroutine, to interact with a dynamic environment, or both, the benefits of having the group use its varied perspectives synergistically outweigh the disadvantages of having to overcome barriers created by those differences. Some examples of these types of work groups include self-managed teams, product development groups, customer service groups, sales teams, and international strategy groups. Although the group may encounter some difficulties, especially at the beginning of its time together, these difficulties can be overcome with explicit attention to group processes (Maznevski, 1995). The team then has the potential to contribute substantially to the organization.

Conclusion

Multinational management requires creativity and breadth of experience. No one person possesses the breadth of experience, knowledge, and perspective needed to handle the full range of situations an MNC faces. The MNC superhero does not exist, and collaboration is unavoidable. Moreover, highly complex collaboration among very different people is unavoidable if real issues are to be addressed rather than postponed. Multicultural teams benefit from the different responses to "what do I know," from members who perceive different parts of an MNC's world; the different responses to "where can I go for help," based on experience in relying on various sources of meaning; and the different responses to "how do I know and how do I respond," based on projecting from different cultural value orientations.

We have sought to provide some basis for anticipating issues that arise in multicultural teams. Much of this discussion is speculative, given the present state of knowledge about national cultures. Much glosses over important variables affecting differences of viewpoint and value apart from national culture. All of our discussion needs to be concertized through knowledge of particular cultures represented by members of multicultural executive groups.

Do we have any useful information from comparative studies of national culture that we can draw on? We would answer with a cautious "yes." People are not computers. When people accept new ways of thinking, their prior way of interpreting situations is not erased. One's first language will always be special, no matter how many languages one learns. The social experiences of one's youth will retain a key place despite any subsequent experiences with cultures quite different from the culture mix of one's first socialization. Scripts and schemas are not immutable, but those long in place shape subsequent modifications. One's cultural background matters.

The ideas presented here are intended to help move the field of international management a step forward from the comparative approach currently dominant in international management research in which cultures are examined separately from each other, toward an approach that takes into account interaction among people from different cultures. This step is a critical one, because the reality faced by managers today is not one of simply importing, exporting, or otherwise working with people from only one other country at a time. Rather, managers face a complex, dynamic reality in which cultures intersect with greater frequency and intensity than ever before. Managers must know how best to work effectively in these situations, and we hope the approach offered here provides some initial guidance.

References

Bartlett, C. A., & Ghoshal, S. (1995). *Transnational management* (2nd ed.). Chicago: Irwin.

Cartwright, D., & Zander, A. (1968). Leadership and performance of group functions: Introduction. In D. Cartwright & A. Zander (Eds.), *Group dynamics* (3rd ed., pp. 301-317). New York: Harper & Row.

Cohen, M. D., March, J. G., & Olsen, J. P. (1972). A garbage can model of organization choice. *Administrative Science Quarterly, 17*(1), 1-25.

DiStefano, J. J., & Maznevski, M. L. (1996). *Managing diversity for competitive advantage.* Unpublished manuscript.

Jackson, S. E., & Dutton, J. (1988). Discerning threats and opportunities. *Administrative Science Quarterly, 33,* 370-387.

Kluckhohn, F. R., & Strodtbeck, F. L. (1961). *Variations in value orientations.* Evanston, IL: Row, Peterson.

Lane, H. W., DiStefano, J. J., & Maznevski, M. L. (1997). *International management behavior: From policy to practice* (3rd ed.). Cambridge, MA: Blackwell.

March, J. G., & Simon, H. A. (1958). *Organizations.* New York: John Wiley.

Maznevski, M. L. (1995). *Process and performance in multicultural teams* (Working paper 95-06). London, Canada: University of Western Ontario, Western Business School.

Maznevski, M. L., & DiStefano, J. J. (1995). *Measuring culture in international management: The Cultural Perspectives Questionnaire* (Working paper 95-39). London, Canada: University of Western Ontario, Western Business School.

Mischel, W. (1973). Toward a cognitive social learning reconceptualization of personality. *Psychological Review, 80,* 252-283.

Nutt, P. C. (1984). Types of organization decision processes. *Administrative Sciences Quarterly, 29,* 414-450.

Peterson, M. F. (1993). *Embedded organizational events and the new situationalism.* Unpublished manuscript, Texas Tech University, Institute for Leadership and Management Research, Lubbock.

Peterson, M. F. (in press). Embedded organizational events: Units of process in organization science. *Organization Science.*

Shoda, Y., Mischel, W., & Wright, J. (1993). The role of situational demands and cognitive competencies in behavior organization and personality coherence. *Journal of Personality and Social Psychology, 65,* 1023-1035.

Sims, H. P., Jr., & Gioia, D. A. (1986). *The thinking organization: Dynamics of organizational social cognition.* San Francisco: Jossey-Bass.

Smith, P. B., & Peterson, M. F. (1988). *Leadership, organizations, and culture.* Beverly Hills, CA: Sage.

Smith, P. B., & Peterson, M. F. (1995, August). *Beyond value comparisons: Sources used to give meaning to work events in 25 countries.* Paper presented at the annual meeting of the Academy of Management, Vancouver, BC.

Weick, K. E. (1995). *Sensemaking in organizations.* Thousand Oaks, CA: Sage.

5

Majority and Minority Perspectives on Cross-Cultural Interactions

SHARON G. GOTO

T wo major economic forces have brought the need to deal with diversity issues to the forefront (Jackson & Alvarez, 1992). First, the U.S. economy has shifted from manufacturing to service work—approximately 78% of all employees work in service industries (Bureau of Labor Statistics, 1991). Service work has been described as a "game between persons" (Bell, 1973). When coupled with the increase in minorities in the United States, this shift has exacerbated difficulties of cross-cultural interactions. Second, the occurrence of international business ventures has increased dramatically. Therefore, companies must now compete for customers with foreign companies both domestically and abroad.

These economic trends increase the number and intensity of intergroup, intragroup, and interpersonal cross-cultural interactions. Although each of these types of interactions is important, interpersonal cross-cultural interactions, or relations between two culturally different individuals, are the focus of this chapter.

Different interactions between diverse people may lead to negative consequences in organizational contexts. For example, Bass and Turner

(1973) found that interpersonal attraction can affect measures of job performance. In a study of the effects of culture on performance ratings, when European American managers rated African American subordinates, the ratings tended to be based on objective measures (e.g., attendance, performance levels). When European American managers rated European American subordinates, however, the ratings tended to be based on interpersonal measures as well. This allowed interpersonal attraction to compensate for poorer objective performance in the European American, culturally congruent dyads. The managers' greater perceived social distance to African American subordinates resulted in fewer recommendations for pay increases.

Perceptions of promotability are also contingent on interpersonal interactions (Fine, Johnson, & Ryan, 1990). In addition to merit, "having friends in the right places" was perceived to lead to promotions for both European Americans and minority group members. Friendships are a product of a series of smooth intercultural interactions. Fine et al. argued that social experiences within the organization differ depending on group membership. In their study, a higher proportion of minority group members reported relationship factors to be important for promotion. Minority group members were more likely to see relational factors as "obstacles" to their advancement.

Donnellon and Kolb (1994) focused on the effects of disputes rising from social diversity. They found that these types of disputes often persist unresolved, and without proper remedy manifest themselves in unacceptable ways. In addition, the unheard disputes can have larger organizational costs, or can inhibit the potential benefits of cultural diversity from being realized.

Indeed, cross-cultural interpersonal interactions are particularly relevant for understanding cross-cultural work groups. Interpersonal interactions often occur within a group context. For example, employees surveyed by Fine et al. (1990) reported that "being a team player" was important for enhancing promotability. Interpersonal relations affect perceptions of team work because teams are comprised of several one-on-one relations, often cross-cultural dyads. Therefore, cultural diversity within the group context can be just as problematic as in the one-on-one situation.

Kirchemeyer and Cohen (1992) found minority group members suffered in heterogeneous groups—they performed more poorly and showed lower attachment to the group than majority group members. If being perceived as a "team player" is an important determinant of promotability, then minority group members, in particular, are at risk.

In addition to issues of promotability, cross-cultural interpersonal interactions have consequences for work group efficiency. Culturally heterogeneous task groups have been found to produce higher-quality solutions than homogeneous task groups (Triandis, Hall, & Ewen, 1965). Orasanu (Chapter 7, this volume) emphasizes that, within airline flight crews, cockpit performance levels increase when the interactions between crew members are smooth. In contrast, cultural differences in verbal and nonverbal communication can be devastating. The high-stakes work environment of aviation certainly exacerbates the effects of cultural differences, but the consequences of cultural differences are also seen in more "ordinary" work contexts.

These studies suggest that when people from different cultures interact with outcomes that are less than satisfying, negative consequences occur. Both the individual and the work group incur these consequences. Costs to the individual include negative perceptions of performance or ability. The work group may not benefit from the maximum input of all group members, and inaccurate or insufficient information may be communicated.

Because cross-cultural interactions are quickly becoming unavoidable, due to increased demographic diversity, these questions emerge: What is the role of culture in interpersonal, cross-cultural interactions? Are perceived cultural differences related to the success of the interaction, the failure of the interaction, or both? And, if so, to what extent?

The Triandis Model for
Dealing With Cultural Diversity

A useful framework for addressing these issues and for understanding the antecedents and consequences of interpersonal relations that cross cultural boundaries was introduced by Triandis (1992; Triandis, Kurowski, & Gelfand, 1993). The model's relevance stems from its explicit inclusion of both cultural and interpersonal variables, and their interrelationships.

The original framework for dealing with cultural diversity is quite complex, consisting of 19 constructs.

In a general sense, the model suggests that cultural variables influence interpersonal-level variables, which in turn influence intrapersonal-level variables. Triandis hypothesized that the primary ingredient for success in handling diversity is contact between individuals of different cultures who perceive each other as similar. This is known as the *contact hypothesis* (see Amir, 1969, for a review).

According to Triandis (1992), many factors contribute to the perceived similarity of the persons interacting, including the absence of a past history of conflict between the cultures, small cultural distance of the individuals, knowledge of the other's culture, equal-status contact, intimacy, and previously successful interactions. Contact between persons who view each other as similar is hypothesized to lead to rewards (i.e., satisfaction), which are amplified within a pluralistic society. The satisfaction derived from the situation, in turn, can lead to many positive consequences, such as positive intergroup attitudes, smaller social distance, the desire for more interactions, and ultimately the actors' sense of control over the social relationship.

Framework of the Present Study

The original model is too complex for a single manageable empirical test. Thus, only a subset of the original variables was used in this study. These include the following: perceived knowledge of culture, perceived cultural distance, perceived history of conflict, perceived similarity, opportunity for contact, satisfaction with interactions, intention to interact, and intergroup attitudes.

These variables were selected because they represent the core of the model—that is, they capture the contact hypothesis. Furthermore, both cultural and interpersonal variables, the two crucial elements of cross-cultural interpersonal interaction, were retained. The variables selected could be roughly divided into the interpersonal variables from classic attraction research (e.g., Byrne, 1971)—(opportunity to interact, perceived similarity, satisfaction with interaction)—and cultural variables (i.e., perceived knowledge of culture, perceived cultural distance, and perceived history of conflict). Most studies of interpersonal relations have focused on the relational qualities between individuals, while neglecting the characteristics of groups, or cultural factors. Therefore, including cultural factors was appropriate. Specifically, an individual's perceptions of various aspects of the target person's cultural group were hypothesized to influence characteristics of the interpersonal relationship.

The relationships posited among the eight selected variables remained consistent with Triandis's larger model, with the exception of an additional path from intergroup attitude to intention to interact (see Figure 5.1). This addition was based on work supporting the theory of reasoned action (Fishbein & Ajzen, 1975).

Constructs

The following brief description of each construct will clarify its scope, and examples of how the constructs have been used in the past will clarify their relevance.

Perceived knowledge of culture. The extent to which an individual is familiar with the other individual's culture defines the construct of "knowledge of culture." In Stephan and Stephan's (1984) investigation of the effects of ignorance on prejudice, this variable was negatively related to prejudice.

Perceived history of conflict. This construct is conceptualized as the degree of past conflict between the cultures of the two persons interacting. Historical evidence, such as the conflict of Turks and Armenians and conflicts in the former Yugoslavia, show this factor to be important. There are conditions, however, where history may not be as important. Brewer and Campbell (1976), in a study of intergroup relations in East Africa, found that "despite a relatively recent history of overt conflict among ethnic groups in our survey sample, respondents apparently feel psychologically closer to a 'familiar enemy' than to a little-known stranger" (p. 142). Perhaps the recency of conflict is a key in determining when history of conflict is important.

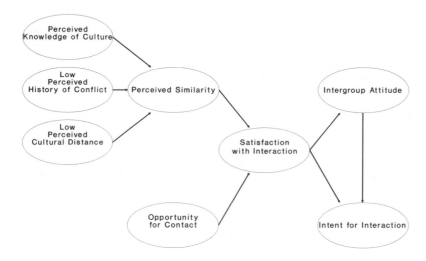

Figure 5.1. An Eight-Variable Subset of Triandis's (1992) Model

Perceived cultural distance. Brewer and Campbell (1976) described convergent boundaries as the perceived degree of similarity between the actor's culture and the target person's culture. When multiple bases for differentiation among groups are evident (e.g., religious, economic, political, language), the cultural distance is said to be high. Cultural distance has been found to be correlated with poor adjustment of foreign exchange students (Babiker, Cox, & Miller, 1980), and with high probability of suicide in a new culture (Furnham & Bochner, 1986).

Perceived similarity. The perceived degree of similarity or difference between the actor and the target person at the individual, rather than cultural, level is "perceived similarity." To the extent that interactions are category based, perceived similarity is likely to be highly influenced by cultural distance. In the attraction paradigm (Byrne, 1971), perceived similarity with respect to attitudes has been found to be positively related to level of attraction.

Opportunity for contact. This construct is conceptualized as the frequency with which the actor finds himself or herself in situations that enable interactions with persons of the other culture.

Satisfaction with interaction. This is the extent to which the actor generally finds interactions with members of the culturally disparate group rewarding (Skinner, 1981).

Intention to interact. This is the extent to which future interactions with members of the other cultural group are anticipated with positive affect.

Intergroup attitude. The affect generally felt by the actor toward members of the culturally disparate group is "intergroup attitude." This is similar to Brewer and Campbell's (1976) conceptualization of intergroup attraction as the direction and intensity of intergroup affect.

Multiple Perspectives in Interactions

The phenomenon of cross-cultural interaction is not one-sided, although the literature would suggest this to be so. Typical studies, especially those on prejudice and stereotyping, focus on the European American as subject and the minority group member as object. The studies that do incorporate both perspectives have typically measured only a few variables, obtaining only a superficial perspective. As Myrdal (1944) and Allport (1954) noted in their now-classic writings, the problems and processes of intergroup relations are dynamic and interactive.

To effectively study cross-cultural interactions, an in-depth study was needed that incorporated both sides as equally involved participants. Thus, in the present study, both African American and European American perspectives on cross-cultural interactions were solicited, and cultural and interpersonal variables were measured. To study one particular aspect of cross-cultural work groups, both cultural and individual variables were used to predict three interpersonal interaction criterion variables: intention to interact, intergroup attitude, and satisfaction with interaction.

Method

Data were collected from written surveys filled out by high school students. Students, like work group members, are frequent participants in groups with structured tasks, where their group performance is evaluated by others. They interact daily, and not exclusively by choice. Furthermore, just as interactions within work groups reflect the cross-cultural dynamics of the larger society, so do interactions within the walls of a high school. For these reasons, high school students were considered similar to work group members for study of this particular phenomenon.

Participants

Participants were recruited from 25 classrooms in 3 midwestern public high schools. The classroom levels ranged from remedial to accelerated, although most data were elicited from average-talent classrooms. Subjects were informed that the information would be reported back to the school administration in group form only, with assurances of anonymity and confidentiality.

There were 549 participants in the study (263 male, 271 female, 15 unreported). The racial breakdown reflected that of the school population; 376 European American, 135 African American, 23 Asian American, 5 American Indian, 7 Hispanic, 2 other, and 1 unreported. Because the other groups were small, only the European American and African American respondents were used in the analyses. The European American sample was 50.5% female and had an average age of 16.2 years. Among the African American participants, 53.8% were female and the average age was 16.6 years.

Measures

In a series of Likert and Semantic Differential items, subjects were asked to indicate their perceptions of various aspects of culture and cross-cultural contact on campus. Approximately half of the scale items were reverse-worded to avoid response bias. Two versions of the questionnaire were developed: (a) for European American respondents with respect to a general African American target, and (b) for African American respondents with respect to a general European American target.

Perceived history of conflict. Although there is an objective level of history of conflict between two cultures, the objective measure would contain no variance, and thus would not be useful for correlational analyses. Therefore, a measure of perceived history of conflict was developed, based on the assumption that the objective history of conflict is reflected in the perceived history of conflict. For the perceived history of conflict and the perceived cultural distance scales, identical sets of items were used for both European Americans and African Americans.

There were nine semantic differential items, rated on a 7-point scale, completing the question: "In the past, relations between blacks and whites in this country have been _____ ." The nine adjectives were *good/bad, pleasant/unpleasant, fair/unfair, wise/foolish, correct/incorrect, unfriendly/friendly, cruel/kind, painful/pleasurable,* and *negative/positive*. The Cronbach's alpha was .96 for the European American sample, and .95 for the African American sample. Higher scores indicated greater perceptions of conflict.

Perceived cultural distance. Babiker et al.'s (1980) measures were modified to create closed-ended measures appropriate for discriminating between cultures with similar physical environments. The basic question was, "To what extent are the _____ different/similar for a typical white and black person?" rated on a 7-point similar/dissimilar scale. Ten social and physical attributes were inserted into the stem: *hours worked per week, clothes, levels of education, food, religious faiths, standards of living, leisure activities, dating patterns,* and *men's roles within the family*. The Cronbach's alpha for the European American and African American samples were .87 and .79, respectively. Higher scores indicated greater perceptions of cultural difference.

For the remaining measures, the items were changed according to the participant's ethnicity. For example, if the participant was African American, the target culture/person would be "white" (e.g., "In general, I would describe my familiarity with white culture as _____ .").

Perceived knowledge of culture. Stephan and Stephan (1984) used items from a culture assimilator designed to teach about Chicano culture. Culture assimilators used to measure this construct are based on the notion that accurate attributions of another group's behavior will lead to smoother intercultural relations (Fiedler, Mitchell, & Triandis, 1971). These training guidebooks typically take the form of a series of scenarios. Each scenario is followed by alternatives for behavioral or verbal responses, only one of which is culturally appropriate. In the absence of a current and validated African American assimilator, however, a series of semantic differentials was used: "In general, I would describe my familiarity with black (white) culture as _____ ." The five adjectives, rated on a 7-point scale, were: *bad/good, foolish/wise, sketchy/thorough, detailed/superficial, smart/ignorant.* The Cronbach's alpha for the European American and African American samples were .89 and .79, respectively. Higher scores indicated greater perceived levels of knowledge.

As checks of actual knowledge, several true-false and multiple-choice items were developed for use in the European American sample. A scale capturing African American values was developed based on a cultural study by Wilson (1986). A sample item is, "The extended family is highly valued by African Americans." Knowledge of African American history was tapped by a series of multiple-choice items. The sum of correct answers on the multiple choice and true-false questions was slightly positively correlated with the semantic differential measure of perceived knowledge of African American culture, $r = .10$; $p < .06$. Despite pretesting efforts, the participants performed poorly on the true-false and multiple-choice scales. The low correlation between the two scales was apparently due either to a ceiling effect on the objective scale or to the overestimation of knowledge of African American culture.

Perceived similarity. A series of semantic differentials assessed the extent of perceived similarity between the self and the other cultural group. For example, "Blacks (Whites) and I are _____ ." Using a 7-point scale, several adjectives completed the sentence: *dissimilar/similar, unlike/alike, identical/different, like each other/ unlike each other.* The Cronbach's alpha on the these scales were .92 for the European Americans and .81 for the African Americans. Higher scores indicated greater perceived similarity.

Opportunity for contact. Several items tapped the frequency of intergroup contact. For example, one item read "I have many opportunities to meet blacks (whites) in my daily activities on campus." Ratings were made on a 7-point "disagree/agree" scale. Cronbach's alpha was .74 for the European American sample, and .62 for the African American sample. Higher scores indicated more opportunity for contact.

Satisfaction with interaction. The scale for satisfaction with interaction included six disagree-agree Likert items. A sample item was: "I am satisfied with my interactions with blacks (whites) on campus." The Cronbach's alpha for the European American and African American samples were .92 and .84, respectively. Higher scores indicated greater satisfaction.

Intergroup attitude. For the European American sample, there were eight 7-point semantic differentials completing the sentence, "In general, black people are _____ ." The adjectives used were *good/bad, pleasant/unpleasant, fair/unfair, wise/foolish, correct/incorrect, unfriendly/friendly, cruel/kind, negative/positive.*

As secondary measures, seven old-fashioned racism items, and seven modern racism items (McConahay, Hardee, & Batts, 1981) were included. The semantic differential scale was significantly correlated with both the old-fashioned racism scale ($r = .57$; $p < .001$), and the modern racism scale ($r = .65$; $p < .001$).

To measure intergroup attitudes in the African American sample, only the semantic differential items were used because old-fashioned and modern racism scales do not exist to tap racism against European Americans. The Cronbach's alpha was .96 for the European American sample, and .95 for the African American sample. Higher scores indicated more positive intergroup attitude.

Intention to interact. The desire for future intercultural interactions was assessed with four items of behavioral intention to interact with persons of the other culture (e.g., "I _____ to get to know more blacks (whites) in the near future," inserting *intend, will, will try, plan*). In addition, three Likert scale items were rated on a 7-point scale ("It is important to me to _____ ." *have black (white) friends, have black (white) teammates, go to racially mixed parties*). For the European American sample the Cronbach's alpha was .93; for the African American sample it was .91. A higher score indicated a greater desire to interact in the future.

Analysis Plan

To examine whether the cultural variables substantially increased the prediction of the three dependent variables beyond the interpersonal-level variables, four sets of hierarchical regression analyses were performed. The African American and European American data were analyzed separately to capture differences in perception or experience by group.

For each sample, the first set of analyses entered the "causal" variables before the "effect variables." Thus, the antecedent variables (i.e., cultural variables) entered the regression equation as Step 1. The mediators (i.e., interpersonal variables) were entered in Step 2.

Recall, however, that the cultural variables were thought to influence the interpersonal variables, which in turn influence satisfaction, intergroup attitude, and intention. The interpersonal-level variables were conceptualized as more immediate predictors of the criterion variables. Therefore, their relationships to the criterion variables should be greater than the relationships between the cultural variables and the criterion variables. In the second set of analyses for each sample, the interpersonal variables were entered first, and the cultural variables were entered as the second step.

Only the variables that preceded the dependent variable in the causal model were included in the regression equations. Thus, for instance, intention to interact was not used as a predictor of intergroup attitude.

Composite scores were created for use as predictor and criterion variables. For each variable, the mean of the items comprised the composite score (see Table 5.1 for descriptive statistics).

Results

Satisfaction

When the cultural variables were entered before the interpersonal variables, Step 1 accounted for 27% of the variance in the European American sample. The inclusion of the interpersonal variables predicted an additional 16% of the variance (see Table 5.2).

When satisfaction with interaction was regressed on interaction variables first, they accounted for 40% of the variance in Step 1 for the European American sample (not shown). The addition of the cultural variables into the equation increased the variance accounted for by only 3%. All predictors were significant, with the exception of perceived history of conflict.

Table 5.1
Descriptive Statistics of Scales

Scale	Mean	SD	Correlations						
			1	2	3	4	5	6	7
European American sample									
1 Perceived similarity	3.36	1.54							
2 Satisfaction with interaction	4.72	1.36	.43						
3 Intention to interact	4.51	1.39	.24	.59					
4 Intergroup attitude	4.29	1.59	.20	.47	.59				
5 Perceived history of conflict	5.57	1.47	-.18	-.09	-.11	-.32			
6 Perceived knowledge of culture	4.68	1.37	.19	.22	.18	-.11	.05		
7 Perceived cultural distance	4.46	1.11	-.47	-.45	-.33	.28	-.22	-.18	
8 Opportunity to interact	5.44	1.28	.20	.44	.45	-.34	.07	-.38	.23
African American sample									
1 Perceived similarity	3.85	1.47							
2 Satisfaction with interaction	4.75	1.46	.57						
3 Intention to interact	4.66	1.50	.56	.59					
4 Intergroup attitude	4.70	1.44	.60	.64	.59				
5 Perceived history of conflict	5.43	1.38	.05	.07	.11	.09			
6 Perceived knowledge of culture	4.29	1.25	.34	.33	.35	-.29	.03		
7 Perceived cultural distance	3.94	1.11	-.56	-.47	-.37	.54	.05	-.26	
8 Opportunity to interact	4.49	1.37	.43	.49	.47	-.32	.03	-.36	.35

$p < .05$ for $r > .17$.

For the African Americans, the cultural variables accounted for 22% of the variance in satisfaction when entered first, and the interpersonal variables at Step 2 accounted for an additional 15% of the variance (see Table 5.2).

In the African American sample, the interpersonal variables (specifically perceived cultural distance) accounted for 32% of the variance when they were entered first (not shown). The addition of the cultural variables increased the predicted variance by 5%.

Intergroup Attitude

The cultural variables accounted for 32% of the variance in intergroup attitudes in the European American sample when entered first. The addition of the interaction variables, opportunity to interact, perceived similarity and satisfaction, increased the predicted variance by 21% (see Table 5.3).

The interaction variables accounted for 49% of the variance in intergroup attitude for the European American sample when entered first (not shown). The addition of the cultural variables increased the variance accounted for in this dependent variable by 3%.

In the African American sample, when intergroup attitude was regressed on the cultural variables first, 15% of the variance was predicted. The interpersonal variables accounted for 17% of additional variance (see Table 5.3). The interpersonal variables accounted for 24% of the variance in the intergroup attitude when they were entered first (not shown). The inclusion of the cultural variables (specifically perceived history of conflict), explained an additional 8% of the variance in this variable.

Intention to Interact

For the European American sample, entering the cultural variables first accounted for 21% of the variance in intention to interact. When the interpersonal variables were included in the equation, the predicted variance was increased by 28% (see Table 5.4).

Table 5.2
Prediction of Satisfaction With Interaction
in the European American and African American Samples

Predictors	European American Satisfaction With Interaction				African American Satisfaction With Interaction			
	Initial		Final		Initial		Final	
	B	β	B	β	B	β	B	β
Step 1:								
Perceived history of conflict	n.s.	n.s.	n.s.	n.s.	n.s.	n.s.	n.s.	n.s.
Perceived knowledge of culture	.28	.24	.11	.09	.15	.15	n.s.	n.s.
Perceived cultural distance	−.53	−.40	−.22	−.16	−.51	−.42	−.32	−.26
Change in R^2				.27*				.22*
Step 2:								
Opportunity to interact			.29	.27			.36	.34
Perceived similarity			.33	.33			.22	.25
Change in R^2				.16*				.15*
Total adjusted R^2				.42*				.34*

NOTE: The total adjusted R^2 is somewhat smaller than the sum of the two unadjusted R^2 figures.
*$p < .001$.

When intention to interact was regressed first on the interpersonal variables, they accounted for 48% of the variance in the European American sample. In the second step, the cultural variables accounted for a significant, but small, 1% of additional variance.

With the cultural variables entered as Step 1 in the analysis for the African American sample, the cultural variables predicted 12% of the variance of intention to interact. The inclusion of opportunity to interact, perceived similarity, intergroup attitude, and satisfaction increased the predicted variance by 38% (see Table 5.4). When the interaction variables were entered first for the African American sample, they accounted for 50% of the variance in intention to interact (not shown). The cultural variables made no additional contribution to prediction.

Table 5.3
Prediction of Intergroup Attitude
in the European American and African American Samples

Predictors	European American Attitude				African American Attitude			
	Initial		Final		Initial		Final	
	B	β	B	β	B	β	B	β
Step 1:								
Perceived history of conflict	n.s.	n.s.	n.s.	n.s.	−.26	−.28	−.27	−.28
Perceived knowledge of culture	.19	.17	n.s.	n.s.	n.s.	n.s.	n.s.	n.s.
Perceived cultural distance	−.64	−.49	−.28	−.22	−.26	−.21	n.s.	n.s.
Change in R^2				.32*				.15*
Step 2:								
Opportunity to interact			−.09	−.09			.18	.17
Perceived similarity			.26	.27			n.s.	n.s.
Satisfaction with interaction			.40	.41			.40	.39
Change in R^2				.21*				.17*
Total adjusted R^2				.52*				.29*

*$p < .001$.

Discussion

The predictor variables accounted for a fairly large portion of variance in the criterion variables, ranging from a low of 29% for prediction of African American attitudes to a high of 52% for European American attitudes. These findings provided support for the portion of Triandis's (1992) model that was tested. As expected, both interpersonal and cultural variables were predictors of intention to interact, intergroup attitude, and satisfaction.

When the cultural variables were entered first, the variance accounted for in the criterion variables ranged from 12% for African Americans' intention to interact, to 32% for European American attitudes. The variance accounted for by the cultural variables, when the interpersonal variables were entered first, paled in comparison, ranging from 0% to 8%. These findings support the notion that the interpersonal-

Table 5.4
Prediction of Intention to Interact in the European
American and African American Samples

Predictors	European American Intention to Interact				African American Intention to Interact			
	Initial		*Final*		*Initial*		*Final*	
	B	β	B	β	B	β	B	β
Step 1:								
Perceived history of conflict	.11	.10	.08	.07	n.s.	n.s.	n.s.	n.s.
Perceived knowledge of culture	.32	.27	.10	.08	n.s.	n.s.	n.s.	n.s.
Perceived cultural distance	−.39	−.29	n.s.	n.s.	−.41	−.29	n.s.	n.s.
Change in R^2				.21**				.12*
Step 2:								
Opportunity to interact			.21	.19			.22	.17
Perceived similarity			.20	.20			n.s.	n.s.
Satisfaction with interaction			.20	.20			.37	.32
Intergroup attitude			.30	.29			.45	.40
Change in R^2				.28**				.38**
Total adjusted R^2				.48**				.48**

$*p < .01; **p < .001.$

level variables mediate the relations between the cultural variables and
the consequences of intergroup interactions. Perceived cultural variables are important, but interpersonal variables have a more direct
influence on intention for future interaction, intergroup attitude, and
satisfaction with interaction.

The role of culture, when it was added to the prediction equation last,
was slightly larger in the African American than in the European American
sample, for the dependent variables of satisfaction and intergroup attitudes. More interesting, differences in the predictors of the dependent
variables depended on the group. Satisfaction with interactions among
European Americans increased with greater perceived knowledge of
culture, lower perceived cultural distance, greater perceived similarity
and more opportunities to interact. For African Americans, similarly,
the predictors included lower perceived cultural distance, greater per-

ceived similarity, and greater opportunity for contact, but perceived knowledge of European American culture was not significant.

Interestingly, with respect to intergroup attitude, lower perceptions of cultural distance were predictive of favorable intergroup attitudes for European Americans, but not for African Americans. In contrast, lower perceptions of history of conflict were related to favorable intergroup attitudes for African Americans but not for European Americans. Perceived knowledge of the other culture was not predictive of intergroup attitudes in either sample. More opportunity to interact was negatively related to favorable European American attitudes but positively related to favorable African American attitudes.

Concerning intentions to interact, perceived history of conflict, perceived knowledge of culture, and perceived similarity were significant positive predictors for European Americans but were not significant for African Americans. Greater opportunity to interact and more satisfaction with interactions were positive predictors of intentions for both groups.

These results should be generalized with caution because students are different from employees—they are younger, and do not work in a for-profit organizational context. As stated earlier, however, there are similarities between commercial organizations and high school environments, particularly concerning processes as "basic" as interpersonal interactions. The pattern of results suggests that the cross-cultural interpersonal dynamics in this sample reflect those of the larger society.

The ethnic-group differences can be understood within the framework of majority and minority group membership, also referred to as dominant versus nondominant group membership (see Berry, Chapter 2, this volume). The African American and European American samples were of equal formal status because both groups were students in public high schools. It is doubtful, however, that the high school walls truly shielded the students from the group power differences that exist in society. The majority group (European Americans), being in a position of power, need not be concerned with changing their behavior in an effort to assimilate, and therefore to gain power. Rather, judgments of similarity are important determinants of intergroup attitudes for the majority group (i.e., "I'll like you, if you're like me"). This conclusion is similar to Leventhal's (1971) finding that European American evaluators tended to base reactions to African American workers on whether the individual was behaving in a socially approved fashion.

Importantly, socially approved standards are defined by the majority group, the European Americans. If African Americans behave according to their own cultural norms, they will be perceived as less similar, which will have a negative impact on all aspects of their interactions with European Americans.

In contrast, from a minority standpoint, the similarity of majority group members is secondary in determining intergroup attitudes. Minority group members recognize that majority standards of culture are somewhat incompatible with their own, due to their immersion in European American culture, therefore, so perceived knowledge of European American culture is not significantly related to their interaction dimensions. More salient are factors that have contributed to their current minority status—the history of past conflict and satisfaction with previous interactions.

Emics and Etics

Both groups (European American and African American) are participants in the same cross-cultural interactions. Thus, it might seem reasonable to expect the interrelations between variables to be similar for the two groups. Differences emerged across groups, however.

One possibility is that these differences may be explained in terms of the power and status differences of the groups in American society. An alternative explanation may lie in an etic-emic distinction. An etic is a general phenomenon that exists across cultures. In contrast, an emic is the particular manifestation of an etic in a given culture. For some variables, such as perceived history of conflict, perceived cultural distance, and perceived similarity, it is reasonable to expect a core of similarity, based on events as well as differences in the perception of these events, across samples. The etics reflect the objective events; the emics reflect the culture-specific interpretation of these events. For example, the general hypothesized model is an etic explanation of intercultural interactions, and the modifications to the model (the different regression coefficients across cultures) are the emics.

The cultural and power/status differentiation explanations are not mutually exclusive. African American culture began and has persisted in the context of a minority status; thus the two are undoubtedly related.

Ogbu (1993) has argued that certain minority groups (involuntary minorities) display two types of cultural differences. The primary factor consists of "ancestral cultural practices," and the secondary factor consists of "responses to the difficult nature of intercultural contact."

Research on interpersonal interactions, and on work groups more specifically, tends to neglect the specific characteristics of groups in favor of studying general processes and adopting a value-free approach. In some respects this approach may be detrimental to our understanding. It seems important for both application and theory to be able to parse issues of culture and power. This may be accomplished by comparing African American intercultural relations with those of "voluntary minority" cultures (e.g., Asian Americans) or by looking at African American and European American intercultural relations in the rare situations where neither group dominates the other.

Implications

Interesting implications for theory, as well as for cross-cultural work groups, stem from the current research. For instance, rather than allowing self-selection of team membership, which often leads to culturally homogeneous groups, membership might be assigned. This would ensure diverse groupings in situations where tasks are likely to be completed successfully and group members are likely to be satisfied, since satisfaction with past interaction predicts desire for future interactions. The caveat, of course, is that these contact experiences must be satisfying for all parties.

Evidence supports the implementation of educational programs to improve cross-cultural work group relations. Several means of improving intergroup contact have been discussed by Triandis et al. (1993). The current results suggest, however, that these must be tailored to the specific goal. Kirchemeyer and Cohen's (1992) findings suggest that work group performance and attachment to the group are related. Therefore, satisfaction with cross-cultural interactions in the group should be fostered. To this end, the current results suggest that knowledge of the other culture per se is not effective. Rather, a better focus would be on encouraging perceptions of similarity, and opportunity for positive interactions.

For improving intergroup attitudes generally, the cultural variables that should be emphasized are contingent on the group being trained. For European American employees, training programs that stress the similarity of African Americans at the cultural level may be effective. Training programs for the African American employees might be aimed at reducing the perceptions of a history of conflict, although this is challenging, because perceptions of a history of conflict may be resistant to change. Improving intergroup attitudes may help increase the perceptions of attachment and team membership in diverse work groups.

Implications also arise for theory. First, the basic aspects of Triandis's (1992) model for dealing with cultural diversity, as tested, were confirmed. That is, the hypothesized predictors were significant and in the direction predicted. Furthermore, the perceived cultural variables did add to prediction of most of the criterion variables beyond the contribution of the interpersonal-level variables, so they should be explicitly included in future studies of cross-cultural interaction.

Future Directions

Future studies are needed of cross-cultural interactions between European Americans and various racial minority groups. Additional racial groups would more adequately reflect the changing U.S. demographics and might help parse the issues of differential power versus differential culture. If the present results do extend to other racial minority groups, then this would support the hypothesis that power/status differences create similar models of intergroup relations for different groups. If the results fail to generalize to other racial minority groups, then the differences in findings may be due to particular aspects of the cultural groups involved, or emics.

Beyond additional samples, an important challenge is to develop a conceptual framework to study the interrelations of several groups conjointly. This would more accurately reflect the emergent population diversity. One possible strategy would be to study the relations between two groups in the context of a third group. Other possibilities certainly should be pursued to more adequately capture the complexity of the issues in cross-cultural work groups.

References

Allport, G. W. (1954). *The nature of prejudice.* Cambridge, MA: Addison-Wesley.

Amir, Y. (1969). Contact hypothesis in ethnic relations. *Psychological Bulletin, 71,* 319-341.

Babiker, I. E., Cox, J. L., & Miller, P. M. (1980). The measurement of cultural distance and its relationship to medical consultations, symptomatology, and examination performance of overseas students at Edinburgh University. *Social Psychiatry, 15*(3), 109-116.

Bass, A. R., & Turner, J. N. (1973). Ethnic group differences in relationships among criteria of job performance. *Journal of Applied Psychology, 58*(2), 101-109.

Bell, D. (1973). *The coming of postindustrial society: A venture in social forecasting.* New York: Basic Books.

Brewer, M. B., & Campbell, D. T. (1976). *Ethnocentrism and intergroup attitudes.* New York: Russell Sage.

Bureau of Labor Statistics. (1991, June). *Employment and earnings.* Washington, DC: U.S. Department of Labor.

Byrne, D. (1971). *The attraction paradigm.* New York: Academic Press.

Donnellon, A., & Kolb, D. M. (1994). Constructive for whom? The fate of diversity disputes in organizations. *Journal of Social Issues, 50*(1), 139-155.

Fiedler, F. E., Mitchell, T., & Triandis, H. C. (1971). The culture assimilator: An approach to cross-cultural training. *Journal of Applied Psychology, 55*(2), 95-102.

Fine, M. G., Johnson, F. L., & Ryan, M. S. (1990). Cultural diversity in the workplace. *Public Personnel Management, 19,* 305-319.

Fishbein, M., & Ajzen, I. (1975). *Belief, attitude, intention, and behavior: An introduction to theory and research.* Reading, MA: Addison-Wesley.

Furnham, A., & Bochner, S. (1986). *Culture shock: Psychological reactions to unfamiliar environments.* London: Methuen.

Jackson, S. E., & Alvarez, E. B. (1992). Working through diversity as a strategic imperative. In S. E. Jackson (Ed.), *Diversity in the workplace: Human resources initiatives* (pp. 13-29). New York: Guilford.

Kirchemeyer, C., & Cohen, A. (1992). Multicultural groups: Their performance and reactions with constructive conflict. *Group and Organization Management, 17,* 153-170.

Leventhal, G. S. (1971). *Equity and reward allocation in social relationships.* Research proposal submitted to the National Science Foundation.

McConahay, J. B., Hardee, B. B., & Batts, V. (1981). Has racism declined in America? It depends on who is asking and what is asked. *Journal of Conflict Resolution, 25,* 563-579.

Myrdal, G. (1944). *An American dilemma.* New York: Harper & Row.

Ogbu, J. U. (1993). Differences in cultural frame of reference. *International Journal of Behavioral Development, 16,* 483-506.

Skinner, B. F. (1981). Selection by consequences. *Science, 213,* 501-504.

Stephan, W. G., & Stephan, C. W. (1984). The role of ignorance in intergroup relations. In N. Miller & M. B. Brewer (Eds.), *Groups in contact* (pp. 229-255). Orlando, FL: Academic Press.

Triandis, H. C. (1992, July). *Creating culture-sensitive organizations.* Paper presented at the meeting of the International Congress of Psychology, Brussels, Belgium.

Triandis, H. C., Hall, E. R., & Ewen, R. B. (1965). Member heterogeneity and dyadic creativity. *Human Relations, 18*(1), 33-35.

Triandis, H. C., Kurowski, L. L., & Gelfand, M. J. (1993). Workplace diversity. In M. D. Dunnette & L. Hough (Eds.), *Handbook of industrial and organizational psychology* (2nd ed., Vol. 2, pp. 769-827). Palo Alto, CA: Consulting Psychologists Press.

Wilson, P. M. (1986). Black culture and sexuality. *Journal of Social Work and Human Sexuality, 4*(3), 29-46.

6

Self and Other
"Face" and Work Group Dynamics

P. CHRISTOPHER EARLEY
AMY E. RANDEL

People interact with and are interdependent on others as they work in organizations. People work together to perform various tasks (e.g., assembly of an automobile) as well as to meet social needs. In this chapter, we examine the importance of a person's self-presentation in a social context, or "face" (Goffman, 1959), in relation to the dynamics of work groups. We pay special attention to applications in work settings such as participative decision making and cooperative work teams.

Overview of Groups and Teams

Gersick (1988, 1989), Guzzo and Waters (1982), Hackman (1990), and McGrath (1984) have applied group research to the study of evolving work teams. The existing literature on work teams has focused on a number of aspects of group dynamics, such as task structure (Steiner, 1972), demographics (Tsui, O'Reilly, & Egan, 1992), process (Gersick, 1988), and collective efficacy (Bandura, 1986; Gibson, 1995; Guzzo & Shea, 1992). Some scholars claim that we cannot understand the dynamics of group development within a laboratory context (Goodman, 1986). Ironically, such critics often neglect cultural context from a societal viewpoint, focusing instead on the "culture" of the organization itself or on emergent norms within the group, as if they arise independently of the cultural context. We argue that this assumption is as limiting to the study of cross-cultural work groups as is overreliance on using a laboratory context.

People interact in a given social context for a variety of symbolic, utilitarian, and pragmatic purposes (Etzioni, 1968). Likewise, a number of motives underlie people's behavior in a work group context. Erez and Earley (1993) outlined three motives of the self—enhancement, efficacy, and consistency—that mediate cultural and management influences on work behavior. It is the first of these motives, enhancement, that serves as a focal point for our discussion in this chapter. By *enhancement,* Erez and Earley meant a person's desire to maintain a positive self-image and view of the self. In placing self-enhancement in a social context, it is possible to improve our understanding of how and why people interact within a work group setting in various cultural contexts.

In this chapter, we describe group and team dynamics by focusing on a person's self-presentation in a social context, or what has been referred to as "face" by a number of scholars (e.g., Goffman, 1959; Hu, 1944). Face refers to a universal aspect of interaction concerning how we present ourselves to others, and it also serves as a basis for individual self-definition. Face regulates social exchange and individual action. It varies systematically according to individual differences as well as societal value-orientations (Redding & Ng, 1982). Although this concept has been attributed predominantly to Asia (Hu, 1944), we will present a universal topology of the construct and discuss its applicability to a variety of cultural contexts.

Organizational "Face" Theory

Recently, Earley (in press) described a conceptual framework for understanding face within an organizational context (see Figure 6.1). The model consists of six basic parts: societal context, organizational context, organizational structure and content, social actor, harmony, and

Distal to Individual

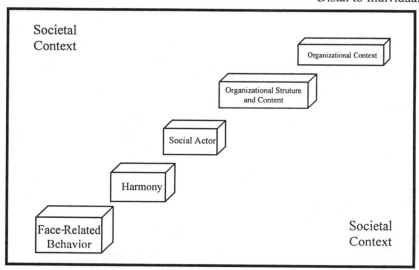

Proximal to Individual

Figure 6.1. Organizational "Face" Theory

face. Societal context is represented by six dimensions of culture: individualism versus collectivism, tight versus loose (sometimes referred to as field dependence versus independence), relationship to nature, power distance, guilt versus shame, and masculinity versus femininity. These dimensions constitute a collage in which face and interpersonal interaction are embedded. Within the societal context, the following five concepts progress from most distal to most proximal to individual actors.

In this model, *organizational context* refers to the general situation in which organizations operate within a given society, such as industry structure. There are a variety of influences on the nature of industrial organization within a given society. These include the following: synergies attributable to collections of organizations of a common type, or what is referred to as the organizational field (Giddens, 1979; Kanter, 1972); ecological forces (Freeman, 1982; Hannon & Freeman, 1977; Wholey & Brittain, 1989); and institutional practices (DiMaggio & Powell, 1983; Meyer & Rowan, 1977).

Organizational structure and content refer specifically to those influences inside of an organization that influence a social actor, such as technology, institutional roles and rules, intraorganizational dependencies, communication systems, and governance structures.

The *social actor* refers not only to the psychological makeup of a person within a society, but also to the various immediate constraints acting on an individual that determine how he or she interacts and behaves. The psychological profile of the social actor is a dynamic structure providing an important link between culture and action, and interpreting the social patterns around it. Long-term attachments and commitments to the social environment help define who people are (Sandel, 1982).

Harmony reflects processes of social exchange, social regulation, and social discourse. It refers to the systems-level, dynamic processes through which face and other behaviors are regulated. The motivation for face regulation in a group context is harmony.

Face is at the heart of this discussion; face refers to both a person's self-identity and social identity.

Overview of the Construct of Face

Face refers to the evaluation of a person based on internal and external social judgments (Earley, in press). Face does not lie completely within or outside of the individual, and it has important implications for an individual's behavior in an organization. For example, a concern for face leads junior executives to purchase expensive cars, throw big parties for the boss, or spend an exorbitant amount on private schools for their children. Face is not mere pride, however, in that it is a consequence of personal and social judgments. It is not enough that the junior executives know their children are at expensive, private schools; their superiors and colleagues must know it as well, for them to receive face. This example illustrates an important point—that face is both given (by others) as well as claimed by the self.

Traditional work on face was presented by Hu (1944), in which he argued that there are two general forms of face, one concerned with moral character (*lian*) and one concerned with reputation and status (*mianzi*) through "getting on in life" (p. 45). Both forms of face have numerous variations, such as individuals having no character (*"bu yao lian,"* or not wanting *lian*), or giving others face (*"gei mianzi"*). Ho (1976, 1994) followed the Hu tradition and provided a discussion of *lian* and *mianzi* in relation to other aspects of self-concept such as standards for behavior, personality variables, honor, dignity, and prestige. Yang (1945) argued that face is not some physical manifestation of a person, but rather it represents the prestige and status a person has attained as well as the moral character of an individual (cf. Chang & Holt, 1994). This idea is captured by Yang's statement that, "When we say that a man wants a face, we mean that he wants to be given honor, prestige, praise, flattery, or concession, whether or not these are merited. Face is really a personal psychological satisfaction, a social esteem accorded by others" (p. 167).

Erving Goffman (1959, 1967) paid the greatest attention to social exchange relevant to face and self-presentation. Goffman argued that people participate in social interactions, or performances, relying on self-presentation and impression manipulation to regulate their self-image. He divided social behavior into two categories, front-stage and back-stage (Goffman, 1959, 1974). Front-stage behavior refers to those aspects of self that others view, and back-stage behavior refers to inner and intimate aspects of self that are private and ego threatening. Face-work reflects the actions taken by a person to make whatever he is doing consistent with face. Face-work also serves to counteract incidents or events that threaten other people's face. Two basic forms of face-work, "avoidance" and "corrective," are used to regulate face. Avoidance means that a person avoids engaging in actions that would threaten the face of others or self. Corrective refers to a proactive reestablishment of someone else's face as a result of an infraction of their face.

In a discussion of politeness and social discourse, Brown and Levinson (1978) described face as the public self-image a person wishes to claim. There are two aspects of face, negative (e.g., basic claim to territories and preserves, reflecting a desire to act unimpeded by others) and positive (e.g., consistent self-images maintained to be socially desirable to others). These authors described a number of face-threatening acts, such as pressuring someone to act in a certain fashion, and expressing disapproval or criticism of others.

Ting-Toomey (1988) described a face theory in relation to conflict management, presenting a general model of communication and negotiation in which face was seen as a core element. Her model borrowed from the dual-concerns approach to negotiation and conflict management. It contrasted positive versus negative face with self-face versus other-face concerns. In addition, she described two cross-cutting dimensions of cultural values, individualism/collectivism and high/low context cultures, from which she made a series of predictions concerning face and conflict management/negotiation styles. According to her model, collectivists are very concerned with the preservation of harmony and maintaining positive self-evaluations. If an in-group member is threatened, the response to such a threat is not due to an individual face response; rather, it is due to the desire to avoid conflict within the in-group context.

According to Earley's (in press) framework, face has two general forms, *lian* and *mianzi*, as well as two sources, internal and external. The resulting 2×2 topology, shown in Table 6.1, illustrates the interplay of face type with source. For example, an employee who steals company supplies answers to his or her conscience as well as a supervisor. From Goffman's perspective, a critical external aspect of face is the symbolic nature of a person's actions within a given social context. Thus, an employee who transgresses may lose face in a company having high moral standards of conduct, but he or she may not in a company for which such actions are ignored or reinforced by peers. Face, then, captures those aspects of self externally presented to one's peers and community, as well as internal standards of actions as defined by oneself and important referent others. This topology encompasses the various existing approaches to face by incorporating internal and external referents as well as social position and moral judgments.

"Face" in an Organization

The importance of face, *lian* and *mianzi*, in an organizational setting can be understood through the model presented in Figure 6.1. Face is regulated so that social actors can interact in an organizational and social context. That is to say, a person's behavior reflects, in part, his or her attempt to establish and maintain face across a range of social settings.

Lian refers to a person's respect derived from a society based on the fulfillment of societal obligations. It is maintained as long as a person acts morally within the dictates of society. For example, according to a

Table 6.1
Taxonomy of Face in Organizations

Sources	Forms	
	Lian	*Mianzi*
Internally enacted	Moral standard of behavior internally referenced. Examples: Feeling of guilt because of a personal failure such as failure to achieve a self-set goal for work.	Personal view of one's accomplishments. Example: Personal status for working at a major work organization.
Externally enacted	Social evaluation of the morality/goodness of a person's actions. Example: Recognition of a person's integrity and honor for engaging in extra-role work performance.	Social recognition of a person's position vis-à-vis other social actors. Example: Recognition of a person's position in a company based on office location, expense account, and so on.

recent report in the *New York Times* (Johnson, 1996), a man who was a top manager for a division of CBS that was going to be closed was asked by an employee whether he thought it was a good time for the employee to buy a house. Even though the top manager knew that the employee soon would be laid off, the manager did not divulge what he knew, because he thought that it was in CBS's best interests for the employee not to suspect any problems. The employee, who bought a house and lost his job shortly afterwards, was subject to severe financial problems that could at least have been minimized if he had received honest advice from the manager. Lying and deception reflect a violation of employees' rights in this example, and the manager lost *lian* as a result. These actions need not be public. An individual who engages in such deception has lost *lian* based on societal standards of moral conduct, even if others do not uncover the deception. It is sufficient that the person knows.

In a culture stressing shame, the standards on which *lian* is based are heavily tied to relationship networks. For example, in Chinese society, immoral acts are harshly judged by one's in-group, and people avoid committing social infractions to avoid the judgments of others. In an internally focused culture such as in the United States, people avoid committing such infractions to avoid the personal experience of guilt or remorse. Thus, *lian* refers to the rules of moral conduct in a given society, and some of these rules are based on universals of morality. In defining moral goodness or character, a number of scholars have provided etic, or universal, standards. Recently, Wilson (1993) has argued for four universal morals (sympathy, self-control, justice, and duty), suggesting that there are universal standards or rules that constitute a person's *lian,* or moral character. The moral value of duty drives such an adherence to social laws and contracts. So, although some people may emphasize duty over sympathy, or self-control over fairness, these standards are prevalent throughout the world. From the perspective of face, people's actions are judged in terms of their impact on, and reflection of, these moral standards.

Mianzi reflects a dynamic interplay of the person in the organizational situation. That is to say, *mianzi* can be gained or lost through ongoing interactions with others, and it can be acquired through a variety of ways. First, *mianzi* is gained as a result of a person's role enacted in an organization. Thus, a maintenance worker has little *mianzi,* whereas a senior executive has a great deal. Status of position in an organizational hierarchy provides face directly through the prestige of a job title, as well as indirectly through organizational "perks" such as a company car or expense account. Second, *mianzi* is gained through physical attributes and characteristics. An attractive man or woman who looks like a model has *mianzi* attributable to physical appearance. Clothes worn, car driven, and personal appearance contribute to *mianzi.* Third, a person can gain *mianzi* by acting "beautifully." Someone who shows him or herself to be generous gains *mianzi* through such actions. For instance, someone might help out a new coworker who has not learned his job and thereby, enhance her own *mianzi.* These factors enhance *mianzi* through an individual's personal actions.

Mianzi also is an exchangeable social currency that can be received from others. For instance, a graduate student gains *mianzi* by having a visiting scholar praise her question at a talk, and an employee gains *mianzi* after receiving company praise for an innovative suggestion. A person gains *mianzi* through instrumental relationships with others such as having a famous relative (e.g., Billy Carter, who gained instant fame much to the chagrin of his presidential brother), or having important friends (e.g., knowing powerful people). Being the victor in friendly competitions (e.g., putting up the largest holiday display in the neighborhood, or giving the biggest cocktail party in the company) can increase one's *mianzi.*

In addition to accumulating *mianzi,* it is possible to lose it, as well. In many respects, this is more important than the benefits one might achieve simply by safeguarding one's accomplishments (Goffman, 1959). There are a number of ways that a person might lose *mianzi.* First, direct criticism, particularly from powerful others, siphons off a person's *mianzi.* Second, the exposure of a person's mistakes or weaknesses dilutes *mianzi.* Third, cruel or stingy people may lose *mianzi* in the minds of others. Interestingly, someone who has less *mianzi* may have the power to adversely affect the *mianzi* of a more powerful individual. For instance, a low-level employee can dilute the *mianzi* of a powerful manager by claiming that the manager has acted disrespectfully toward the employee. By not affording the employee reasonable respect, the manager loses respect (*mianzi*) from others. *Mianzi* can also be lost through poor investment decisions, economic troubles, and so forth.

There are several important differences between *lian* and *mianzi.* Although *mianzi* is conceptualized as a currency of self-status, to be lost or gained, *lian* refers to a moral conduct expected of all citizens. A new job incumbent has *lian* as a right of organizational membership; only an experienced employee may earn *mianzi* from his or her work colleagues. A second and perhaps more important distinction is that *lian* involves relatively stable attributions of individuals. For instance, an employee who steals will be branded as immoral, and so must be monitored by his or her organization. In this sense, one's actions forge moral character, and can lead to a fall from grace. The reason that the loss of *lian* is not comparable to a loss of *mianzi* (i.e., is not easily recovered) is that it denotes a violation of societal rules for conduct. In essence, loss of *lian* signals that a person does not want to be a member of society, and so other people have reason to mistrust this person in the future. Of course, intentionality must be assumed for such an interpretation to be made.

Another difference between *lian* and *mianzi* is that *lian* cannot be given to someone by another person. A manager cannot "give" her subordinate *lian*; the subordinate must earn it. *Lian* is acknowledged and affirmed by fellow group members, however, and is "given" in this sense. Interestingly, the two forms of face may be interrelated. For instance, if a subordinate gives proper respect to her superior, then the superior maintains *mianzi*. In doing so, the subordinate also has reaffirmed a natural chain of command, and has demonstrated her *lian*.

Using Face to Understand Work Groups and Teams in Organizations

What is the relative significance of each form of face to social interaction in work groups and teams? This is a question best addressed by examining the nature of the interdependence of a person in his or her social context. The importance of each form of face is influenced by the strength and character of the relationship ties that comprise teams and work groups. According to the model proposed by organizational face theory, work groups and teams are embedded in the first three elements of the model (societal context, organizational context, and organizational structure and content) and depend on the last three components of the model (social actor, harmony, and face) for their essence.

Face and Interpersonal Ties

In this analysis, we use forms of social ties described by Foa and Foa (1974) and Hwang (1987)—expressive versus instrumental versus mixed. An expressive tie refers to a relationship characterized by shared affection, warmth, and respect, such as is expected in a family context, where the tie itself is an end rather than a means. An instrumental tie refers to a relationship in which individuals focus on maintaining their personal attributes, material position, and possessions; relationships are established to provide an individual with personal gain. Finally, a mixed tie is a relationship in which individuals seek to influence others through varied means; although some trust and mutual support exists, individuals do not view the relationship itself as an end. In mixed ties, people share common characteristics (e.g., come from the same town or region) and some common goals, but each person views himself or herself as the central point of the interaction. Although an expressive tie is relatively stable and long lived, a mixed tie may be somewhat short lived, and an instrumental tie can be quite short lived, such as a single exchange between a shopkeeper and an out-of-town visitor in need of supplies.

The significance of these three forms of interdependencies lies in the nature of how face is maintained, gained, or lost. *Mianzi* can be traded or exchanged, analogous to a physical product, in a variety of these interdependence structures. Although *mianzi* can be exchanged in any of the three ties, it will be most heavily emphasized in an instrumental or mixed tie because it can provide individuals with desirable gains that are immediately measurable. For example, a person might ingratiate himself by complimenting his boss's golf game to gain a promotion from a boss or to get a desired assignment. Whereas an instrumental tie is characterized by a strong norm of reciprocity and equity (Hwang, 1987), a mixed tie is characterized by an increasing emphasis on the relationship itself as an important outcome. In a mixed tie, *mianzi* may be exchanged as a means of further strengthening the relationship for future interactions, rather than simply obtaining an immediate outcome or reward. For instance, a subordinate might ingratiate herself to facilitate a relationship with her boss as well as to obtain a desired raise. In this circumstance, a good relationship (i.e., friendship) becomes an important outcome. Thus, a subordinate may give *mianzi* to her superior to foster a stronger social relationship with the superior. *Mianzi* is relevant to relationships characterized by expressive ties insofar as *mianzi* is given to promote social harmony within an in-group. Gaining *mianzi* in the name of one's group in the presence of individuals external to the group enhances group harmony.

Lian is more relevant for expressive and mixed ties rather than instrumental ones. Why is this? In both expressive and mixed ties, *lian* becomes increasingly important because of the implied longevity of the relationship. In other words, *lian* is important because it assures both parties that the other is sincere and dedicated to mutual interests. In brief interactions with strangers, the only rules that need to be endorsed are those that affect and regulate exchange. Questions of character are minimized through emphasis and dependence on rules of exchange (e.g., equity or reciprocity), and the market becomes a surrogate for moral character (Homans, 1961; Williamson, 1975; Wilson, 1993). For longer term relationships such as an expressive tie, *lian* is more critical for several reasons: first, people are concerned with maintaining and promoting the relationship as an end; and second, a violation of moral principles threatens the existence and stability of the collective. Thus, although market forces may govern an instrumental relationship, an expressive one is regulated through personal integrity and devotion to the good of the relationship.

Although any of these three types of ties can be found in teams, mixed ties probably are most frequently found in organizational teams. The extreme individual-oriented concerns representative of instrumental ties interfere with the benefits of work performed by a team. Expressive ties may be found in organizations that foster devotion and commitment. For example, the life-long employment and social connectedness between Japanese companies and their employees encourage expressive ties, and this implies a heavy emphasis on *lian*. In the mixed tie relationships more commonly found in U.S. organizations, *mianzi* becomes relevant as individuals negotiate their roles in terms of both personal and group goals. Although people working in teams share common work goals, individual desires for prestige and status may motivate people to attempt to gain *mianzi* from their group members. The common interests that group members share, however, can also lead to *mianzi* that is sought on behalf of the group's prestige.

Within a cross-cultural team, the form that mixed ties take may differ in ways that are determined by the various cultures that comprise the team. Although all mixed ties share the characteristic that each person involved views himself or herself as the focal point of social interaction, how people relate to others during the interaction can be influenced by culture. How culture affects interaction styles can be illustrated with face. For example, power distance, or the extent to which inequality is accepted within a culture (Hofstede, 1980), has been found to be positively related to, but independent from *mianzi* (Randel, Lewis, & Earley, 1996). In a cross-cultural team in which different levels of power distance are represented, different levels of emphasis could be placed on gaining *mianzi*. Not only might the pursuit of *mianzi* vary within such a team, but also the manner in which gaining *mianzi* is considered acceptable could differ for each team member. Attempting to earn *mianzi* in the name of one's group may be the only acceptable form of *mianzi* for some team members, whereas gaining *mianzi* as an outcome of a competition with other team members might be considered to be a viable way of enhancing group performance by others.

In the next two sections of this chapter, we use the concept of face and social ties to explore several aspects of work groups and teams in organizations.

Applying Face to Work Teams

A great deal of attention has been focused on the use of individual-based versus group-based job design (Hackman & Oldham, 1980; Tannenbaum, 1980; Trist & Bamforth, 1951). The focus of much of this work has been on the sociotechnical approach to job design (Thorsrud & Emery, 1970). In this approach, emphasis is placed on maintaining intact work groups by integrating the methods of production with the needs of a group. The benefits to group members are to allow them more discretion in their work, provide them control over their nonwork activities, and so on. The advantage of this approach for group-oriented cultures is that these work groups are maintained so that workers do not experience alienation. The basic features used in the famous Saab engine factory experiment included (a) assembly groups rather than assembly lines; (b) assembly of a whole engine by a group; (c) determination by group members of how work was to be allocated within the group; (d) a cycle time of 30 minutes rather than 1 8/10s minutes that was typical of the assembly line; and, (e) selection of work mates by team members (Tannenbaum, 1980). Rubenowitz (1974) provided a summary of several of the Scandinavian experiments in sociotechnical systems and he reported favorable reactions to the system by managers and employees. This approach is clearly consistent with the motives of growth and self-presentation reflecting collectivistic values of group togetherness and functioning.

From a face perspective, the Saab experience illustrates an interesting point about work structure versus group context. To some extent, the introduction of automated assembly technology has the potential to remove direct, interpersonal contact and the type of interactions that are related to face. In the Saab experiment, the means of production were altered to provide an opportunity for continuing social relationships among work group members. By maintaining group structure, *lian* was supported through in-group loyalty. Also, the opportunity to keep an intact group provided group members with the chance to further develop *mianzi*. An interesting aspect of *mianzi* is that it has greatest significance if given by a friend rather than a stranger. Thus, the motivational influence of *mianzi* is enhanced by the use of intact work groups in production.

A second area of work teams that has received considerable attention is participation in goal setting. Participation in decision making and goal setting is an effective way to enhance a group member's attachment to a goal. Work by a number of researchers (e.g., Erez, 1986; Erez & Earley, 1987) has demonstrated that participation in goal setting has a positive impact on goal commitment and performance, and that the effects differ somewhat across cultural settings. An analysis using face suggests that goal-setting interventions may be useful because they provide an opportunity for individuals to regulate face. For instance, Erez and Earley (1987) described a study of kibbutz members in Israel. During an initial stage of their experiment, Erez noted that the participative goal condition group initially set very low group goals, among the lowest of any of the three samples. The researchers found that the kibbutz members sought to establish a goal sufficiently low to ensure that all group members would achieve it. In face terms, the kibbutz members set a goal level such that *mianzi* (tied to performance competence) would not be threatened. In contrast, members of an American sample tended to set quite high goals for themselves. This was attributable, in part, to a desire to appear competent in front of others. In the case of the kibbutz, a tight-knit group of people who endorsed egalitarian values, face was preserved through the maintenance of equality among group members. For the individualistic Americans, face was maintained and strengthened by asserting inequality through interpersonal competition. In both the American and kibbutz examples, *mianzi* was an important facet of participation in setting performance goals.

Another type of work group is the Japanese management quality circle (Cole, 1980; Lincoln, Olson, & Hanada, 1978; Tannenbaum, 1980; Triandis, 1989). In this approach, quality control techniques are taught to all employees, and all employees have opportunities to participate in quality circles. The basic principle of the quality circle is the provision of group-based suggestions for the improvement of the work environment and production (Cole, 1980). Although some critics suggest that quality circle participation is coercive (Cole, 1980), the system does afford participants personal prestige, occupational opportunities, and limited financial incentives through bonuses. What is unique about the quality circle system is that it appears to enhance worker commitment and loyalty to an organization through a participative system of work involvement.

When we use the concept of face to analyze quality circles, we find that face maybe useful in a number of different cultures for different reasons. The success of the quality circle technique is consistent with the ideological orientation of the Japanese. It reaffirms an individual's sense of group membership and it provides an important opportunity for establishing one's face in relation to others in the in-group. It is particularly effective because it provides workers with an opportunity to reaffirm face within a group context. An effective quality circle is acknowledged by other quality circles, the general workforce, and the organization, and this enhances the face of each quality circle member.

American managers have asked to what extent these methods can be adopted. Although American workers may not have such a strong in-group identity as Japanese workers, quality circles may be useful in the United States if organizations focus on an individual's sense of personal image, or face. As individualistic Americans work within a quality circle, there are opportunities to demonstrate personal competence in front of others and thus to earn *mianzi*. Furthermore, the cooperative context underlying a quality circle provides group members with occasions for giving face to others in their group if they are effective performers.

Applying Face to Group Decisions

The largest stream of cross-cultural research on group decision making was stimulated by Lewin's (1951) field theory. The essence of his approach was that participation in the decision-making process will enhance individuals' acceptance of, and commitment to, a decision. In follow-up work using Lewin's framework, Misumi and his colleagues (e.g., Misumi, 1984; Misumi & Haraoka, 1960; Misumi & Shinohara, 1967) have shown group decision methods to be highly effective in inducing attitude and habit changes for Japanese workers. Misumi found that the influence of participation was more effective when using natural groups than ad hoc ones. A more naturalistic form of decision making for the Japanese work environment is referred to as the *ringi-sei* system (Erez, 1994; Nakane, 1970; Triandis, 1989). In this consensus system, decisions are made "anonymously," and subordinates and leaders are bound together in obligations and loyalty. Decisions are made according to a bottom-up procedure: A subordinate sends a tentative solution or decision to some problem, proceeds to "clear it" through increasing levels of superiors, and adjusts the decision according to each level's suggestions. By the time the decision makes it to the top, it has been altered and endorsed by all individuals who will be involved in its implementation. This system reflects a strong emphasis on group loyalty and commitment. It also reflects a ritualistic style of decision making that reinforces a strong hierarchy within a particular social structure.

In a cultural context where strong norms encouraging group conformity exist, the *ringi-sei* group decision-making system may derive strength from its ability to decrease the likelihood that participants' face will be threatened. As group's decision-making process moves from an initial state in which there is a lack of consensus, to a final agreement, there are numerous risks to group harmony. In group interactions involving face-to-face contact, an imbalance in harmony may be beneficial for decision-making outcomes such as innovativeness, but it will be detrimental if it comes at the cost of group members' face. The *ringi-sei* system provides a structure that encourages contribution of individual input to decisions while minimizing the threat posed to group members' face. The highly participative nature of the *ringi-sei* system results in decisions that are formulated and approved by the entire organization. Approval for the decision is demonstrated by the written form of the *ringi sho* (distributed decision proposal) accompanied by the stamp of organization members at all levels of the firm's hierarchy (Lincoln, 1991; Jun & Muto, 1995). The collective effort put forth in forming a decision, and the written endorsement of the decision by firm members, offer confirmation of the interdependent self that is based on relationships with others (Markus & Kitayama, 1991). As the term implies, the interdependent self consists of a conception of the self as part of a relationship network among two or more people. Recall that a person's face makes reference to both self-identity and social identity. Through *ringi-sei,* the interdependent aspect of the self, which relies on interpersonal relationships, and the social identity derived from group interaction are both emphasized and fortified.

A criticism that has been made against the *ringi-sei* system is that the source of an idea is difficult to distinguish, because decisions are made anonymously through "silent" participation (Johnston, 1981). It is, however, this anonymous feature of *ringi-sei* that allows groups, particularly in collectivist cultures, to function without disrupting group harmony. The Japanese adage, "the nail that stands out gets pounded down," applies here, indicating the desire not to distinguish individuals from the group. Group members are able to verify that they are worthy of *lian,* which can be maintained by demonstrating concern for in-group harmony. An advantage of the *ringi-sei* system is that individual input to decisions is made acceptable in contexts in which individuals do not want to be distinguished from the rest of their group members.

The assumption that individuals who have contributed to a group decision should be differentiated from group members who have not, is based on the individualist assumption of high concern for *mianzi*. Individuals may earn prestige and the respect of their group members (*mianzi*) by demonstrating that it was they who contributed to the group decision. Research conducted in the United States has indicated the "equity norm" whereby employees expect to receive rewards in proportion to their contribution (Mowday, 1991). When minimizing group conflict is the goal, however, as would be expected in a collectivist context, the distribution of rewards based on equality norms is thought to be more appropriate (Leung & Bond, 1984; Mowday, 1991). When rewards are allocated based on equality norms, group members receive rewards based on group membership rather than on contribution. The *ringi-sei* system is aligned with equality norms and places less emphasis on *mianzi* than equity-based group-decision processes, although *mianzi* can be earned by group members via the *ringi-sei* system by performing competently as a group.

The *ringi-sei* system is beneficial for the face of those at the top level of an organizational hierarchy. Relative to those of lower status, high-status individuals are thought to have *lian* that is more vulnerable because they are expected to attain greater self-control in their behavior (Hu, 1944). By the time that a *ringi sho* (decision proposal) makes its way upward through the hierarchy, those at the top level typically approve the decision in a fairly automatic fashion (Jun & Muto, 1995). The structure of the *ringi-sei* system thus encourages the deferral of high-level managers to the group for the decision content while still ensuring that these managers are included in the decision by virtue of their stamp of approval. Although top-level managers may pose a threat to group harmony by virtue of the fact that they may be distinguished from other organization members by their position in the hierarchy, this threat is minimized through the *ringi-sei* system. Decision-making power is diffused throughout the hierarchy in *ringi sei* (Lincoln, 1991). Thus, the *ringi-sei* system has built into it a mechanism that downplays the hierarchical distinction of top managers; the self-control of those in top management levels becomes less necessary and the vulnerability of their *lian* decreases through the use of *ringi-sei*.

The outcomes that have been demonstrated to result from the use of *ringi-sei* systems in collectivistic cultures—increased job satisfaction and organizational commitment (Lincoln, 1991)—seem quite logical from the perspective of face. Through successful use of the *ringi-sei* system, the *lian* of fellow group members can be assured. The motive of the interdependent self to be incorporated into a system of interpersonal relationships may be realized (Markus & Kitayama, 1991). If positive self-definition on the job results from effective group functioning and assurances of *lian,* outcomes in the form of satisfaction and commitment can be expected to be projected onto one's job and organization, because they are the sources of such positive self-affirmation.

Implications

The assumption of organizational face theory, that individuals try to maintain their self-definition across a range of social situations, implies that teams become increasingly effective as a result of their relation to team members' self-definitions. Team members' self-definitions depend both on the cultural context in which the team is founded and on an individual's self- concept. For example, because an individualist strives to gain the status and prestige indicated by *mianzi,* opportunities for individualists to acquire *mianzi* as a result of membership in a group should increase the importance of the group to the individual, as well as the individual's willingness to exert effort for the benefit of the group. In contrast, those who derive their self-definition from *lian,* or adherence to social rules, should thrive in a team environment that allows team members to confirm their commitment to ascribed moral standards. When implementing teams or work groups in organizations, the most appropriate group format can be indicated by consideration of face and of the other components of the model proposed by organizational face theory. Individuals are motivated to affirm their self- and social-identity, or face, and group structures that allow them to do so, while recognizing the context in which face is found, should meet with success.

The examples provided in this chapter illustrate the different contextual influences that affect face in work teams. For instance, the comparison of American and kibbutz goal-setting groups demonstrates the effect of societal context, specifically the varying degrees of emphasis placed on equality/inequality, on the preservation of face. The Saab experiments were concerned with integrating groups and production methods, to use the beneficial motivational effects of intact work groups and in-group loyalty in the organization's production structure. When harmony is important or norms for group conformity exist, *ringi-sei* systems have been shown to be beneficial. Recognizing the role of face, in conjunction with the context in which it exists, can suggest how individuals can work best in a cross-cultural team environment.

References

Bandura, A. (1986). *Social foundations of thoughts and action: A social cognitive theory.* Englewood Cliffs, NJ: Prentice Hall.

Brown, P., & Levinson, S. (1978). Universals in language use. In E. N. Goody (Ed.), *Questions and politeness* (pp. 56-289). Cambridge, UK: Cambridge University Press.

Chang, H. C., & Holt, R. G. (1994). A Chinese perspective on face as interrelational concern. In S. Ting-Toomey (Ed.), *The challenge of facework: Cross-cultural and interpersonal issues* (pp. 95-132). Albany: State University of New York Press.

Cole, R. E. (1980). *Work, mobility, and participation: A comparative study of American and Japanese industry.* Berkeley: University of California Press.

DiMaggio, P. J., & Powell, W. W. (1983). The iron cage revisited: Institutional isomorphism and collective rationality in organizational fields. *American Sociological Review, 48,* 147-160.

Earley, P. C. (in press). *Face, harmony, and social structure: An analysis of organizational behavior across cultures.* New York: Oxford University Press.

Erez, M. (1986). The congruence of goal-setting strategies with sociocultural values and its effect on performance. *Journal of Management, 12*(4), 83-90.

Erez, M. (1994). Toward a model of cross-cultural industrial-organizational psychology. In H. C. Triandis, M. D. Dunnette, & L. M. Hough (Eds.), *Handbook of industrial-organizational psychology* (2nd ed., Vol. 4, pp. 559-607). Palo Alto, CA: Consulting Psychologists Press.

Erez, M., & Earley, P. C. (1987). Comparative analysis of goal-setting strategies across cultures. *Journal of Applied Psychology, 72,* 658-665.

Erez, M., & Earley, P. C. (1993). *Culture, self-identity, and work.* New York: Oxford.

Etzioni, A. (1968). *The active society.* New York: Free Press.

Foa, U. G., & Foa, E. B. (1974). *Societal structures of the mind.* Springfield, IL: Charles C Thomas.

Freeman, J. H. (1982). Organizational life cycles and natural selection processes. In B. Staw & L. L. Cummings (Eds.), *Research in organizational behavior* (pp. 1-32). Greenwich, CT: JAI.

Gersick, C. J. G. (1988). Time and transition in work teams: Toward a new model of group development. *Academy of Management Journal, 31*(1), 9- 41.

Gersick, C. J. G. (1989). Making time: Predictable transitions in task groups. *Academy of Management Journal, 32,* 274-309.

Gibson, C. B. (1995). *Determinants and consequences of group-efficacy beliefs in work organizations in the U.S., Hong Kong, and Indonesia.* Unpublished doctoral dissertation, University of California, Irvine.

Giddens, A. (1979). *Central problems in social theory: Action, structure, and contradiction in social analysis.* Berkeley: University of California Press.

Goffman, E. (1959). *The presentation of self in everyday life.* Garden City, NY: Doubleday.

Goffman, E. (1967). *Interaction ritual: Essays in face-to-face behavior.* Chicago: Aldine.

Goffman, E. (1974). *Frame analysis: An essay on the organization of experience.* New York: Harper & Row.

Goodman, P. S. (Ed.). (1986). *Designing effective work groups.* San Francisco: Jossey-Bass.

Guzzo, R. A., & Shea, G. P. (1992). Group performance and intergroup relations in organizations. In M. D. Dunnette & L. M. Hough (Eds.), *Handbook of industrial and organizational psychology* (2nd ed., Vol. 3, pp. 269-314). Palo Alto, CA: Consulting Psychologists Press.

Guzzo, R. A., & Waters, J. A. (1982). The expression of the affect and the performance of decision-making groups. *Journal of Applied Psychology, 67*(1), 67-74.

Hackman, J. R. (1990). Introduction. In J. R. Hackman (Ed.), *Groups that work (and those that don't)* (pp. 1-14). San Francisco: Jossey-Bass.

Hackman, J. R., & Oldham, G. R. (1980). *Work redesign.* Reading, MA: Addison-Wesley.

Hannon, M. T., & Freeman, J. H. (1977). The population ecology of organizations. *American Journal of Sociology, 82,* 929-964.

Ho, D. Y. F. (1976). On the concept of face. *American Journal of Sociology, 81,* 867-884.

Ho, D. Y. F. (1994). Face dynamics: From conceptualization to measurement. In S. Ting-Toomey (Ed.), *The challenge of facework: Cross-cultural and interpersonal issues* (pp. 269-286). Albany: State University of New York Press.

Hofstede, G. (1980). *Culture's consequences: International differences in work-related values.* Beverly Hills, CA: Sage.

Homans, G. C. (1961). *Social behavior: Its elementary forms.* New York: Harcourt, Brace & World.

Hu, H. C. (1944). The Chinese concepts of "face." *American Anthropologist, 46,* 45-64.

Hwang, K. (1987). Face and favor: The Chinese power game. *American Journal of Sociology, 92,* 944-974.

Johnson, K. (1996, March 7). In the class of '70, wounded winners: The downsizing of America. *New York Times,* A1, A12-14.

Johnston, J. (1981). *Ringi*-decision-making, Japanese style. *Management World, 10*(5), 16-18, 44.

Jun, J. S., & Muto, H. (1995). The hidden dimensions of Japanese administration: Culture and its impact. *Public Administration Review, 55*(2), 125-134.

Kanter, R. M. (1972). *Commitment and community: Communes and utopias in sociological perspective.* Cambridge, MA: Harvard University Press.

Leung, K., & Bond, M. (1984). The impact of cultural collectivism on reward allocation. *Journal of Personality and Social Psychology, 47,* 793-804.

Lewin, K. (1951). *Field theory and social science.* New York: Harper.

Lincoln, J. R. (1991). Employee work attitudes and management practice in the United States and Japan: Evidence from a large comparative survey. In R. M. Steers, L. W. Porter Morris, & C. W. Morris (Eds.), *Motivation and work behavior* (pp. 326-341). New York: McGraw-Hill.

Lincoln, J. R., Olson, J., & Hanada, M. (1978). Cultural effects on organizational structure: The case of Japanese firms in the United States. *American Sociological Review, 43,* 829-847.

Markus, H. R., & Kitayama, S. (1991). Culture and the self: Implications for cognition, emotion, and motivation. *Psychological Review, 98,* 224-253.

McGrath, J. E. (1984). *Groups: Interaction and performance.* Englewood Cliffs, NJ: Prentice Hall.

Meyer, J. W., & Rowan, B. (1977). Institutionalized organizations: Formal structure as myth and ceremony. *American Journal of Sociology, 83,* 340-363.

Misumi, J. (1984). Decision making in Japanese groups and organizations. In B. Wilpert & A. Sorge (Eds.), *International perspectives on organizational democracy* (pp. 92-123). New York: John Wiley.

Misumi, J., & Haraoka, K. (1960). An experimental study of group decision making (III). *Japanese Journal of Educational Social Psychology, 1,* 136-153.

Misumi, J., & Shinohara, H. (1967). A study of effects of group decision on accident prevention. *Japanese Journal of Educational Social Psychology, 6,* 123-134.

Mowday, R. T. (1991). Equity theory predictions of behavior in organizations. In R. M. Steers & L. W. Porter (Eds.), *Motivation and work behavior* (pp. 111-131). New York: McGraw-Hill.

Nakane, C. (1970). *Japanese society.* Berkeley: University of California Press.

Randel, E. A., Lewis, K. M., & Earley, P. C. (1996, August). *Face and concepts of efficacy: Linking social presence with social capability.* Paper presented at the annual meeting of the Academy of Management, Cincinnati, OH.

Redding, S. G., & Ng, M. (1982). The role of "face" in the organizational perceptions of Chinese managers. *Organization Studies, 3,* 201-219.

Rubenowitz, S. (1974). *Experiences in industrial democracy and changes in work organizations in Sweden* (Report No. 1). Goteborg, Sweden: University of Goteborg, Department of Psychology.

Sandel, M. J. (1982). *Liberalism and the limits of justice.* Cambridge, UK: Cambridge University Press.

Steiner, I. D. (1972). *Group process and productivity.* New York: Academic Press.

Tannenbaum, A. S. (1980). Organizational psychology. In H. C. Triandis & R. W. Brislin (Eds.), *Handbook of cross-cultural psychology* (Vol. 5, pp. 281-334). Boston: Allyn & Bacon.

Thorsrud, E., & Emery, F. E. (1970). Industrial democracy in Norway. *Industrial Relations, 9,* 187-196.

Ting-Toomey, S. (1988). Intercultural conflict styles: A face negotiation theory. In Y. Kim & W. Gudykunst (Eds.), *Theories in intercultural communication* (pp. 213-235). Newbury Park, CA: Sage.

Triandis, H. C. (1989). Cross-cultural studies of individualism and collectivism. In J. Berman (Ed.), *Nebraska symposium on motivation* (Vol. 37, pp. 41-133). Lincoln: University of Nebraska Press.

Trist, E. L., & Bamforth, K. W. (1951). Some social psychological consequences of the longwall method of coal getting. *Human Relations, 4*(1), 3-38.

Tsui, A. S., O'Reilly, C. A., III, & Egan, T. D. (1992). Being different: Relational demography and organizational attachment. *Administrative Science Quarterly, 37,* 549-579.

Wholey, D. R., & Brittain, J. (1989). Characterizing environmental variation. *Academy of Management Journal, 32,* 867-882.

Williamson, O. E. (1975). *Markets and hierarchies.* New York: Free Press.

Wilson, J. Q. (1993). *The moral sense.* New York: Free Press.

Yang, M. C. (1945). *A Chinese village.* New York: Columbia University Press.

7

Cross-Cultural Barriers to Effective Communication in Aviation

JUDITH ORASANU
UTE FISCHER
JEANNIE DAVISON

**Tenerife, Canary Islands,
March 3, 1977**

A bomb explosion at Las Palmas (Canary Islands) Airport closed that airport and caused a number of international flights to be diverted to Los Rodeos (Tenerife) Airport. The large number of flights diverted to Tenerife caused overcrowding on the apron, making it very difficult for aircraft to maneuver. Two B-747s were directed to back taxi on the active runway (RW12), first a KLM aircraft, followed several minutes later by a PanAm flight. Low clouds were blowing intermittently across the runway at the time, making it impossible for the crew members of the two aircraft to see each other. On reaching the departure end of RW12, the KLM crew requested clearance to take off and performed their pretakeoff procedures. The Tenerife Tower controller gave the KLM

AUTHORS' NOTE: We wish to acknowledge support for the research on which this chapter was based from NASA, Code UL, and the FAA, Office of the Chief Scientific and Technical Advisor for Human Factors, AAR-100. In addition, we would like to thank Malcolm Brenner and Barry Strauch of the National Transportation Safety Board and Robert Woodhouse of the International Air Transport Association for their invaluable assistance in locating information for this chapter.

134

crew their departure clearance (but NOT the takeoff clearance), which they read back, ending with "We are now at takeoff."

Unbeknownst to the controller, the captain began advancing the thrust levers for takeoff while the first officer (F/O) was finishing the readback. In response, the controller said: "OK, Stand by for takeoff . . . I will call you," but the KLM crew only heard the "OK." On hearing the KLM crew say they were "at takeoff," the PanAm crew called the tower to remind him that they were still taxiing on Runway 12. On the KLM flight deck, there was a squeal on the radio at this time, so they did not hear the PanAm transmission. As the KLM captain was advancing the power levers for takeoff, the following dialogue took place in the KLM cockpit:

Flight Engineer: *Is he not clear, then?*

Captain: *What do you say?*

Flight Engineer: *Is he not clear that PanAmerican?*

Captain: *Oh, yes.* (emphatic)

The KLM flight continued its takeoff roll in the fog toward the PanAm aircraft, which was still taxiing on the same runway. By the time the crews of the two aircraft could see each other, it was too late to avert the collision that resulted in 583 fatalities, the worst disaster in airline history (Ministerio de Transportes, 1978; National Transportation Safety Board [NTSB], 1977).

Communication is the glue that binds participants together in group interaction or team tasks. It is a transparent medium through which group work is organized and accomplished. Participants may be inches apart, may not be in the same room, or may be hundreds of miles distant. For tasks requiring interaction and coordination among multiple players, communication is the central issue. It is through communication that we make our intentions known to others, request and provide information, invite others to share their thoughts and suggestions, direct others to take actions, and manage social relations among participants (Kanki & Palmer, 1993).

Effective and efficient communication is especially critical in high-risk environments that require coordination among team members. This is especially true when emergency conditions impose time pressure and present considerable ambiguity concerning the nature of the problem. Examples of these environments include the hospital operating room or shock trauma center, offshore oil platforms, nuclear power plants, fire fighting and police sites, space shuttles, and military theaters of operation.

This chapter specifically addresses communication in commercial aviation, a highly proceduralized domain that involves coordination not only among pilots on the flight deck, but between the flight crew and cabin attendants, and between flight crew and controllers, dispatchers, and maintenance personnel on the ground. Aviation is a challenging field for analysis of discourse because much communication is highly routinized, especially among the flight crew and between the flight crew and air traffic control (ATC). That is, much of the communication has been standardized: Formulaic utterances are part of check lists and standard operating procedures performed by pilots (standardized callouts during takeoff, at certain altitudes, and during descent and landings). Communication with air traffic control to request clearances or when checking in at sector boundaries, and clearances given by controllers to flight crews, are—or should be—grounded in rigorous, standardized, explicit language, with variation coming primarily in the numbers (e.g., altitudes, speeds, headings, and runways). This standardization of communication is intended to reduce communication errors. Why it doesn't always work is the topic of this chapter.

In addition to discussing failures of communication in aviation, we will describe features of effective communication and what can be done to enhance communication success. These issues will be addressed from the perspective of what we have learned about communication from flight crews talking within the flight deck and between pilots and ground personnel (primarily air traffic controllers), both within the United States and in other countries. The feasibility and appropriateness of "exporting" U.S.-developed training approaches will also be discussed.

The Importance of
Communication to Flight Safety

Successful flight operations require much more from air crews than the complex skills necessary to fly the aircraft. Flight safety has repeatedly been jeopardized by poor crew communication or poor communication between crews and ATC (for a review of accident investigations and recommendations by the National Transportation Safety Board, see Kayten, 1993). To illustrate the importance of communication to aviation, let us first consider two crashes in which language problems of some type contributed to the crash.

Kuala Lumpur, Malaysia, February 18, 1989 (B-747)

A Flying Tigers 747 cargo flight was preparing for landing in Kuala Lumpur. Fog obscured visibility in the mountainous terrain. The following clearances and acknowledgments were recorded:

ATC: . . . *Descend to two seven zero zero (2,700).*

Pilot: . . . *Roger—Cleared to twenty seven hundred—we're out of forty-five.*

ATC: . . . *Descend two (to?) four zero zero—cleared for NDB approach 33.*

Pilot: . . . *OK—four zero zero.*

The intended clearance was 2,400 ft., but what the pilots heard and read back was 400 ft. The aircraft's altitude alert signaled at about 1,300 ft. (approximately 1,000 ft. above the 400 ft. set in the computerized landing system) and the ground proximity warning sounded at about 500 ft. Sixteen seconds later the flight crashed into a mountain (NTSB, 1989).

Cove Neck, NY (JFK), January 25, 1990 (DC-8)

Avianca flight #052 had departed Medellin, Colombia with sufficient fuel for the planned flight to New York's JFK airport, plus 1 hour and 28 minutes of reserve fuel. Repeated periods of holding totaling 1 hour and 17 minutes, however, left them in a critical fuel state when they reached their destination. The first time the Avianca crew mentioned their critical fuel situation to the controllers was when the first officer (F/O) said: "I think we need priority." There was some discussion about how long they could hold and what their alternate was, but the crew never informed the controller that they were declaring an emergency. A request for priority has no meaning in the ATC vocabulary. The flight received normal handling for the next 39 minutes, and the crew still did not inform the controllers that they were in trouble.

Due to wind shear in the JFK area, the crew was forced to do a missed-approach on their first attempt, and the captain told the first officer, "Tell them we are in emergency." While reading back the ATC instructions, the F/O added: "Ah, we'll try once again, we're running out of fuel." The captain again told the F/O to: "Advise them we are in emergency," and the F/O replied "Yes, sir, I already advised him." The captain told the F/O a third time to "Advise him that we don't have fuel." Again the F/O merely ended a routine readback with, "We're running out of fuel, sir." During this time, the Avianca flight was handled by more than one controller, so the repeated statements about their fuel were not all directed to a single controller.

After the missed approach, the controller informed the flight that he was going to "bring you about 15 miles northeast and then turn you back for the approach. Is that fine for you and your fuel?" The F/O replied, "I guess so, thank you very much." When the captain asked what had been said, the F/O said, "The guy is angry." At 21:32 Avianca 052's engines flamed-out and the aircraft crashed a minute later, approximately 15 miles from the airport. There were 73 fatalities as a result of the crash (NTSB, 1991).

All of the examples illustrate cross-cultural misunderstandings in which language may have played a role. In the KLM/PanAm crash, the primary language of the KLM crew was Dutch; the controllers' primary language was Portuguese. All were speaking English. Use of a second language may have contributed to a lack of precision in communication along with a willingness to overlook nonstandard terminology. A similar problem occurred in the Kuala Lumpur situation: It appears the controller used a nonstandard format for giving the clearance. When the pilot incorrectly read back the clearance, the controller did not correct him. Was this because he didn't hear the error, or did he assume that the pilot had the correct information?

In the Avianca case, language plus other cultural factors contributed to the problem. The flight crew's primary language was Spanish, whereas the New York controllers spoke English. The first officer's English was much better than the Captain's and he conducted most of the communication with ATC, frequently translating English clearances for the Captain. In addition to possible English problems, culture appears to have contributed to the failure of this crew to request assistance. Colombia is a highly masculine, high power distance, and collectivist country (Hofstede, 1980). The crew may have been reluctant to request assistance from contract dispatchers while en route concerning weather or possible refueling sites, or to reject suggestions from the controllers concerning routing (Helmreich, 1994).

Communicating effectively with participants who all speak the same language is difficult enough. Many aircraft crashes in the United States have involved communication between people whose native language was English. When a task involves individuals or groups who do not share the same idiomatic language and culture, although they may ostensibly speak a common language, the possibility for miscommunication is enormous. With the rapid expansion of airlines in developing countries, this situation is becoming increasingly common in aviation. Due to a lack of trained native pilots, many airlines in the Middle East and Pacific areas are hiring expatriate pilots from the United States, United Kingdom, Australia, or other Western countries while they train local pilots. This results in a cross-cultural melange in the cockpit, creating uncertain consequences. Moreover, increased international traffic means that pilots are communicating with air traffic controllers with whom they do not share a native language (despite the requirement that worldwide air traffic communication is to be in English).

Kinds of Cross-Cultural Communication Problems in Aviation

To obtain a broad view of the types of communication problems experienced by flight crews, we examined a sample of reports submitted to the Aviation Safety Reporting System (ASRS). The ASRS is a non-jeopardy system run by NASA, supported by the FAA, that provides limited immunity to pilots who report events that might result in a possible violation or a threat to safety. *Culture* and *communication problems* were the key words used in our search.

Table 7.1 illustrates the distribution of problems encountered in a random sample of 100 reports. Notice that the total number of cases is greater than 100 because more than one problem could occur per report. Initially, Cushing's (1994) taxonomy was used to classify the problems listed in Table 7.1. We found, however, that a large number of cases did not fit easily into his categories, so we added two more, Language/Accent and Dual Language Switching. These two categories alone accounted for nearly half of the problems reported. Language/ Accent refers to difficulty in understanding clearances issued by controllers, mostly during takeoffs and landings. This resulted in missed information or errors in interpretation. Partial Readback, the second most commonly reported problem, refers to confusions arising because only a portion of the clearance issued by the controller was read back by a pilot, leaving the referent ambiguous. For example, if a controller says "Cleared to 240," and the readback is "240," this could refer to a heading, speed, or altitude, leaving other pilots in the dark and the controller not sure that the message was understood. The third most frequent category, Dual Language Switching, refers to the practice of air traffic controllers outside the United States speaking English to foreign pilots and speaking the local language to local pilots. This practice can result in loss of "party-line" information, which may alert pilots to conditions awaiting them. Unfamiliar Terminology refers to use of local jargon rather than standardized terminology approved by the International Civil Aviation Organization (ICAO). An example that has caused recent confusion is, "Line up and hold." Does this mean to hold short of the active runway or to taxi into position on the runway and hold prior to takeoff clearance? Speech Act confusion results when an utterance intended to be one speech act is interpreted as another, for example, a declarative taken as an imperative: "Traffic at 2 o'clock, 3 miles, level at 6,000, to pass under you." The phrase "level at 6,000" referred to the traffic, but was interpreted as a directive and the pilot leveled off at 6,000 feet.

From these examples and the remaining cases in Table 7.1, we can discern at least three different ways in which communication can go wrong. First, a message may suffer in its transmission, resulting in information not getting through to the addressee. Language/Accent problems and Dual Language Switching would fall into this category. In these instances, language itself is an impediment to transmission. Second, a message may be transmitted accurately, but not be understood as intended. These cases of misunderstanding may be grounded in various types of ambiguity or use of jargon. Partial Readbacks, Unfamiliar Terminology, and Speech Act confusions fall under this category. In the third type of communication failure, messages are transmitted accurately and understood as intended, but there is a failure of conversants to build a shared understanding of the situation. This type of problem is more difficult to detect and is not evident in Table 7.1.

Table 7.1
Frequency of Language-Based
Aviation Safety Reporting System (ASRS) Reports

Language Category	Frequency
Language/accent	47
Partial readback	24
Dual language switching	23
Unfamiliar terminology	17
Speech acts	12
False assumptions	9
Homophony	7
Unclear hand-off	5
Repetition across languages	4
Uncertain addressee	3
Lexical inference	1

Consequences of Communication Failure

The consequences of communication failures can be deadly. First of all, accurate and unambiguous transmission of ATC clearances is essential to prevent flight errors. Safe flight depends on correct information about flight altitude, speed, heading, barometric pressure, winds, and radio frequencies. Standard language formats have been designed to facilitate this type of communication. Yet errors occur, as is evident in the Kuala Lumpur confusion of "two" and "to."

Communication is also essential for maintaining accurate situation awareness during flight. Situation awareness refers to awareness of the condition of one's aircraft systems and one's location in relation to the intended course of flight, weather en route and at the destination, terrain, runway conditions, and traffic, both in the air and on the ground. Much of this information originates with air traffic controllers, especially information concerning weather, airports, and traffic. Despite the requirement that ATC communication must be in English, not all controllers around the world are fluent, and their messages to pilots, no matter what their native tongue, may not be readily understood, as reflected in the frequency of problems listed in Table 7.1.

Situation awareness is also supported by what has been called "party line" information. In addition to receiving clearances and other flight-relevant information from ATC, pilots typically pick up communication between ATC and other pilots on open radio channels. Midkiff (1992) found that U.S. pilots rely on party-line information, particularly in terminal areas during departures and arrivals, for information about wind shear, turbulence, weather, and other traffic. If pilots cannot understand these communications, a valuable source of information that enhances their situation awareness is lost.

A situation that reduces party-line information is Dual-Language Switching (see Table 7.1). In parts of the world where English is not common, controllers do not always use English, especially when talking with noncommercial local pilots whose English may be poor or nonexistent. In those cases, the controller may try to be accommodating and to foster safety by using a local language, with exactly the opposite results. At least one midair collision has resulted from such a loss of party-line information. A Mexico City controller gave approach and landing clearances to the pilot of a small aircraft in Spanish, which the pilots of a U.S. aircraft could not understand. The U.S. pilots were unaware of the location of the small plane and collided with it in midair.

Successful communication is also essential for building a shared understanding about flight-related problems among crew members and with personnel on the ground who may be helpful in resolving the problem. When a problem arises on board an aircraft, such as a system malfunction, a fuel problem, or a medical emergency, personnel on the ground can provide assistance. They may have deeper expertise and a broader perspective on the problem than the flight crew.

For resources on the ground to be helpful to crews in the air, however, the nature of the problem and the crew's goals must be understood by all parties. This understanding comes about through communication, which is especially critical because the various participants are physically separated and do not share all the relevant primary data about the problem. A shared understanding of the problem enables all participants to contribute appropriately to its solution (Orasanu, 1994).

In the Avianca case described previously, the flight crew and the several controllers with whom they interacted during their approach to JFK never appeared to have established a shared understanding of the Avianca fuel situation. Clearly, the captain was fully aware of the critical fuel condition, and repeatedly instructed the first officer to communicate this status to the controllers and to declare an emergency.

The first officer in turn told the controllers that they were running out of fuel, a true but inadequate description of the situation. Most of the aircraft flying into New York that day were also running low on fuel because of extensive holding due to bad weather on the East Coast. Without the magic word "emergency," no special handling was provided to the Avianca flight and the first officer was unable to impress the various controllers who handled their flight with the severity of their condition.

Similarly, in the Tenerife crash, the crews of the two jumbo jets and the air traffic controllers did not have a shared understanding of the location of each aircraft and its movements, which was essential for safe coordination on the busy runways. Just prior to the crash there was low-blowing fog. The controller could not see either aircraft nor could they see each other, increasing the importance of clear communication to establish a shared understanding of the situation. The ambiguous utterance, "We are at takeoff," did not clearly tell the controller that the KLM flight was in the process of taking off.

From both the accident examples and ASRS reports, we can see that communication problems may occur in several different ways. In the next section of this chapter we will discuss in more detail what causes crew communication to fail.

Causes of Communication Failure

Human communication is a joint activity involving at least two people that is intrinsically goal directed. We want to get things done with words (Austin, 1962). Succeeding in our efforts depends critically on our addressees' understanding what we mean and on their compliance with our intentions (Searle, 1969). Moreover, understanding spoken discourse presupposes that addressees correctly heard what was said (Clark & Schaefer, 1987). If any one of these requirements is not met, communication may fail.

Culture can affect communication success at each of these levels. Even if a message is accurately transmitted and the meaning of the words is understood, the addressee may not "understand" the message or comply with the speaker's intentions. In this section we will address potential causes of communication failures at each level: transmission, understanding, and compliance. As we shall see, although miscommunications arising at the transmission or understanding levels may be most common, the most difficult to detect and correct are probably at the social or compliance level.

Problems in the Transmission of Information

Discourse on the flight deck and between flight crew and ground controllers frequently co-occurs with other tasks and may thus be impeded by distractions. Pilots may simply not hear what was said because something else demanded their attention. Flight deck-ground communications are transmitted by radio and thus susceptible to disruptions and distortions. For instance, in the KLM/PanAm accident described at the beginning of this chapter, part of the miscommunication was due to inaudible and noisy radio connections between pilots and controllers. In addition, unfamiliar accents may lead to errors in transmission and requests for repetition, which may or may not lead to successful transmission of the message.

Problems Concerning the Content of Communication

When is communication sufficiently informative for an addressee to understand what the speaker intended? This question cannot be answered in absolute terms because communication is highly contextualized. What speakers say not only has to be understood in the context of the immediate situation and the conversants' familiarity, but also has to be interpreted in light of the social conventions and cultural values that define types of social interactions and determine acceptable ways of communicating.

Speakers normally take for granted that this background knowledge is shared by their addressees (Clark & Marshall, 1981; Sperber & Wilson, 1986). For the aviation environment the common ground presupposed by the participants has three parts:

- Knowledge and assumptions about the current situation
- Professional knowledge about each participant's roles and responsibilities (pilot, controller, dispatcher, cabin attendant, and so on), standard operational procedures, and standardized vocabulary and phraseology (Cannon-Bowers, Salas, & Converse, 1993; Orasanu, 1994)
- Cultural knowledge, that is, knowledge, beliefs, norms, and values prevalent in a particular culture (Clark, 1994)

Sometimes speakers make wrong assumptions about the knowledge they have in common with their addressees, and consequently do not provide sufficient information to establish mutual understanding. From the point of view of the addressees, understanding may be impaired because too little information or ambiguous information was given, or because expected standards of talk were violated. For example, in the following accident the controller and flight crew may have differed in their problem understanding.

Everglades, FL,
December 29, 1972 (L-1011)

While approaching Miami International Airport for landing, the crew of an L-1011 noticed that one of the landing gear lights did not illuminate. They requested a holding pattern away from the airport to determine if the light was just burned out or if they actually had a problem with their landing gear. While attempting to identify the problem, the auto pilot was accidentally disconnected, allowing the aircraft to begin a slow descent. When the controller noticed that the aircraft was not at its assigned altitude, he asked: "How are things comin' along out there?" The crew, thinking that he was inquiring about the landing gear problem, replied that they were fine and would like to return to the approach. One of the crew members finally noticed that they were losing altitude, and while they were trying to figure out what happened, the aircraft continued its descent. By the time they added power, it was too late to prevent the crash (NTSB, 1973).

While the flight crew was focusing on its landing gear, the Miami controller was focusing on the flight's decreasing altitude when he asked, "How are things comin' along out there?" The word "things" was sufficiently ambiguous that a different message was heard than was intended, with tragic results.

Ambiguous or incomplete information threatens mutual understanding but does not inevitably lead to misunderstanding. As long as addressees sense that there is something problematic about the message or about their understanding, they can request clarification. The resulting repair sequence may thus restore mutual understanding (Clark & Schaefer, 1987; Fischer, 1995). Use of local jargon, colloquialisms, or nonstandard phraseology may trigger a query. For example, a clearance was given as, "Join the localizer at five evens"; a traffic advisory included the admonition, "Keep your eyes peeled"; a radio check yielded, "your radio's stepped on by another call"; and a pushback clearance included, "Cleared to push and put your back to the northeast" (Captain C. M. Kang, personal communication, September 11, 1995). Presumably, controllers assume that all pilots will understand these colloquialisms, which may be true for local native-English speakers, but may be unfounded for pilots who are not native-English speakers who also are flying in their airspace.

Unfortunately there are situations like the Everglades crash in which problems go by unnoticed and unrepaired, resulting in misunderstanding. We call this "illusionary understanding." The speaker and addressee both believe they have communicated successfully, but in fact the message received was not identical to the message intended.

The illusion of understanding need not always be symmetrical across the speaker and addressee, as in the previous example. Instead, one participant may recognize that ambiguous or incomplete information has been communicated and may attempt to clarify it, but to no avail. The repair efforts may fail because the other party believes that mutual understanding has been achieved and that there is no communication problem. This situation is illustrated in communication between the captain and the first officer in the Avianca accident. The captain had repeatedly asked the first officer to advise ATC that they were low on fuel and that they were in an emergency. The first officer assured the captain that he had done so and that ATC understood their problem. The first officer, however, had never used the term "emergency" (NTSB, 1991). Although the captain apparently suspected that the first officer did not communicate appropriately with ATC, he failed to convey this to his first officer. The first officer, on the other hand, presumably thought that he had understood what the captain wanted him to do and had properly carried out his request.

Another kind of misunderstanding concerns the transmission of wrong information that remains undetected and unrepaired, despite the aviation system's emphasis on redundancy. Flight crews are required to read back directives and clearances given by controllers, and controllers in turn are expected to verify pilot readbacks. Uncorrected misinformation may either result in a shared misunderstanding of a given situation, that is, both parties misrepresent the situation, or it may lead to different representations between participants when addressees unknowingly "correct" their interpretation of what they've heard (without ever correcting the speaker). This may have been the case in the Tenerife controller's interpretation of the KLM captain's utterance, "We are now at takeoff." The controller expected the KLM crew to be at the takeoff point, waiting for takeoff clearance, not to be taking off. He may well have "adjusted" the nonstandard phraseology to fit his expectations. Making allowances of this sort is probably more likely when speakers and addressees do not speak the same native language (cf. comprehension errors based on readers' schemata, Brewer & Nakamura, 1984; Kahneman & Miller, 1986).

Problems Arising From
Social Interaction Style

When parties to a conversation are from different cultures, miscommunication based on different conceptions of the organization and structure of professional interactions is likely to occur. Culture determines norms of interaction—what can be said, how, and by whom. When conversing in a second language, moreover, individuals tend to follow the conversational routines and norms of their first language (Scollon & Scollon, 1981).

Cultural anthropologists and psychologists distinguish between two major cultural systems that have been linked to distinct conversational styles (Gudykunst, Ting-Toomey, & Chua, 1988; Hall, 1976; Hofstede,1980) and attitudes toward leadership (Merritt & Helmreich, 1993; Redding & Ogilvie, 1984). Cultural *individualism,* by stressing the self, personal choices, and achievements, is believed to promote a conversational style that is explicit, unambiguous, brief, goal directed, and first-person oriented. In contrast, talk in *collectivistic* cultures has been characterized as elaborate, often indirect, and role centered in accordance with the cultural emphasis on group harmony and group success.

Cultures also differ in the extent to which power distance between individuals is accepted and expressed in their interactions (Hofstede, 1980). Using a questionnaire to tap into attitudes toward preferred leadership and communication styles, Merritt and Helmreich (1993) observed that pilots from Anglo cultures tend to prefer leaders who are consultative rather than authoritarian. In emergencies, even junior crew members expect to contribute to the decision making. Pilots from non-Anglo cultures tend to prefer leaders who are authoritative, take command of the aircraft in emergencies and tell other crew members exactly what to do.

Power distance between conversants influences the communication strategies of members in both individualistic (Fisher, 1984; Linde, 1988; Mehan, 1985; Maynard, 1991) and collectivistic cultures (Holtgraves & Yang, 1992). Lower-status conversants are generally found to be more indirect in their communications toward high-status conversants than high-status conversants are to lower-status ones. Cross-cultural work, moreover, suggests that status effects are even more pronounced in collectivistic cultures (Holtgraves & Yang, 1992).

Cross-cultural differences highlight the critical tension between communicating information related to flight safety while preserving "face" (see Earley & Randel, Chapter 6, this volume). This issue is just as relevant in the United States as it is in other cultures, despite our more egalitarian values. Status differences are evident in the communications between captains and first officers in U.S. crews, and are reflected in different politeness strategies. Brown and Levinson (1987) have developed a theory of politeness that maintains that the degree of politeness expressed in an utterance will vary as a function of three factors: status differences, familiarity between speakers, and degree of imposition conveyed by an utterance. Greater politeness will be used when addressing someone of a higher status than the speaker, a person not familiar to the speaker, or when the request makes a great imposition on the addressee.

Linde (1988) has characterized conversational politeness in terms of "mitigation," or the degree to which an utterance is softened by several markers, including informal vocabulary, use of modals ("would you, could you"), use of agreement tags ("is it?," "do you think?"), and use of "we" instead of "I." In an analysis of "black box" conversations from eight U.S. aircraft accidents and a NASA full-mission simulator study, Linde (1988) found greater mitigation (politeness) in communications from the first officers to captains than from captains to first officers.

Unfortunately, when first officers used mitigated talk, they ran the risk of not being taken seriously. Linde observed that captains were more likely to act on suggestions from first officers when they were more direct than mitigated.

In an analysis of 37 accidents in which crew behaviors played a causal role, the National Transportation Safety Board (1994) found 31 cases that involved failure of one crew member to monitor and challenge the other. These were all secondary errors. That is, one crew member committed an error (of procedure, decision making, and so forth), and the other crew member did not correct it, either because he or she did not notice it, chose not to say anything about it, or expressed concern in an ineffective manner. We can only speculate about the degree to which these communication failures resulted from concerns about preserving face. Consider the following accident that occurred during a driving snowstorm.

Washington, DC,
January 13, 1982 (B-737)

An Air Florida aircraft had been de-iced, but 45 minutes had elapsed before it was cleared for takeoff. The captain had little experience flying in winter weather. While awaiting their takeoff clearance, the following conversation took place:

First Officer: *Look how the ice is just hanging on his, ah, back, back there, see that? (. . .)*

First Officer: *See all those icicles on the back there and everything?*

Captain: *Yeah.*

After a long wait following de-icing, the first officer continued:

First Officer: *Boy, this is a, this is a losing battle here on trying to de-ice those things, it (gives) you a false feeling of security, that's all that does.*

Shortly after being given clearance to take off, the first officer again expressed his concern:

First Officer: *Let's check those tops again since we been setting here awhile.*

Captain: *I think we get to go here in a minute.*

Finally, while they were on their takeoff roll, the first officer noticed that something was wrong with the engine readings.

First Officer: *That don't seem right, does it?*

[three second pause] *Ah, that's not right. . . .*

Captain: *Yes, it is, there's 80.*

First Officer: *Naw, I don't think that's right.*

[seven-second pause] *Ah, maybe it is.*

Captain: *Hundred and twenty.*

First Officer: *I don't know.*

The takeoff proceeded, and 37 seconds later they crashed into the Potomac River due to excessive snow and ice on the aircraft and a frozen indicator that gave them a false engine power reading (NTSB, 1982).

In this unfortunate situation, the first officer made frequent references to the dangerous conditions affecting both their own aircraft and others. He seemed to be aware that the engine condition did not appear to be normal during the takeoff roll, but did not succeed in getting the captain to take these concerns seriously or to act on them.

We are currently conducting a research project that attempts to understand how first officers can effectively challenge the actions of captains in situations like the above, and how first officers' strategies differ from captains' strategies. In addition, we will study whether pilots from different cultures have distinct notions of what constitutes effective challenging behavior in flight contexts. Our initial analyses of U.S. pilots' responses to scenarios describing in-flight errors by the other crew member (captain or first officer) confirmed Linde's (1988) observations. Captains were more likely than first officers to use unmitigated commands ("Go back down to 9,000 ft.!"), or obligation statements ("You need to correct back to the right."). First officers' preferred strategies were suggestions ("Let's level off here until we clarify our present position and clearance, OK?") or other indirect means such as stating a problem and asking about the captain's intentions ("That looks like a pretty bad cell up ahead. Which direction would you like to vector around that cell?").

Features of Effective
Crew Communication

To try to reduce miscommunication in critical flight situations, we need to identify features of effective communication as a model. What constitutes effective team communication in high-risk situations? Is there a universal model, or are there several, culturally bound models? Grice (1967/1989) argued that rational, cooperative communication adheres to the following maxims: Be informative, be relevant, and be perspicuous. Accordingly, we would hypothesize that effective team members are explicit about what to do, when it should be done, and who should do it. Empirical support for this hypothesis comes from research on communication in U.S. air transport crews. Effective crews were found to have higher levels of communication overall, more normative patterns, and more acknowledgments or closed-loop communication (Billings & Reynard, 1981; Foushee & Manos, 1981; Kanki, Lozito, & Foushee, 1989). Effective crews were also more explicit in allocating and structuring tasks. Orasanu and Fischer (1992), who analyzed crew communication and performance in two NASA full-mission simulator studies, noted that effective airline captains stated more plans and strategies than their less effective counterparts. First officers, as mentioned earlier, were generally less directive and instead tended to use indirect strategies to suggest plans.

In contrast to Orasanu and Fischer's (1992) findings, in a different simulator study Linde (1988) observed that more successful crews used higher levels of mitigation in their speech than less successful crews. How can we account for this apparent contradiction? Mitigation or indirectness on the part of captains is an affiliative strategy used to build a positive team atmosphere among crew members. A positive team atmosphere may well have contributed to effective team work when it was required to meet the demands of an abnormal situation. (Higher-ranking persons can choose to be more or less formal; lower-ranking persons' choices are more limited. Linde did not describe the levels of mitigation used by captains and first officers, so it is not possible to know the contribution of each speaker to these results.)

A key difference between Linde's (1988) findings and Orasanu and Fischer's (1992) work is that the latter analysis examined the functions and content of utterances, whereas the former addressed their form. As

Watzlawick, Beavin, and Jackson (1967) have pointed out, every utterance has two components: the referential, which makes some direct predication about the world, and the relational, by which we signal something about our social relationship to the listener. Communication is not just a matter of what we say; it is how we say it that determines the received message. The Air Florida example (NTSB, 1982) highlights the tension between the safety requirement to communicate essential information in a direct way (the referential component) versus the social requirement of communicating with the appropriate level of politeness. Linde (1988) noted:

> It might at first appear desirable to train crew members to speak as directly as possible. . . . However, in some situations, a subordinate's speaking directly might be seen as challenging the hierarchical relationship of crew members. If this is so, simple training in the direct expression of matters of concern would not be sufficient. It would also be necessary to train in forms of communication that can challenge a superior's assessment of a situation, while indicating respect for the superior's position. (p. 396)

At this point we can only suggest that the most effective U.S. crews are those that address problem-relevant content (and build shared mental models for emergent problems), but do it in an affiliative manner. This ideal poses a challenge for cross-cultural communication within a flight deck, whether the personnel are culturally homogenous or diverse, and between flight crews and air traffic command around the world.

What Can Be Done to Enhance Communication Success?

Needless to say, the goal of communication in aviation is accurate and timely transmission of information, along with successful communication in situations requiring local or distributed team problem solving or decision making. The different types of communication problems described previously demand different types of solutions.

Correcting Transmission and
Content Errors

Aviation industry regulatory bodies and associations have recognized the problems of information errors and missing information and have taken steps to correct them. Standardized formats, terminology, phraseology, and procedures have been implemented to reduce or eliminate these problems. The FAA gives new controllers a course on listening and remembering that emphasizes the importance of using standardized formats for clearances and of avoiding local jargon or slang. There should be no confusion about whether an aircraft is or is not cleared onto an active runway when a crew member hears, "Line up and hold." And a flight crew must know that ATC will accommodate them when they use the standard phrase, "Fuel emergency." The International Civil Aviation Organization has established standardized phraseology that is used worldwide for communication of routine information between controllers and pilots.

A second approach to assuring accurate transmission of information is the readback. On receiving a clearance from ATC, a pilot is supposed to read back the clearance to assure that the information has been received completely and accurately. Although this procedure would seem to catch most transmission or reception errors, it requires the controller to monitor the readback for errors.

Obviously, this procedure sometimes fails, as it did in the case of the Flying Tigers crash in Kuala Lumpur. Communication failures are most likely when the controller is busy and tries to pack many information components into one clearance, thereby reducing his or her workload (i.e., only one radio transmission rather than two). As Morrow and Rodvold (1993) have shown, more receptive errors on the part of the pilots are likely when clearance messages include three or more elements of information (heading, altitude, speed, climb rate, restrictions, traffic, and so on) than when they are shorter. These errors are evident as readback errors by pilots. Thus, strategies that reduce workload for controllers increase workload for pilots and vice versa. Moreover, cross-language or culture-based misunderstandings are not necessarily eliminated by readback procedures.

To overcome information transmission errors, new technology called "datalink" will be used to transmit clearances digitally from the controller to the flight deck, where the message will appear on a computer screen. Work will still be required to transmit and to receive the message, but certain classes of errors, like the confusion between "two" and "to" ("descend two [to?] four zero zero") are likely to be reduced by this technology. The incidence of messages not getting through because of radio transmissions being "stepped on" or not heard should also be reduced. On the other hand, the possibility of typing errors will be introduced! Datalink, however, will eliminate party-line information that has been found to be so useful. How to make up for that loss of valuable information has not yet been determined.

Overcoming Interpretation/
Compliance Failures

Overcoming misunderstanding based on inadequate communication strategies or cultural differences is the most difficult problem. How to assure that two individuals, even those who speak the same language, have a shared understanding of their task environment so that they can work together effectively is not well understood. In addressing this problem we must deal with language on several levels—form, function, and content. To say that one does or does not understand the meaning of an utterance is not a straightforward all-or-none proposition. Although technology may fix other types of communication problems, the solution for this problem must be at the human level.

Because problems in communication and coordination have repeatedly been found to be contributing factors in aircraft accidents, the NTSB has called for crew training in effective communication and coordination skills (Kayten, 1993). The industry's response has been the development of crew resource management (CRM) training programs (see Wiener, Kanki, & Helmreich, 1993, for a review of recent work in this area). These courses train crew members to work together more effectively. Communication is an important component of all CRM courses (along with team building, leadership, situation awareness, decision making, planning and task/workload/stress management). Captains are taught to encourage open communication among crew members (first officers, flight engineers, and flight attendants). First officers are taught to be more assertive and to advocate their positions when they see something that might compromise safety. These courses have been adopted by all major U.S. carriers and are expanding to U.S.

regional and commuter airlines, as well as to major foreign carriers. According to recent evaluations, crew performance has improved since these programs have been put into place (Helmreich & Foushee, 1993).

But how do such programs fare when injected into crew training in South America, the Far East, or the Middle East? CRM programs have been accepted and have succeeded in the United States because they are compatible with our cultural norms. The United States is an egalitarian society that values individual effort. In Hofstede's (1980) terms, the United States is a highly individualistic and moderately low power distance culture. This means that all crew members are expected to participate in responding to problematic situations and that junior crew members can volunteer information and suggestions.

In cultures that are high power distance, it would be unthinkable for a person of lower status to challenge or question the judgment of a higher-status person. Similarly, collectivist cultures value group harmony over individual achievement. In highly collectivist cultures, one's success or failure comes from the success or failure of the group rather than one's own efforts. Challenges or pointing out mistakes made by the captain would be seen as highly face-threatening, not just to the captain, but to the first officer as well. Given the need to communicate critical information, a junior crew member in such a culture experiences a conflict between safety and maintaining face and harmony on the flight deck. No simple answer to this dilemma is readily available (Johnston, 1993).

Merritt (1995) described some initial efforts to tailor training programs to the social norms of various cultures by finding the appropriate "culture comfort zone." Strong cultural models are adopted as the framework for crew training. For example, in one high power distance/collectivist culture, the crew is represented as a family business. Although the captain is the head of the business, the first officer is the elder son who has to learn the business so that he will be qualified eventually to take over. Thus, it is important for the "son" to ask questions and to participate, while the "father" must nurture him. First officers are asked to imagine that the other crew member (the captain) is a brother or a friend to provide practice in assertiveness. In contrast, to sensitize crew members from highly individualistic, low power distance cultures, power distance is increased by asking pilots to imagine that the copilot is the company president.

Consider a further complication: What if one crew member is from a high power distance/collectivist culture and the other is from a low power distance/individualistic culture? If the captain is from the high power distance culture and the first officer is from a low power distance culture, the captain may feel that the first officer is not according him the respect he deserves because of his status. Conversely, if the captain is from a low power distance culture and the first officer is from a high power distance culture, the captain may feel like the Lone Ranger, waiting for active input from the first officer, who in turn is waiting for the captain to tell him or her what to do.

Merritt (1993) reported several difficulties associated with culturally diverse flight crews. The primary one was a language barrier that increased the workload simply to communicate basic information. Because of the cultural distance, greater politeness was evident and the atmosphere was more formal. Anglo captains felt they could not joke around with first officers from high power distance cultures. Also, they had to be more explicit about their expectations for how to do business on the flight deck because they could not assume a shared understanding of procedures.

Cultural Aspects of Communication Problems

In this chapter we have reviewed several ways in which communication can fail and how cultural factors can contribute to those failures. Three distinct problem areas have emerged:

- Communication between pilots and air traffic controllers around the globe, in which the official language is English but both pilots and controllers may speak different native languages.
- The legitimacy of extending training practices and theories of effective communication based on U.S. flight crews to cultures that differ from the United States in terms of power distance and collectivism.
- How to train flight crews to operate in culturally diverse crew contexts.

Considerable progress has already been made by ICAO and other international bodies to standardize the language of air traffic control, to create a lingua franca to assure that all personnel can communicate effectively using formulaic agreed-on utterances. The advent of datalink will eliminate certain classes of errors. As long as pilots and controllers interact using nonstandardized language, however, the possibility for miscommunication will exist. Sensitizing both controllers and crews to the possibility of miscommunication and its various types may help.

With respect to exporting U.S.-made CRM programs, theories that describe culturally bound forms of social interaction are bound to fail in some, if not all, ways when transported beyond the boundaries of the culture in which they were developed. Some general principles may travel well, however, such as the need to assure that all crew members understand the nature of a system malfunction or other emergency that requires crew coordination and decision making. The challenge is to identify, for each specific culture, appropriate ways of accomplishing certain crew tasks. How to communicate "bad news" or to call attention to an error with safety consequences in a manner that preserves "face" is a dilemma. Local rather than general solutions are likely to emerge.

Finally, the problem of culturally diverse crews is perhaps most difficult. At this point all we can suggest is sensitizing crew members to the potential for cultural mismatches and the cultural significance of certain ways of interacting. The problem is that pairings of individuals are generally ad hoc, with pilots from a variety of cultures being absorbed by rapidly expanding airlines in certain parts of the world. Local efforts to identify problems and to develop training programs that provide tools for interaction are the only solutions that can be offered at this point.

In all of these situations it is critical that crew members work together and with air traffic controllers to assure safety in flight. Learning how to foster effective teamwork within a single culture has been the goal driving researchers for the past decade. Now the challenge is to test the utility of their findings and theories in a broader multicultural context. The safety of global aviation will depend on it.

References

Austin, J. (1962). *How to do things with words*. Oxford, UK: Clarendon.

Billings, C. E., & Reynard, W. D. (1981). Dimensions of the information transfer problem. In C. E. Billings & E. S. Cheaney (Eds.), *Information transfer problems in the aviation system* (NASA Tech. Paper 1875). Moffett Field, CA: NASA-Ames Research Center.

Brewer, W. F., & Nakamura, G. V. (1984). The nature and functions of schemas. In R. S. Wyer & T. K. Srull (Eds.), *Handbook of social cognition* (Vol. 1, pp. 119-160). Hillsdale, NJ: Lawrence Erlbaum.

Brown, P., & Levinson, S. C. (1987). *Politeness: Some universals in language usage.* Cambridge, UK: Cambridge University Press.

Cannon-Bowers, J. A., Salas, E., & Converse, S. (1993). Cognitive psychology and team training: Training shared mental models of complex systems. *Human Factors Society Bulletin, 33*(12), 1-4.

Clark, H. H. (1994). Discourse in production. In M. A. Gernsbacher (Ed.), *Handbook of psycholinguistics* (pp. 985-1021). San Diego, CA: Academic Press.

Clark, H. H., & Marshall, C. R. (1981). Mutual understanding. In A. K. Joshi, B. Webber, & I. A. Sag (Eds.), *Elements of discourse understanding* (pp. 10-63). Cambridge; UK: Cambridge University Press.

Clark, H. H., & Schaefer, E. F. (1987). Collaborating on contributions to conversations. *Language and Cognitive Processes, 2(1),* 19-41.

Cushing, S. (1994). *Fatal words.* Chicago: University of Chicago Press.

Fischer, U. (1995). *Does status affect conversational repair?* Unpublished manuscript, NASA-Ames Research Center, Moffett Field, CA.

Fisher, S. (1984). Institutional authority and the structure of discourse. *Discourse Processes, 7,* 201-224.

Foushee, H. C., & Manos, K. L. (1981). Information transfer within the cockpit: Problems in intracockpit communications. In C. E. Billings & E .S. Cheaney (Eds.), *Information transfer problems in the aviation system* (NASA Tech. Paper 1875). Moffett Field, CA: NASA-Ames Research Center.

Grice, P. (1989). Logic and conversation. In P. Grice (Ed.), *Studies in the ways of words* (pp. 3-143). Cambridge, MA: Harvard University Press. (Original work published in 1967)

Gudykunst, W. B., Ting-Toomey, S., & Chua, E. (1988). *Culture and interpersonal communication.* Beverly Hills, CA: Sage.

Hall, E. T. (1976). *Beyond culture.* New York: Doubleday.

Helmreich, R. L. (1994). Anatomy of a system accident: The crash of Avianca flight 052. *International Journal of Aviation Psychology, 4,* 265-284.

Helmreich, R. L., & Foushee, H. C. (1993). Why crew resource management? Empirical and theoretical bases of human factors training in aviation. In E. Weiner, B. Kanki, & R. Helmreich (Eds.), *Cockpit resource management* (pp. 3-45). San Diego, CA: Academic Press.

Hofstede, G. (1980). *Culture's consequences: International differences in work-related values.* Beverly Hills, CA: Sage.

Holtgraves, T., & Yang, J.-N. (1992). Interpersonal underpinnings of request strategies: General principles and differences due to culture and gender. *Journal of Personality and Social Psychology, 62,* 246-256.

Johnston, N. (1993). CRM: Cross-cultural perspectives. In E. Wiener, B. Kanki, & R. Helmreich (Eds.), *Cockpit resource management* (pp. 367-398). San Diego, CA: Academic Press.

Kahneman, D., & Miller, D. T. (1986). Norm theory: Comparing reality to its alternatives. *Psychological Review, 93(2),* 136-153.

Kanki, B. G., Lozito, S. C., & Foushee, H. C. (1989). Communication indices of crew coordination. *Aviation, Space, and Environmental Medicine, 60(1),* 56-60.

Kanki, B. G., & Palmer, M. (1993). Communication and crew resource management. In E. Wiener, B. Kanki, & R. Helmreich (Eds.), *Cockpit resource management* (pp. 99-136). San Diego, CA: Academic Press.

Kayten, P. J. (1993). The accident investigator's perspective. In E. Weiner, B. Kanki, & R. Helmreich (Eds.), *Cockpit resource management* (pp. 283-314). San Diego, CA: Academic Press.

Linde, C. (1988). The quantitative study of communicative success: Politeness and accidents in aviation discourse. *Language in Society, 17,* 375-399.

Maynard, D. W. (1991). On the interactional and institutional bases of asymmetry in clinical discourse. *American Journal of Sociology, 92,* 448- 495.

Mehan, H. (1985). The structure of classroom discourse. In T. A. Van Dijk (Ed.), *Handbook of discourse analysis: Vol. 3. Discourse and dialogue* (pp. 119-131). London, UK: Academic Press.

Merritt, A. C. (1993, August). *What our cross-cultural studies have taught us about CRM.* Paper presented at the CRM Industry Workshop, Atlanta, GA.

Merritt, A. C. (1995, March). *Cross-cultural issues in CRM/LOFT training.* Proceedings of the International Air Transport Association Human Factors in Aviation Seminar. Montreal: IATA.

Merritt, A. C., & Helmreich, R. L. (1993). *Human factors on the flight deck: The influence of national culture.* Unpublished manuscript, University of Texas, Austin.

Midkiff, A. (1992). *Identification of important "party line" information elements and the implications for situational awareness in the datalink environment.* Unpublished master's thesis, Massachusetts Institute of Technology, Cambridge.

Ministerio de Transportes Y Communicaciones, Subsecretaria de Aviacion Civil. (1978). *Colision Aeronaves, Boeing 747 PH-BUF de K.L.M. y Boeing 747 N736PA de PANAM, Los Rodeos, Tenerife, March 27, 1977.* Madrid, Spain: Author.

Morrow, D., & Rodvold, M. (1993). *The influence of ATC message length and timing on pilot communication* (NASA Contractor Report 177621). Moffett Field, CA: NASA-Ames Research Center.

National Transportation Safety Board. (1973). *Aircraft accident report: Eastern Air Lines, Inc. L-1011, N310EA, Miami, Florida, December 29, 1972* (NTSB-AAR-73-14). Washington, DC: Author.

National Transportation Safety Board. (1977). *Aircraft accident report: Tenerife, Canary Islands, March 3, 1977.* Washington, DC: Author.

National Transportation Safety Board. (1982). *Aircraft accident report: Air Florida, Inc., Boeing 737-222, N62AF, collision with 14th Street bridge, near Washington National Airport, Washington, DC, January 13, 1982* (NTSB-AAR-82-8). Washington, DC: Author.

National Transportation Safety Board. (1989, June). *Safety recommendation (A-89-44 through -49).* Washington, DC: Author.

National Transportation Safety Board. (1991). *Aircraft accident report: The Airline of Colombia, Boeing 707-321B, HK2016, fuel exhaustion, Cove Neck, New York, January 25, 1990* (NTSB/AAR-91/04). Washington, DC: Author.

National Transportation Safety Board. (1994). *A review of flight crew-involved, major accidents of U.S. air carriers, 1978-1990* (NTSB/SS- 94/01). Washington, DC: Author.

Orasanu, J. (1994). Shared problem models and flight crew performance. In N. Johnston, N. McDonald, & R. Fuller (Eds.), *Aviation psychology in practice* (pp. 255-285). Brookfield, VT: Ashgate.

Orasanu, J., & Fischer, U. (1992). Distributed cognition in the cockpit: Linguistic control of shared problem solving. In *Proceedings of the Fourteenth Annual Conference of the Cognitive Science Society* (pp. 189-194). Hillsdale, NJ: Lawrence Erlbaum.

Redding, S. G., & Ogilvie, J. G. (1984, October). *Cultural effects on cockpit communications in civilian aircraft.* Paper presented at the Flight Safety Foundation Conference, Zurich.

Scollon, R., & Scollon, S. B. K. (1981). *Narrative, literacy, and face in interethnic communication.* Norwood, NJ: Ablex.

Searle, J. R. (1969). *Speech acts: An essay in the philosophy of language.* Cambridge, UK: Cambridge University Press.

Sperber, D., & Wilson, D. (1986). *Relevance: Communication and cognition.* Cambridge, MA: Harvard University Press.

Watzlawick, P., Beavin, J., & Jackson, D. D. (1967). *Pragmatics of human communication.* New York: Norton.

Wiener, E. L., Kanki, B. G., & Helmreich, R. L. (Eds.). (1993). *Cockpit resource management.* San Diego, CA: Academic Press.

PART III

MANAGEMENT OF
CROSS-CULTURAL GROUPS

8

International and
Intranational Diversity

ROSALIE L. TUNG

Thereare important similarities and differences in the processes and dynamics associated with managing *international* and *intranational* diversity (Tung, 1993). The former refers to managing the interface between expatriates and host country nationals. Intranational diversity, on the other hand, refers to dealing with the realities of a multiethnic workforce and the increasing participation of women in professional and managerial ranks within a domestic context. This chapter suggests that the skills and core competencies traditionally required of executives on international assignments will also be required of managers in a domestic context. This argument is based on several major developments in the past decade that have necessitated fundamental changes in the nature and qualifications of people who will staff managerial positions in the next millennium.

The chapter examines these major developments/factors and identifies the core competencies required of managers in both international and domestic contexts in the 21st century. These skills and core competencies are discussed in the context of cross-cultural group interactions. In addition, the chapter discusses how these core competencies can be developed. It illustrates these points with case studies of how two companies, Hong Kong Bank and the Bank of Montreal, have tried to meet this challenge.

Factors Contributing to
Growing Convergence of Core Competencies

Six major factors/developments have contributed to the growing convergence of core competencies required of international and domestic managers. These are (a) globalization of industries, (b) increasing incidence of global strategic alliances formed between entities from different countries, (c) quantum advances in telecommunications and data processing, (d) organizational restructuring, (e) growing diversity in the domestic workforce, and (f) increasing mobility of the workforce across international boundaries. Each factor is examined briefly.

Globalization of Industries

This development implies that corporate decisions with regard to sourcing, allocation of resources, and production of goods and services will be made disregarding national boundaries. Hence domestic operations will become part of a global industry/organization, and decisions at the domestic level will become inextricably intertwined with those that are designed to coordinate and integrate worldwide strategy and planning.

Formation of Global
Strategic Alliances

Closely connected with the globalization of industries is the increasing formation of cooperative agreements between entities from two or more nations. There is growing recognition among international firms that, to compete effectively, they may have to collaborate with their competitors. International firms, such as IBM, Phillips, and Nippon Telegraph and Telephone, which were once averse to such collaborative efforts, have been quickly entering into such arrangements ("Hands across Europe," 1987). This implies that there will be (a) a growing number of foreign nationals on assignment in the United States or Canada, and (b) a growing number of Americans and Canadians working for North American subsidiaries of foreign-based multinational corporations. In the United States alone, there are an estimated 400,000 Americans working for the U.S. subsidiaries of Japanese firms. In the case of Canada, traditionally both its inward and outward foreign direct investment (FDI) were with the industrialized West. This profile is changing, however. By the late 1980s, the most important countries of destination for Canada's outward FDI included Singapore (third) and Indonesia (seventh); and, Japan and Hong Kong had emerged as the fourth and ninth most important countries of origin for inward investment in Canada (Phillips, 1994). The conclusion of the North American Free Trade Agreement also translated into more trade and business agreements between Canada and Mexico.

In the past, when the majority of Canada's outward and inward FDI was with the United States and the United Kingdom, countries that are culturally similar to Canada, managing and/or working with nationals from the host societies presented fewer significant problems. With the changing composition in countries of destination and origin for outward and inward FDI, there is an urgent need to develop among Canadian managers a new repertoire of skills and abilities to manage, work with, or both, peoples whose culture and value systems can be significantly different from those at home. Research has shown, for example, that the mindsets of East Asians toward business, including the way they define cooperation and competition, are significantly different from those in North America (Tung, 1994). Despite the closer geographic proximity of Mexico, there are significant cultural differences between Canadians and Mexicans. The basis for business transactions in Mexico is personal relations as opposed to legal contracts in Canada, and the relationship between superior and subordinate can be characterized as paternalistic in Mexico but bureaucratic in Canada (Paik & Teagarden, 1995).

Quantum Advances in Telecommunications and Data Processing

These technological developments mean that it is now possible to gain almost instantaneous access to a wide variety of data and information from disparate corners of the world. This capability has facilitated the globalization of industries and the formation of global strategic alliances, discussed earlier, and organizational restructuring, discussed next.

Organizational Restructuring

Due in part to the quest for high performance and the global recession of the late 1980s, many organizations have resorted to organizational restructuring, including the establishment of network organizations and organizational downsizing. Several industry leaders have been moving in the direction of a network structure. Jack Welch, chairman and CEO of General Electric, for example, has simplified the corporate organizational structure by dismantling the groups and sectors within the company and eliminating several layers of senior management. The 14 business units in GE now report directly to Welch himself or to one of his two vice-chairman. Welch has coined the term *boundarylessness* to characterize this new organizational form. The objective is to remove the real and imaginary boundaries (barriers) to communication and teamwork created by traditional vertical and hierarchical structures. The four essential boundaries to be spanned include vertical (hierarchical levels), horizontal (specialization and compartmentalization), internal/external, and geographic/cultural. With boundarylessness, the organization seeks to leverage critical firm resources through speed, flexibility, integration, and innovation (Ashkenas, Ulrich, Jick, & Kerr, 1995; Tichy & Charan, 1989).

Another example can be seen in Eastman Chemical Co., a spinoff of Eastman Kodak Co. When it was formed in January 1994, the first order of business for the new company was reorganizing the vertical structure into a network. President Ernest Davenport, Jr., described the new organizational structure as follows:

> Our organization chart is now called the pizza chart because it looks like a pizza with a lot of pepperoni sitting on it. We did it in a circle to show that everyone is equal in the organization. No one dominates the other. . . . Making the "pizza" work meant replacing several of the company's senior vice presidents in charge of key business functions with self-directed work teams . . . it makes people take off their organizational hats and put on their team hats. It gives people a much broader perspective and forces decision making down at least another level. (Sullivan, 1996, p. 3595)

**Growing Diversity in the
Domestic Workforce**

According to the 1995 Federal Glass Ceiling Commission report, *Good for Business: Making Full Use of the Nation's Human Capital,* African Americans account for 12.1% of the population in the United States, and women constitute one half of the productive workforce. In their book, *Kiki: Dangers and Opportunities—The Crisis Facing U.S.-Based Japanese Companies,* Lipp and Clarke (in press) document the problems Japanese managers face in managing American employees in the United States. In general, Japanese managers are more indirect in their communication and tend to adopt a holistic approach in evaluating an employee's performance. Americans, on the other hand, are more direct in their communication and prefer to be assessed along discrete dimensions. In the area of gender differences, research has shown that there can be significant differences in communication patterns and styles of leadership between males and females (Rosener, 1990; Tannen, 1990). According to Tannen, talk between women and men is "cross-cultural communication."

Thomas Kochan (1995), in his presidential address to the 10th World Congress of the International Industrial Relations Association, called for the launching of a renaissance in industrial relations research. In his opinion, the existing paradigms in industrial relations/human resource management are designed for a traditionally white male workforce who are full-time employees. New paradigms should be developed that can account for workplace diversity in its broadest sense. Traditional paradigms in industrial relations assume that there are only two distinct interest groups: labor and management. Current workplace diversity extends beyond race and gender to encompass other forms of differences, however, such as those between full-time and part-time workers, single versus multiple job holders, and so on. With diversity, a whole range of workplace conflicts comes to the fore—discrimination/harassment on the basis of race, gender, and other social affiliations; breakdowns in communication attributable to cultural differences; and work and family issues. These new types of workplace conflicts "are not easily resolved through the formal system of negotiations, grievance handling, or legal enforcement procedures that assume a clear labor-management dividing line." According to Kochan (1995), workplace diversity challenges organizations to "develop new processes and institutions for legitimating differences arising from personal diversity and resolving conflicts and solving problems" (p. 3).

Increasing Mobility of the Workforce
Across International Boundaries

Because of the general aging of the workforce in the industrialized West and the increasing elimination of immigration barriers across countries, there is a growing migration of workers from the developing to the developed economies. Johnston (1991) has coined the term *global workforce 2000* to refer to this phenomenon. In the case of Canada, for example, visible minorities currently account for 6% to 9% of the population but are projected to increase to 20% by the year 2000. Of these visible minorities, many are immigrants. In 1993, over 70% of immigrants to Canada came from Asia, Africa, and the Caribbean. In 1982, fewer than 10,000 immigrants came from Africa and the Middle East. In 1992, this number increased more than four-fold to over 40,000. The most significant increase, in absolute numbers, has come from the Asia-Pacific region. In 1982, less than 40,000 immigrants arrived from this region; in 1992, over 120,000 immigrants were admitted from this region (Taylor, 1995).

As one example, in Richmond, British Columbia, nearly 40% of the population is Asian, more specifically Hong Kong Chinese. In the Hong Kong Bank branch in Richmond, this change in ethnic mix of the local community has meant a dramatic shift in its staffing. Five years ago, the branch had 35 employees, 2 of whom were non-Caucasians. Now the branch has 73 employees, 65% of whom are Asians. This change in recruitment policy responds to the fact that virtually all new accounts opened in that branch now are with Asian clients.

Managerial Skills and
Core Competencies in the 21st Century

In light of the these developments, the managers of the 21st century, both domestic and international, will have to possess a different set of skills and core competencies to enable them to function effectively in the new situation of global competition. According to a 1989 survey of a sample of U.S. executives, the CEO for the year 2000 "must have a multienvironment, multicountry, multifunctional, maybe even multicompany, multi-industry experience" (Bennett, 1989, p. 1). These requirements were elaborated in "21st-Century Report: Reinventing the CEO" (1989) and in a separate study by IBM & Towers Perrin (1992).

The new breed of managers, both domestic and international, must possess specific attributes. Because of the different job contexts, some of these competencies will undoubtedly be more salient for international managers. The factors that drive toward convergence of core competencies, however, clearly support the need for domestic managers to possess such attributes as well. The attributes include (a) an ability to balance the conflicting demands of global integration versus local responsiveness; (b) an ability to work in teams comprised of people from multiple functions/disciplines, different companies, and diverse industry backgrounds; and (c) an ability to manage and/or work with peoples from diverse racial/ethnic backgrounds.

An Ability to Balance the Conflicting Demands of Global Integration Versus Local Responsiveness

Beginning in the 1980s, multinational companies have had to contend with two conflicting trends: the globalization of industries, on one hand, and regional economic integration and localization policies, on the other. At the interface between corporate headquarters and disparate operations around the world, international managers constantly have to perform a delicate balancing act of satisfying the objectives of corporate headquarters and those of its worldwide subsidiaries when the objectives of the two groups may often diverge (Bartlett & Ghoshal, 1989). This balancing act has been referred to as the "art of being local worldwide" (Sullivan, 1996).

An expatriate who tries too hard to adapt to local ways of relating to host country employees—such as speaking the local language and adopting local human resource management practices—may be accused of having "gone native." Corporate headquarters may doubt the expatriate's loyalty to the home office and, hence, call into question the international manager's continued usefulness to the home office. In contrast, the manager who makes no local adjustments is unlikely to succeed in meeting headquarter-set business goals.

Although this competency is undoubtedly more crucial to international executives, managers who function in a primarily domestic context still need to be sensitive to this conflicting requirement. In light of the growing interdependence in the world economy, it is virtually impossible to identify an industry or a segment of a country's economy that is totally unaffected by the decisions of managers from other nations. Consequently, domestic managers need to transact business with international managers and, therefore, have to understand the latter's perspective. Through greater sensitivity to, and knowledge of, the conflicting demands confronting international firms, host country managers who relate to expatriates can better understand the "why" and "how" of the latter's decisions and actions.

An Ability to Work in Teams Comprised of Peoples From Multiple Functions/Disciplines, Different Companies, and Diverse Industry Backgrounds

In light of the emergence of the network structure and the growing incidence of strategic alliances among entities from different sectors and across international boundaries, it is important that both domestic and international managers possess this competency. A manager has to be mindful of the variation in values, attitudes, and behaviors attributable to the multiple forms of culture (cross-national, corporate, professional, and industry) and be open to different points of view.

Corporate or organizational culture can differ significantly across companies and affects the behavior and values of employees in a given organization. Corporate culture refers to the "shared beliefs top managers in a company have about how they should manage themselves and other employees, and how they should conduct their business(es)" (Lorsch, 1986, p. 95). Likewise professional culture, the code of ethics and other commonalities shared by members of a given professional group, also influences the norms and behaviors of people who belong to a particular occupational group. Behaviors and norms also tend to vary across industries. Managers who operate in strategic alliances involving personnel from these multiple forms of culture have to appreciate how people from diverse functional, industry, and company backgrounds may possess different mindsets that influence their strategies and modus operandi.

In global strategic alliances, the domicile of the manager (whether at home or abroad) is inconsequential, because the person becomes part of an international team. Even domestic managers who work for companies that do not belong to such global alliances are not completely exempt from the latter's influence because they will undoubtedly have business dealings with other organizational entities that are part of such cooperative arrangements.

An Ability to Manage and/or Work With Peoples
From Diverse Racial/Ethnic Backgrounds

Traditionally, the ability to manage, work with, or both, people from different racial/ethnic backgrounds has been required of international managers. With "workforce 2000" and "global workforce 2000" it is now equally important that domestic managers possess these skills. In the international arena, it is imperative that the international manager adapt, to a certain extent, to the host culture to avoid charges of ethnocentrism—for example, being the "ugly American." In the domestic context, there is increasing evidence that valuing diversity has become an economic imperative. Domestic managers who are adept at managing and/or working with peoples from different ethnic/cultural backgrounds are better able to serve their customers/clients through new product development, and to improve relations with their employees, thus reducing labor costs (McEnrue, 1993; Wheeler, 1994). In a 1994 Conference Board of Canada study of 115 companies, 63% of the respondents felt that their organizations had derived economic benefits from valuing diversity (Taylor, 1995).

The three competencies identified previously resemble, to some extent, the attributes called for in an ideal international manager:

> [The international manager] should have the stamina of an Olympic runner, the mental agility of an Einstein, the conversational skill of a professor of languages, the detachment of a judge, the tact of a diplomat, and the perseverance of an Egyptian pyramid builder. . . . And if he [*sic*] is going to measure up to the demands of living and working in a foreign country he should have a feeling for culture; his moral judgments should

not be too rigid; he should be able to merge with the local environment with chameleon-like ease; and he should show no signs of prejudice. (Heller, 1980, p. 48)

Unfortunately, many of these attributes do not appear to be the forte of most North Americans. Our ethnocentric tendency can inhibit our ability to think globally. Our proficiency in a second language is sorely lacking. Similarly, our tendency to specialize and compartmentalize can hinder our abilities to develop broad-based knowledge of a variety of disciplines and industries. In addition, our strong emphasis on individualism can limit our ability to engage in team work, and in particular, to manage and/or collaborate with people whose value systems and attitudes are significantly different from our own.

To acquire these core competencies, it is imperative that managers possess superior technical and human relations skills. Traditionally, organizations have emphasized the development of technical skills as opposed to human relations skills. This is no longer adequate. In fact, human relations skills, more particularly the ability to develop effective group dynamics to facilitate teamwork, are pivotal to the acquisition of such core competencies. In the case of balancing the conflicting demands of global integration versus local responsiveness, managers have to be sensitive, on one hand, to the unique political, economic, institutional, and societal-cultural characteristics of a particular country. On the other hand, managers must be able to integrate and coordinate effectively the company's operations in disparate corners of the world.

Developing These New Skills
and Core Competencies

The new skills and core competencies identified previously can be developed through a combination of the following measures: (a) undertake overseas assignments, (b) develop communication competency, (c) acquire proficiency in other languages, (d) hone negotiation skills, (e) raise consciousness/awareness of differences, and (f) restructure the curriculum at business schools. These mechanisms involve didactic (cognitive) and experiential learning. Didactic learning is premised on the assumption that "interaction among people from different cultures will be more effective when there is a reciprocal understanding of others' culture." Although effective in the provision of information, by itself didactic learning is "not sufficient to cultivate cross-cultural sensitivity" (Ferdman & Brody, 1996, p. 295). Experiential learning goes a step further by actively engaging the trainees to participate in the process.

Undertake Overseas Assignments

Increasingly, international assignments are not used primarily to fill positions abroad. Rather, a growing number of companies consider them as part of overall career development for those people with potential for advancement to senior management positions. Tung (1988) referred to these individuals as the new breed of expatriates. This includes those people whose careers will primarily be in the home country, that is, domestic managers. Overseas assignments can serve multiple purposes, including:

1. development of a global orientation. An international assignment can sensitize the executive to the limitations of an ethnocentric approach. The person will be exposed to different mindsets, ways of conducting business, and doing things in general.
2. provision of greater opportunities for the expatriate to assume broader responsibilities. Because the overseas operation is usually smaller in size than corporate headquarters, the international executive is required to undertake a broader range of activities with their commensurate responsibilities and authority. Closely associated with this is greater exposure to a more diverse range of disciplines and industries (Tung & Miller, 1990).

Overseas assignments involve both didactic and experiential learning. To maximize their learning potential, managers should be provided with adequate predeparture training to minimize the incidence of failure abroad. Black and Mendenhall (1991), building on Tung's (1981) contingency framework of selection and training for international assignment, have applied social learning theory to identify the types of cross-cultural training programs suitable for different categories of overseas positions. The factors that guide the selection of the appropriate type of training include (a) the degree of culture novelty (i.e., cultural distance), (b) the degree of job novelty (i.e., difference between requirements of the international assignment and previous positions), and (c) the degree of interaction with host country nationals.

Develop Communication Competency

Miscommunication occurs when the message intended by the sender deviates from the message perceived by the receiver. This gap between intention and perception can stem from the different fields of experience of the sender and the receiver, including the meanings and interpretation assigned to specific words and the encoding/decoding of messages on either side (Howell, 1982; Ronen, 1986). These different fields of experience are largely culture based. Peoples from high-context cultures (such as Japan, Latin, and Mediterranean countries) thrive on implicit messages, whereas members from low-context societies (such as the United States and northern European countries) emphasize directness. An estimated 70% of the world's population is high context (Hall, 1976). To compound the problems of communication, Hall noted that only 30% of communication is verbal. Thus, various cultures attribute different meanings and interpretations to nonverbal communication, that is, the silent language.

The five-stage model of communication competency developed by Howell (1982), and subsequently adapted by Ting-Toomey (1992), has been applied to the process of international and intranational communication (Tung, 1993). The five levels of communication competency are:

1. unconscious incompetence;
2. conscious incompetence;
3. conscious competence;
4. unconscious competence; and
5. unconscious super-competence.

Unconscious incompetence, at the low end of the continuum, may stem from ignorance—that is, a member of one group may unintentionally insult members of another group without being aware that he or she has done so. An example of unconscious incompetence in an international setting is referring to Korea as the "second Japan." Although the sender may think he or she is paying a compliment to the receiver, an ethnic Korean, the latter will feel insulted because of the bitter feelings that many Koreans still harbor toward the Japanese as a result of cruelty during the 40-year Japanese annexation of Korea. An example of unconscious incompetence in an intranational setting was Ross Perot's referring to African Americans as "you people" during his bid for the U.S. presidency in 1992.

A person with unconscious super-competence, on the other end of the continuum, becomes truly bicultural and bilingual (in the international context) and moves with spontaneity between one set of cultural norms and another. A desirable goal of managing international and intranational diversity is to attain Level 3 (conscious competence) and, hopefully, Levels 4 (unconscious competence) and 5 (unconscious super-competence).

Advancing to the higher levels of communication competency involves both didactic and experiential learning.

Acquire Proficiency in
Other Languages

Although knowledge of the host society's language does not necessarily guarantee effective interaction and communication with local nationals, it does promote greater understanding of the subtleties and innuendos of the culture and the norms of the target country. Referring to the Japanese language, for example, Cramer (1990, pp. 89-90) noted the following:

> Japanese is more than a language—it is a window into a way of thought and action that is very different from our own. . . . It's what you don't say that's sometimes more important than what you do say. It's how you say it. . . . In a multiparty negotiation, those participants who do speak [Japanese] have some cultural fluency that allows them to measure the flow of the negotiations with a great deal more sensitivity.

In a 12-country study of almost 3,000 executives (IBM & Towers Perrin, 1992), executives from Europe, Asia, and South America perceived knowledge of a foreign language as critical to a firm's competitive advantage. Only respondents from the four English-speaking countries (United States, Canada, United Kingdom, and Australia) deemed such skills as unimportant.

Tannen (1990) has shown that there can be significant differences between male and female communication patterns in the United States. She found that women, similar to members of high-context cultures, tend to use qualifiers and tag questions and make more indirect requests. In her opinion, these do not stem from insecurity or insincerity; rather, such usage is largely a function of their subgroup or cultural upbringing. Tung (1993) showed the parallels between *genderlect* (the term coined by Tannen to describe the significant differences in communication patterns between males and females) and cross-national communication between the stereotypical American and the stereotypical Japanese. According to Tung, the communication pattern associated with the stereotypical American parallels the typical U.S. male, whereas that of the stereotypical Japanese is parallel to the typical female.

Although studying another language involves primarily didactic learning, an effective way to acquire proficiency is to experience the culture where that language is indigenous.

Hone Negotiation Skills

Senior executives were asked to identify and rank-order the 10 most important skills required of chief executive officers for two time periods: 1988 (present) and the year 2000 (future). Negotiation/conflict resolution skills were ranked fourth in importance in 1988 and third in 2000 ("21st-Century Report," 1989). The formation of global strategic alliances, the emergence of network structures, and the global workforce 2000—all made it increasingly important for executives of the future to possess strong negotiation and conflict resolution skills. These developments necessitate greater and more intensive interaction among people of different societies and systems, thus substantially increasing the incidence of conflict and tension among the groups.

Acquisition of negotiation skills involves both didactic and experiential learning.

**Raise Consciousness/Awareness
of Differences**

Although most people prefer the familiar and fear the dissimilar (Ibarra, 1992), in valuing diversity it is important to look beyond the differences to capitalize on the attributes that make each individual/subgroup unique and distinct. Langer (1989) coined the term *mindfulness* to refer to raising consciousness/awareness so that we can free ourselves from traditional mindsets to innovate and make progress. The opposite of mindfulness is *mindlessness,* a pattern "determined in the past, [in which] we blot out intuition and miss much of the present world around us" (Langer, 1989, p. 118). With mindfulness, we can become more innovative and flexible through "less *indiscriminate* discrimination" (Langer, 1989, p. 168).

In international diversity, the objective of many cross-cultural briefing programs is to sensitize participants to the fact that a person's behavioral patterns, values, and attitudes are products of the unique cultural and environmental milieu in which that person was raised. To quote Allan Hall (Tung, 1988, p. 30), deputy director of the Center for International Briefing at Farnham Castle (United Kingdom), "it is useless, stupid, unnecessary, and beside the point to say that [one's culture] is *better* than that [of the host nationals]; it is merely *different*."

In intranational diversity, the objective of such consciousness/awareness-raising programs is to make managers "mindful" of the fact that women and members of other subgroups, because of their upbringing, may espouse different values and assumptions, which can affect the way they lead, cooperate, compete, communicate, plan, organize, and are motivated. For example, Rosener (1990) found that men typically espouse a transactional leadership style (i.e., "view performance as a series of transactions with subordinates"), whereas females characterize their style as transformational (i.e., "getting subordinates to transform their own self-interest into the interest of the group through concern for a broader goal").

Awareness-raising programs involve both didactic and experiential learning. Ferdman and Brody (1996, p. 296) cited the efficacy of "perception exchange," a program developed by Kaleel Jamison Consulting Group to sensitize participants to subgroup differences. During "perception exchange," participants are asked to draw pictures to describe their perceptions of the organization and "the experiences of different groups in it." When these pictures are discussed with the entire group, comprising Caucasians, ethnic minorities and women, many participants realize for "the first time . . . that not everyone experiences the work environment in the same way they do and that the variations are often connected to racial, ethnic and gender identities" (p. 296).

Restructure the Curriculum at Business Schools

To develop the skills and core competencies identified in the previous section, many business schools are restructuring their curriculum to emphasize teamwork, communication skills, greater awareness of other cultures and knowledge of other languages. An increasing number of business schools are using a team-taught curriculum in the first year of the two-year MBA program to replace the traditional department-based course design. Many business schools are also moving to a greater emphasis on language and visits abroad. This is a reversion to an earlier practice; for instance, several European languages (French, German, and Spanish) were included as part of the curriculum in Harvard Business School's 1908-1909 calendar.

The Case of Hong Kong Bank

In the course of my research on managing international and intranational diversity, I have come across a program that holds promise for developing many of the aforementioned skills and core competencies. This is the international officers (I/Os) program at the Hong Kong Bank. Despite its name, the Hong Kong Bank is a United Kingdom-based multinational and is one of the largest banking groups in the world, with year-end 1993 total assets in excess of 206 billion pounds sterling. The Hong Kong Bank group has grown through a series of acquisitions, including the Midland Bank and Marine Midland Bank. The group employs a total of 100,000 people in 65 countries.

The I/Os program is comprised of a small but elite corps of 300 to 400 people. The future general managers of the bank are drawn from this pool because the members have broad-based banking knowledge and experience developed through years of rotation through various banking functions in different countries of the world. The bank feels that this broad-based perspective, coupled with knowledge of its worldwide operations, can help provide the cohesion and strategic direction at the top to integrate its disparate subsidiaries and branches around the world.

Who are these I/Os? What kinds of backgrounds do they come from and what types of training programs do they undergo? International officers are recruited from around the world and, in general, share the two following characteristics:

1. All of them are university graduates with strong analytical, verbal, and quantitative skills.
2. They must be adaptable and flexible. Most of them have traveled extensively or lived abroad in their childhood or early youth. In the bank's recruitment literature for the I/Os program, prospective applicants are asked to assess themselves against a list of criteria to help determine whether they have the necessary attributes to succeed in the program. For example, that I/Os "cannot choose where (they) want to work," and in theory, can be assigned to any region of the world at a moment's notice. They "must be able to cope not only with a wide range of cultures, nationalities, and languages, but also with an ever-changing circle of friends—not to mention unexpected events, frustrating situations, and, at times, uncomfortable conditions." (Hong Kong & Shanghai Banking Corp., n.d., p. 11).

Each year, there are many applicants for the limited number of openings in the I/Os program because of the career prospects with a major multinational bank. On average, only 2% of the applicants are successful in obtaining a position with the bank. The successful applicants are selected through a rigorous process that assesses them along many dimensions, including leadership abilities, level of motivation, degree of emotional stability, and communication competency.

On recruitment, the trainees undergo a 3-month residential program in the United Kingdom. This residential program is also attended by regional officers from the bank's operations around the world. Unlike the I/Os, a regional officer's career is in a given country, usually the country the person is recruited from. With the diversity in geographic and cultural backgrounds of the regional and international officers, the trainees in the I/Os program experience and work with peoples of other cultures from the outset. During this 3-month program, they take technical skills courses, such as foreign exchange management and trade financing. The program also includes outward-bound skills courses that foster a spirit of camaraderie among the new recruits. Through this intensive 3-month interaction, many I/Os develop lifelong friendships with other I/Os and regional officers. This facilitates the formation of effective networks, which are useful in their later careers. For example, if a client in San Francisco has a problem in Seoul, South Korea, an I/O can easily solicit the assistance of a fellow I/O in Seoul.

After the 3-month residential program, the I/Os become part of a junior officers development program that spans 5 years. During this time, they are rotated through the five functions of the bank's business in various countries. Despite the frequent rotation from country to country, the attrition rate is low—under 5%. The I/Os appear to be truly committed to their careers, even at the expense of their personal lives. The frequent rotation from country to country sometimes takes its toll in the form of marital breakups.

Although the I/Os program at the Hong Kong Bank is intended for international assignments and there are obvious drawbacks to the program, such as possible casualties in its members' family lives, other organizations can draw from components of that program in their search for ways and means to develop skills and competencies required of managers in the 21st century.

The Case of Bank of Montreal

In 1989, the senior management at the Bank of Montreal, a leading Canadian bank, established workforce diversity and workplace equality as business priorities. A task force on the advancement of women was formed in 1990 to address the issue of disproportionate representation of women in management-level positions. Despite the fact that three quarters of the bank's 28,000 employees (full-time and part-time) were women, only 9% of its executives were female. The task force identified five commonly held myths about the underrepresentation of women in management:

- Women at the bank are either too young or too old to compete with men for promotions.
- Women are less committed to their careers because they have babies and leave the bank while their children are young.
- More women need to be better educated to compete in significant numbers with men.
- Women don't have "the right stuff" to compete effectively with men for more senior jobs.
- Time will take care of women's advancement to senior levels of the bank (Bank of Montreal, 1991, p. 6)

Citing facts and figures, the task force went on to dispel each of the five myths. In response to the findings and recommendations of the task force, the bank adopted new programs and policies to redress the imbalance in the representation of women at the executive level. These programs and policies included the following:

1. The introduction of an awareness training program, titled "Women and Men as Colleagues," to address "how traditional and often-unconscious attitudes distort the selection, development, and promotion of women" (Bank of Montreal, 1991, p. 12). By the end of 1993, 90% of the bank's executives had participated in this training program. The didactic and experiential learning acquired through the workshops was reinforced through a quarterly news video and internal news magazine containing information about the bank's latest efforts to attain workforce diversity and workplace equality.

2. The institution of corporate and community sponsorship programs to support the education and career development of women employees. This initiative was later extended to ethnic minorities and people with disabilities.

3. The establishment of flexible work arrangements (flexitime, flexible work week, permanent part-time, job sharing, and flexplace) to accommodate employees with multiple commitments. In addition, a 24-hour free phone referral service was established to address the issues pertaining to child care and elder care. The bank also instituted "people care days" to allow its employees to take time off during the work day to attend to personal matters. Leaves of absence for up to 2 years are also permitted to enable employees to devote full-time to education and family exigencies.

The Bank of Montreal's efforts in this regard paid off. In 1994, it won a Catalyst Award, an annual award given to those companies that have done an outstanding job in promoting the cause of women within their respective organizations. Buoyed by the success of the task force on the advancement of women, the bank has subsequently established other task forces, including one on the advancement of aboriginal employment, another on employment of people with disabilities, and yet another on the advancement of visible minorities.

Summary and Conclusions

This chapter challenges organizations to reassess the skills and core competencies required of managers in the 21st century. Specifically, it proposes that, due to six major factors or developments, the distinction between international and domestic assignments is becoming less clear-cut. The attributes traditionally required of successful executives on international assignments will increasingly be required of managers who operate in a domestic context. The managers of the future, both domestic and international, must have the aptitude and ability to (a) relate to peoples in different functional areas, companies, and industries; (b) cooperate with peoples from different countries and cultural backgrounds; and (c) understand and balance the conflicting demands between global integration, on one hand, and local responsiveness, on the other.

In short, specialization and compartmentalization, which were characteristic of efficient organizations in the past, will prove dysfunctional in the future. International and domestic managers can no longer assume homogeneity in the multiple constituencies they have to contend with in their work and personal lives. Suppliers, customers, business partners, and coworkers may espouse different values and attitudes attributable to their distinct cultural, professional, company, and industry backgrounds. To function effectively and efficiently in this new environment, versatility and adaptability become essential. Thus, the contemporary successful manager can be described as a "person for all seasons" who can move with ease and alacrity from one environment to another.

The chapter has presented some programs to develop these skills and core competencies. These include the use of the following: (a) international assignments for career development purposes; (b) programs to develop communication competency to facilitate interaction across gender ("genderlect") and cultures; (c) language training programs to facilitate cross-cultural communication, and to promote greater understanding of the subtleties and innuendos surrounding another culture; (d) programs to hone negotiation skills to prepare managers for the diverse range of workplace conflicts; (e) programs to raise consciousness/awareness of diversity among subgroups so that managers can be "mindful" of the differences that distinguish peoples from the opposite gender and race/ethnic groups; and (f) efforts to restructure the curriculum at business schools, to meet the challenges of the 21st century.

The experiences of two major financial institutions in managing diversity illustrate how these practices can be applied. The international officers program at the Hong Kong Bank provides an example of how a multinational financial institution grooms a cadre of internationally oriented and mobile executives. The initiatives at the Bank of Montreal illustrate how a company was willing to confront the issue of underrepresentation of women in executive positions directly by dispelling the popular myths about women in management and by adopting policies and practices to redress the situation. To compete successfully in the 21st century, companies will have to recognize and anticipate the challenges ahead and adopt policies and programs that are in tune with the intranational and international diversity requirements of the times.

References

Ashkenas, A., Ulrich, D., Jick, T., & Kerr, S. (1995). *The boundaryless organization.* San Francisc: Jossey-Bass.

Bank of Montreal. (1991). *Task force on the advancement of women in the bank.* Montreal: Author.

Bartlett, C., & Ghoshal, S. (1989). *Managing across borders: The transnational solution.* Cambridge, MA: Harvard Business School Press.

Bennett, A. (1989, February 27). The chief executives in year 2000 will be experienced abroad. *Wall Street Journal,* p. 1.

Black, J. S., & Mendenhall, M. (1991). A practical but theory-based framework for selecting cross-cultural training methods. In M. Mendenhall & G. Oddou (Eds.), *Readings and cases in international human resource management* (pp. 177-204). Boston: PWS-Kent.

Cramer, B. A. (1990). Developing competitive skills: How American business people learn Japanese. *Annals of the American Academy of Political and Social Sciences, 511,* 85-96.

Federal Glass Ceiling Commission. (1995). *Good for business: Making full use of the nation's human capital.* Washington, DC: Author.

Ferdman, B. M., & Brody, S. E. (1996). Models of diversity training. In D. Landis & R. S. Bhagat (Eds.), *Handbook of intercultural training* (pp. 282-303). Thousand Oaks, CA: Sage.

Hall, E. T. (1976). *Beyond culture.* Garden City, NY: Anchor/Doubleday.

Hands across Europe: Joint ventures will help companies compete against Japan and the U.S. (1987, May 18). *Business Week.*

Heller, J. E. (1980, May-June). Criteria for selecting an international manager. *Personnel,* 47-55.

Hong Kong & Shanghai Banking Corp., Ltd. (n.d.). *Graduate career overseas with Hong Kong bank.* United Kingdom: Author.

Howell, W. S. (1982). *The empathic communicator.* Prospect Heights, IL: Waveland.

Ibarra, H. (1992). Homophily and differential returns: Sex differences in network structure and access in an advertising firm. *Administrative Science Quarterly, 37,* 422-447.

IBM & Towers Perrin. (1992). *Priorities for competitive advantage.*

Johnston, W. B. (1991, March-April). Global workforce 2000: The new world labor market. *Harvard Business Review,* pp. 115-127.

Kochan, T. A. (1995, June). *Launching a renaissance in international industrial relations research.* Presented as the presidential address at the meeting of the International Industrial Relations Association, Washington, DC.

Langer, E. J. (1989). *Mindfulness.* Reading, MA: Addison-Wesley.

Lipp, D., & Clarke, C. (in press). *Kiki: Dangers and opportunities—The crisis facing U.S.-based Japanese companies.* Chicago: Intercultural.

Lorsch, J. (1986). Managing culture: The invisible barrier to strategic change. *California Management Review, 28*(2), 95-124.

McEnrue, M. P. (1993). Managing diversity: Los Angeles before and after the riots. *Organizational Dynamics, 22*(1), 18-29.

Paik, Y., & Teagarden, M. B. (1995). Strategic international human resource management approaches in the maquiladora industry: A comparison of Japanese, Korean, and U.S. firms. *International Journal of Human Resource Management, 6,* 568-587.

Phillips, A. (1994, February 7). Lessons of Vancouver. *MacLean's,* 26-31.

Ronen, S. (1986). *Comparative and multinational management.* New York: John Wiley.

Rosener, J. B. (1990, Nov.-Dec.). Ways women lead. *Harvard Business Review,* pp. 119-125.

Sullivan, D. (1996). Organization structure in multinational corporations. In M. Warner (Ed.), *International encyclopedia of business and management* (pp. 3573-3597). London, UK: Routledge.

Tannen, D. (1990). *You just don't understand: Men and women in conversation.* New York: Ballantine.

Taylor, C. L. (1995). *Dimensions of diversity in Canadian business.* Toronto: Conference Board of Canada.

Tichy, N., & Charan, R. (1989, Sept.-Oct.). Speed simplicity, self-confidence: An interview with Jack Welch. *Harvard Business Review,* pp. 112-120.

Ting-Toomey, S. (1992, April). *Cross-cultural face negotiation: An analytical overview.* Paper presented at the Pacific Region Forum, Simon Fraser University, Burnaby, BC.

Tung, R. L. (1981, Spring). Selection and training of personnel for overseas assignments. *Columbia Journal of World Business,* pp. 68-78.

Tung, R. L. (1988). *The new expatriates: Managing human resources abroad.* Cambridge, MA: Ballinger.

Tung, R. L. (1993). Managing cross-national and intranational diversity. *Human Resource Management, 32,* 461-477.

Tung, R. L. (1994, Spring). Strategic management thought in East Asia. *Organizational Dynamics,* pp. 55-65.

Tung, R. L., & Miller, E. L. (1990). Managing in the 21st century: The need for global orientation. *Management International Review, 30*(1), 5-18.

21st-Century report: Reinventing the CEO. (1989). Korn/Ferry and Columbia Graduate School of Business. New York: Columbia University, Columbia Graduate School of Business.

Wheeler, M. (1994). *Diversity training: A research report* (Report No. 1083-94-RR). New York: Conference Board.

9

Cross-Cultural Socialization of Asian Employees in U.S. Organizations

CHERLYN SKROMME GRANROSE

During the past 10 years many Asian nationals have become managers of American subsidiaries in Asia (Gillespie, 1989). This practice increases cultural sensitivity and local responsiveness to Asian customs while reducing the use of costly expatriates (Dowling & Schuler, 1990; Tung, 1987). When U.S. multinational organizations attempt to develop policies for subsidiaries in Asia, however, they confront the dilemma: Should we use consistent, efficient policies across the organization that may not fit local practices, or should we implement decentralized, local policies that may be difficult to integrate efficiently with home office practices? Choices made in response to this dilemma have a major impact on organizational effectiveness (Rosenzweig & Singh, 1991). This chapter seeks to identify how organizations can socialize employees from many cultures into a single multinational corporation (MNC) in ways that retain national-culture-specific knowledge and that maintain sufficient internal coherence to be effective.

Many organizations address these countervailing pressures (differentiation vs. integration) by developing a strong organizational culture. Strong organizational cultures yield similarity in employee values, goals, and behavior; facilitate integration; and enhance efficiency by increasing employee motivation, commitment, and identification with the organization (Allaire & Firsirotu, 1983; Schein, 1990). To build a strong organizational culture, firms socialize newcomers and continuing employees to adopt common organizational ways of thinking and doing things. Multinational organizations have problems, however, when organizational socialization threatens to require that specific cultural groups of employees give up, or substantially change, characteristics they consider central to their group identity to be accepted as valued employees or to fit individual goals to organizational goals.

To address this problem, this chapter examines three different streams of research: cross-cultural social science, organizational socialization, and intergroup contact. After integrating information from each perspective, the chapter proposes a model of organizational socialization to enhance perceptions of individual-organizational fit for different cultural groups in organizations. The model is then compared to empirical data on socialization of Asian managers employed by U.S. firms in Taiwan, Hong Kong, Singapore, Thailand, and Japan. Results suggest socialization mechanisms that multinational firms might use to promote individual-organizational fit while preserving national or ethnic group identity.

Culture and Identity

The term *culture* refers to a particular group's shared system of socially transmitted behavior patterns, beliefs, and the shared artifacts needed for the group to use the resources of the environment and to survive (Keesing, 1974). A group of people of any size who share basic beliefs and behavioral patterns may be referred to as having a common culture: Ethnic cultures can extend across national boundaries, or a specific culture can exist within a single organization or department (Schneider, 1988).

Organizational Culture

Shared organizational cultural beliefs usually address the organization's mission, core tasks, goals, strategies, membership boundaries, norms, and criteria for results (Schein, 1990). Organizational culture can be developed by founders and leaders, and is perpetuated by selection, socialization, shared rites, myths, and critical incidents.

Strong organizational cultures may reduce other organizational boundaries (Schein, 1990; Van Maanen & Barley, 1985). Hirschhorn and Gilmore (1992) claim, however, that as contemporary formal organizations become more structurally boundaryless, other boundaries such as ethnic, functional, or gender boundaries are apt to assert themselves. For example, the larger the number of nations or cultural groups that a MNC includes as it spans geographic boundaries, the greater the probability of attitudinal, normative, and linguistic differences among employees. If the MNC tries to promote a culturally homogeneous organization, resistance of subgroup members to preserve their cultural identity may lead to polarization, prejudice, increased intraorganizational boundaries, and decreased effectiveness.

Identity

In organizations, the self can serve as the link between the values of each person's multiple cultural groups and his or her behavior (Erez & Earley, 1993). In this self-defining process, cultural information is used to interpret appropriate goals, rewards, and relationships in a work setting. Individuals may vary, however, on several dimensions of cultural characteristics—for example, the variety of cultural groups to which each person belongs, the centrality of each group to an individual's self-concept, the perceived cultural content of each group, and the importance of each cultural group for mediating work-related values, norms, attitudes, and behaviors (Cox, 1991; Ferdman, 1995). Thus, the extent to which the cultures of an employee's other group memberships are consistent, supportive, or conflicting with an organizational culture has an important effect on the extent to which employees feel that they fit an organization and can meet their personal goals within the organization. The extent to which a comfortable fit can be achieved is discovered by new and continuing members during the process of organizational socialization.

Organizational Socialization

Socialization is the formal and informal process whereby organizations select new employees and teach them appropriate role behaviors, skills, and values (Greenhaus & Callanan, 1994). In addition to the socialization of new members, ongoing socialization also occurs with continuing organizational members as organizations and individuals change over time. Employees accommodate to some of these organizational influence attempts and also seek to have the organization accommodate to their individuality in a process of mutual negotiation (Feldman, 1988; Hackman, 1992; London & Stumpf, 1982; Moscovici, 1980; Pascale, 1985; Schein, 1978). It is especially common, however, for organizational members to reject any form of deviance when it is displayed by a demographic minority member (Clark & Maass, 1988).

Organizational socialization practices are of two major types (Jones, 1986; Van Maanen & Schein, 1979). Institutional socialization practices are formal training and feedback systems that are sequential, time limited, and conducted in a group. These practices include modeling of specific desired behavior, and experiences designed to break ties with former groups and rebuild a self-concept focused on membership in the present organization. Individual socialization practices are more often informal, random, disjunctive, and variable in length. Typically, they focus on positively confirming and affirming the self-concept of the individual as a valued organizational member.

Outcomes of Socialization

Several scholars have investigated the relationship between particular types of socialization and organizational outcomes. Because important issues of cross-cultural organizational socialization involve the extent to which individuals adopt organizational membership as part of their self-concept, I will focus only on research addressing (a) the relationship of socialization to a member's commitment to organizational values or organizational culture, and (b) inclusion of organizational membership into a member's self-concept.

Socialization and commitment. Jones (1986) proposed that institutional socialization practices should produce more conforming and committed organizational members, whereas individual socialization practices should lead to more role innovation and creativity. His hypotheses were largely supported in predicting conformity; however, affective organizational commitment has been related both to formal socialization and also to self-affirming organizational socialization practices common in individual socialization (Allen & Meyer, 1990a, 1990b). The existence of clear rewards and available career paths has been related to behavioral commitment, that is, remaining with the organization (Caldwell, Chatman, & O'Reilly, 1990).

Socialization and identity. Arnold and Nicholson (1991) found, during the first year of a longitudinal study, that many people did perceive that their self-concept had changed regardless of the individuals' tenure in the organization. But they found no evidence of an *increase in similarity* between self and others in the organization during the socialization period. These authors concluded that it was not necessary to feel similarity to be enthusiastic about an organization, but that perceiving a "calculative fit" or a positive answer to "What's in it for me?" did contribute to positive feelings about the organization. Additionally, those who discovered they were similar to their superiors were more committed to the organization.

Hebden (1986) examined the extent to which 31 graduate trainees in 2 organizations adopted values of the organizational culture during their first 5 years in their organizations. In a comparison of 8 individual and organizational value orientations, newcomers differed from their organizations on 2 dimensions from the start, and became increasingly different on the other 6 value dimensions as time passed. The author concluded that organizational socialization practices did not change individual values toward a greater fit, but did teach members what the organizational values were and acceptable ways to cope with value differences. To cope, some of the trainees found a fit in some values and worked to achieve personal and organizational goals within the system, others distanced themselves psychologically from what they perceived to be a "foreign culture" while pursuing individual goals within the organization, and some who perceived a misfit left the organization.

The Role of Fit in Socialization

One objective of individual and organizational socialization mechanisms is to promote a fit on some dimensions that enable organizations and individuals to meet their goals through mutually beneficial interactions (Muchinsky & Monahan, 1987). Individual-organizational (I-0) fit usually includes similarity of type of personality and environment, goals, or values (Chatman, 1989; Dawis & Lofquist, 1984; Holland, 1985; Vancouver & Schmitt, 1991). This perspective asserts that when an individual with particular values, goals, skills, and strategies finds an environment with similar values, compatible and similarly prioritized goals, and structures designed to reward his or her likely behaviors, I-O fit and mutual satisfaction will result (Dawis & Lofquist, 1984; Judge & Ferris, 1992; Vancouver & Schmitt, 1991).

Research exploring these dimensions of fit reveals substantial links between fit and various aspects of organizational effectiveness, including greater employee commitment, motivation, prosocial behavior, and involvement, as well as lower turnover and absenteeism (Blau, 1987; Chatman, 1989; Granrose & Portwood, 1987; Judge & Ferris, 1992). The role of individual-organizational fit in organizational effectiveness, however, is less clear for Asian managers in U.S. organizations. Because of cultural differences, Asian managers may not perceive their values, goals, or priorities to be congruent with U.S. organizations (Hofstede, 1980; Meindl, Hunt, & Lee, 1989). For multinational organizations to reap the benefits of I-O fit, they need to socialize multiple national groups into a single organization within which each member can find a fit.

Almost nothing exists in the international management literature on socialization of managers into organizational cultures that differ from their own in the predominant ethnicity or nationality represented by the home country of the organization. Fortunately, much has been written on cross-cultural intergroup contact. We can use this information to develop a model of socialization of multiple ethnic groups into a global organization.

Cross-Cultural
Intergroup Contact

Individuals or groups involved in acculturation to a nation may try to retain characteristics of their previous culture or may change values, identity, behaviors, and attitudes, depending in part on the permanence, purpose, voluntariness, and normative strategies of the cross-cultural contact. Groups may use different acculturation strategies, including (a) assimilation, (b) integration, (c) separation, (d) marginalization, (e) alternation of cultural expression in different circumstances, and (f) fusion to form a unique new culture (Berry, Chapter 2, this volume; Ferdman, 1995). Because in the United States the term *integration* has acquired some negative connotations from difficult black-white interactions, I will use the term "subtractive assimilation" to refer to assimilation in which one culture is given up in favor of the dominant culture and "additive multiculturalism" (Triandis, 1995) to refer to the situations that Berry describes as *integration,* when individuals or groups add characteristics of a new culture without giving up cultural characteristics of former group memberships.

Regardless of what strategy is advocated, in many social situations little assimilation occurs, because contact may be superficial or intermittent, may involve multiple groups simultaneously, may be highly regulated by norms for specific roles, or all of these (cf. Boyacigiller, Kleinberg, Phillips, & Sackmann, 1996; Taylor & Moghaddam, 1994). In these circumstances, individual change may be minimal, "felt conflict" may not be expressed, and separation may be the primary strategy for interaction.

If separation is not total, groups may interact in ways to preserve their cultural characteristics rather than lose their identity (Buck, 1978; Keefe, 1992). In particular, social identity theory emphasizes the need for members of cultural groups to believe that their group status is equal to or better than the status of other groups (Ferdman, 1992; Tajfel & Turner, 1986). If cultural group membership is the primary basis for the interaction, relationships are likely to be competitive rather than cooperative. Empirical findings suggest that groups that strive to preserve ethnic identity may congregate in certain departments or offices, use their native language, retain important ethnic symbols and intra- or extraorganizational relationships to promote group identity and positive group status, and use their collective political power to position ethnic group leaders in positions of leadership in the organization. This may lead either to employees becoming alienated from the organization as a whole rather than becoming socialized into organizational membership, or to subgroups pursuing goals that hinder rather than help organizational goal attainment. Because these alternatives do not contribute to a strong organizational culture, we must consider other facilitators of intergroup interactions.

Research on outcomes of cross-national acculturation suggests that less stressful and more positive acculturation results occur when additive multiculturalism is the strategy (Berry, Poortinga, Segall, & Dasen, 1992), when pluralism is tolerated or encouraged by the dominant group (Murphy, 1965), when contact is voluntary, when interaction is between individuals and groups of equal status, when interaction provides valued rewards, and when various social supports are available (Berry & Kim, 1988). Similar evidence from intranational intergroup contact indicates that positive interactions occur when there is similarity on a dimension other than those unique to ethnic or national group membership, agreement on mutually valued superordinate goals, and equality of power or status (Taylor & Moghaddam, 1994).

Cross-Cultural Intraorganizational Interaction

Traditional organizational acculturation adopts a subtractive assimilation strategy to create one homogeneous organizational culture (Dülfer, 1995). In contrast, additive multiculturalism perspectives assert that it is possible to encourage interactions among two or more cultural groups in an organization in ways that contribute to increased creativity and innovative problem solving, more effective marketing, and greater employee satisfaction (Brown, 1983; Cox, 1991). This viewpoint recommends that organizations support equality in all aspects of organizations; promote equal organizational identification regardless of cultural identification; offer cross-cultural training; recognize cultural group integrity; pursue superordinate goals; and reward acceptance of diversity (Brislin, 1981; Brown, 1983; Ferdman, 1992).

Triandis (1995) presents a model of intergroup interactions that integrates these perspectives on intergroup interaction and organizational diversity, and reveals the complex nature of the predictors of positive organizational intergroup interactions. He proposes that more positive interactions will occur if groups have a history of positive relationships in a setting that values pluralism; have a smaller cultural distance (that is, are similar on more dimensions and are familiar with each other's cultures); share superordinate goals; perform cooperative, structured tasks with equal-status others; are rewarded for task accomplishment and for positive interaction; and have overlapping social networks. Triandis and his colleagues currently are gathering empirical support for this model, and one example is reported by Goto (Chapter 5, this volume). Some of these recommendations are relevant for MNC socialization. MNCs do have common purposes and some shared superordinate goals, which are often included in socialization processes. Likewise, socialization of employees might be structured to include learning more about other cultures, affirming the positive characteristics and equal statuses of each cultural group, and setting forth a norm for a positive acculturation strategy such as additive multiculturalism. In addition, informal socialization mechanisms might be able to affirm similarity of employees on job-relevant dimensions other than cultural group membership and to reward employees for good performance on these dimensions. These characteristics of positive cross-national group interactions are important to incorporate into a model of cross-cultural organizational socialization.

A Proposed Model of Cross-Cultural Organizational Socialization

If we integrate the national and organizational culture information, the socialization and I-O fit information, and the intergroup contact information, we can obtain a picture of the characteristics of cross-cultural socialization that would promote valued organizational outcomes. As shown in Figure 9.1, the literature on culture proposes that cultural content, in particular the cultural distance or the extent to which the cultures of employees' specific group memberships are consistent or conflicting with the cultures of other organization members and with the organizational culture, has an important effect on the

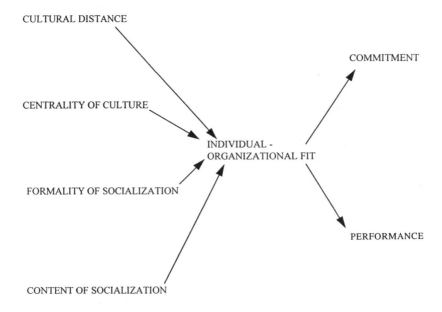

CULTURAL DISTANCE

COMMITMENT

CENTRALITY OF CULTURE

INDIVIDUAL -
ORGANIZATIONAL FIT

FORMALITY OF SOCIALIZATION

PERFORMANCE

CONTENT OF SOCIALIZATION

Figure 9.1. Cross-Cultural Organizational Socialization

extent to which individuals feel that they fit an organization. Also, the centrality or importance of cultural group memberships for each person's identity may influence the extent to which employees find a fit in an organization.

The socialization literature suggests that "institutional" socialization that is formal, includes role models, and has sequential learning activities, increases the probability that employees will discover whether or not they fit a particular organization and can become committed to it. Both socialization and intergroup contact research suggest that if the content of socialization includes a (a) focus on shared superordinate organizational goals and values, (b) the availability of rewards for desired behaviors, and (c) self-affirmation that includes affirmation of different cultural group memberships as well as affirmation of organizational membership (that is, additive multiculturalism), then fit and commitment will be increased. The literature on I-O fit suggests that higher commitment and performance will occur if individuals find they fit the organization in similarity of goals and values.

Applying the Model to Asian
and U.S. Managers in U.S. Firms

The findings reported in this chapter are part of a larger study of the careers of Asian managers. For these analyses, data were obtained from Asian managers working in Asia for U.S. firms and U.S. managers working in the United States for U.S. firms. The four firms in Asia included two manufacturers, one of durable and the other of nondurable goods; the insurance and financial services subsidiaries of one large service firm; and a petrochemical firm. In the United States, three of the four firms in Asia and one other firm participated. Industry sectors represented were the same in the United States and Asia.

Method

Data were collected in two steps. First, the country CEO or senior human resources (HR) manager was interviewed. In this interview, basic company demographic information and human resource policies as implemented in each location were identified, and a list was obtained of a minimum of 10-20 managers who had worked for the firm at least one year, drawn from all departments and all managerial levels. The selected managers then filled out a structured questionnaire and participated in a follow-up interview to clarify any questions they had about the structured questionnaire and to obtain more extensive answers to open-ended questions. Interviews and questionnaires for this part of the sample were in English, because these managers needed English in their everyday interactions in the U.S. firms. All respondents were given the opportunity to have a translator present if they desired. They were assured that the information would be reported to their firms only in aggregated form, and their trust increased noticeably as the interview progressed.

Sample

In Asia, line manager interviews were conducted with Asian managers working in Hong Kong ($n = 18$), Singapore ($n = 29$), Taiwan ($n = 19$), Thailand ($n = 24$), and Japan ($n = 30$). There were not enough managers from each country to detect meaningful country differences

Table 9.1
Demographic Characteristics of the Sample

Demographic Variables*	Chinese (n = 66)	Japanese (n = 30)	Thai (n = 24)	United States (n = 65)
Age	40	44	36	51
Percentage women	27	17	33	19
Percentage married	86	79	54	91
Religion				
Percentage Christian	23	4	8	78
Percentage Buddhist	25	41	88	0
Percentage other	52	55	4	22
Levels from the top	1.52	2.65	4.52	2.75
Organizational tenure	6.55	12.25	7.43	14.18

* Significantly different, $p < .01$.

among the Chinese samples (Hong Kong, Singapore, and Taiwan). Although these national groups were different on other dimensions, on dimensions relevant for this study they were more like each other and more different from the Thai and Japanese, so the three Chinese samples were aggregated. In the United States, 65 line manager interviews were conducted.

According to the group means shown in Table 9.1, the Thai managers were slightly younger and the U.S. managers were older than the others. The Thai and Chinese managers had less organizational tenure, but the Chinese managers were about one level closer to the top of their organizations than other managers, whereas the Thai managers were farther from the top of their organizations. Japanese and U.S. managers were less likely to be women, and Thai managers were less likely to be married. Marital status, level, gender, age, and organizational tenure were included in all analyses to account for these differences. Although there were significant differences in religion, religious heritage was considered to be one aspect of national culture and was not included as a separate predictor in analyses also containing nationality.

Measures

Demographic variables. The demographic variables were measured using single items. Most questions were worded "What is your _____?" Gender was coded 1 = *male,* 2 = *female;* marital status was coded

1 = *single, divorced, or widowed,* 2 = *married.* Nation was coded as three dummy variables with 1 = *member of the target nation,* 0 = *member of another nation.* The United States was the omitted category. Age was calculated by subtracting the response to "What year were you born _____ ?" from the year of the interview, after transforming the answers into the Gregorian calendar from the Thai and Chinese calendars used in some responses. Organizational level was measured by responses to the question "How many levels are there between you and the most senior person in this organization in this country?" Organizational tenure was calculated from a job chart in which line managers listed various characteristics of each job they had held.

Centrality. The centrality of national membership to a person's identity was measured by the question "When you think about yourself, how important is it to see yourself as a citizen of your country?" (1 = *not very important,* 5 = *very important*).

Socialization process. Socialization process was measured using a list of human resource management programs, and summing the number of programs a person indicated were available to him or her. The programs were ones that represented "institutional" socialization and included skill training, job rotation, coaching and mentoring, performance appraisal, and career planning workshops.

Socialization content. Three aspects of socialization content were measured. For each, the managers rated how much the organization used various tactics to try to influence employees to meet organizational goals (1 = *very little,* 5 = *very much*). The three organizational influence tactics were "refers to management culture or mission," "offers appreciation," and "sets performance goals and rewards those who meet them." The three were not summed into a single scale because each represented a different aspect of an organization, which might promote positive intergroup interaction. The first represented promoting superordinate goals; the second represented self-affirmation; and the third represented positive reinforcement for relevant organizational characteristics not related to group membership. Although these items were not exactly the ones a researcher might design if socialization was the primary goal of the research project, they represented the best available indicators in the data set.

I-O fit. Individual-organizational fit focused on career fit rather than values fit, because it included both goal congruence and situations in which individual and organizational goals did not match but individuals were able to progress toward their goals within the organization—the "what's in it for me?" approach. Fit was measured by three items asking how likely "your career goals match your organization's goals for you," "your career timetable matches your organization's timetable for you," "your career strategies match the strategies this organization has for you" (1 = *very unlikely,* 5 = *very likely;* alpha = .89).

Organizational commitment. Organizational commitment was measured by three items "This organization means a lot to me," "I am not part of this organizational family" (reversed), "I do not belong to this organization" (reversed), (1 = *strongly disagree,* 5 = *strongly agree;* alpha = .79).

Expected tenure. Behavioral commitment was measured by the question "How long do you expect to continue working for this organization?" coded in years.

Results

The means, standard deviations, and correlations of study variables are shown in Table 9.2. Correlational analyses do not take into account sample differences in demographic characteristics, however, and they give little information about the network of relationships between national identity, socialization, organizational affect, and expected tenure.

To test the proposed model, stepwise regression analyses were conducted, and standardized regression weights are displayed in Table 9.3. The first analysis used I-O fit as the dependent measure. Independent variables included age, gender, and marital status as indicators of individual identity; organizational tenure and level as measures of probability of equal-status interactions; nationality and centrality of nationality as indicators of cultural distance and the role of national culture in identity; and formal socialization process and the three

Table 9.2
Means, Standard Deviations, and Correlations of Study Variables

Variable	Mean	SD	1	2	3	4	5	6	7	8	9	10	11	12	13	14	15	16
1. Age	44.00	9.74	—															
2. Gender	1.23	.43	-05	—														
3. Marital status	1.82	.38	23	-32	—													
4. Level from top	2.14	2.52	16	-01	06	—												
5. Organizational tenure	10.20	8.22	43	-19	16	03	—											
6. Japanese	.13	.34	-32	09	-29	-10	-13	—										
7. Chinese	.36	.48	-29	07	08	-18	-34	-29	—									
8. Thai	.16	.34	00	-06	-04	09	11	-17	-33	—								
9. Nationality centrality	3.27	1.15	-01	24	-02	03	-08	06	21	-10	—							
10. Formal socialization	3.20	1.33	26	-05	-13	18	10	-10	10	-16	04	—						
11. Organizational culture	3.37	.99	07	-04	19	-01	10	06	-19	16	21	20	—					
12. Appreciation	3.26	.98	-11	04	02	-01	-13	08	25	-09	12	06	39	—				
13. Reward goals	3.52	1.10	14	-00	17	01	-04	-13	22	-04	17	19	35	47	—			
14. I-O fit	2.90	.92	-02	-16	03	01	14	01	17	01	-02	-21	23	34	18	—		
15. Commitment	2.44	.50	08	00	-08	02	10	-03	-20	-02	01	-05	-05	19	-21	-23	—	
16. Expected tenure	8.04	6.25	13	-25	15	08	14	-15	-19	04	-11	24	01	07	21	02	25	—

NOTE: See text for a description of variables. Correlations over .14 are significant, $p < .05$. Decimal points have been omitted in correlations.

Table 9.3
Relationships Between Identity and Socialization Variables
and I-O Fit and Commitment

Independent Variable	Dependent Variable		
	I-O Fit Beta	Commitment Beta	Expected Organizational Tenure Beta
Step 1			
Age	.08	−.01	−.11
Gender	−.27**	−.01	−.21*
Marital status	−.14	−.07	.08
Level from top	.06	−.09	−.01
Organizational tenure	−.11	−.04	.01
Japanese	.11	−.36**	−.28*
Chinese	.20	−.43**	−.32*
Thai	.08	−.13	−.12
National centrality	−.04	.24*	−.03
Formal socialization	.18*	−.00	.07
Organizational culture	.18	.09	−.02
Appreciation	.38**	−.17	−.09
Reward goals	−.05	−.14	.06
R^2	.36**	.26**	.20*
Step 2			
I/O fit	—	−.04	.23*
Total adjusted R^2	.28**	.15**	.12*
F	4.24**	2.38**	2.10*

$*p < .05; **p < .01.$

measures of socialization content, as aspects of socialization likely to promote positive intergroup contact.

Being male, having formal, institutionalized socialization practices, and receiving appreciation were significant predictors of I-O fit. The predictors together explained a significant amount of variance in fit (adjusted $R^2 = .28$, $F = 4.24$, $p < .01$). In the second regression, with organizational commitment as the dependent measure, the identity and socialization variables were entered in Step 1 and I-O fit was entered in Step 2. Japanese and Chinese managers were significantly less committed to their organizations than U.S. managers, and those whose nationality was more central to their identity were more committed ($R^2 = .26, F = 2.58, p < .01$). When I-O fit was added to these analyses in Step 2, I-O fit did not account for a significant amount of the variance in commitment (total adjusted $R^2 = .15, F = 2.38, p < .01$). This does not support the model's claim that the effects of socialization on commitment are mediated by I-O fit.

The third regression analysis used expected organizational tenure as the dependent variable. Again, identity and socialization variables were entered in Step 1. Gender and nationality predicted a significant amount of variance ($R^2 = .20, F = 1.88, p = .04$). Women and Japanese and Chinese employees expected to remain with the organization shorter lengths of time. I-O fit, added in Step 2, was a significant predictor and did account for a small, significant change in the dependent variable ($R^2 = .03, F = 4.13, p = .04$; total adjusted $R^2 = .12, F = 2.10, p < .02$).

Discussion

For male managers, more structured socialization that was accompanied by affirmative rather than self-destructive interactions increased perceptions that individuals fit their organizations and in particular that their career plans matched the plans their organizations had for their future. Perceived fit also increased expected organizational tenure, the amount of time that managers believed they would remain with the organization, that is, their behavioral organizational commitment, but not their affective organizational commitment. Japanese and Chinese managers were less likely to be committed in behavior or emotion, and women were less likely to be committed in behavior. Thai nationality was not significantly related to either commitment or fit.

These findings are important because they provide empirical evidence of a link, not only among U.S. managers working for U.S. firms, but also among Asian managers working for U.S. firms, showing that socialization processes can positively affect perceptions of individual-organizational fit. In addition, they support the idea that perceptions of career fit influence how long managers expect to remain with a firm. This is particularly noteworthy because many Asian managers do not intend to remain with their U.S. organizations as long as U.S. managers do. In data collected from HR managers in this same study, unwanted employee turnover was listed as an important HR problem in every country. These findings suggest that instituting positive formal socialization programs in Asian locations may be one mechanism that firms can use to reduce this turnover and increase their competitiveness.

Findings of negative relationships between Chinese and Japanese nationality and affective commitment, however, indicate that significant problems in cross-cultural socialization are prevalent. In important dimensions of organizational life, some Asian managers and women feel separated from their employers. The interview responses suggested some of the foundations for these problems.

None of these organizations had a specific policy advocating pluralism or additive multiculturalism as part of their stance toward employees of non-U.S. nationalities, although all used standard phrases of nondiscrimination on the basis of ethnicity, gender, or national origin, somewhere in their human resources publications. Statements appearing in strategic plans and policy documents were more likely to affirm the importance of human resources in general, rather than specific integration strategies. For example:

Firm A: "People are our number one asset and our only sustainable advantage."
Firm B: "We will pursue . . . the welfare of our policy holders, agents, employees, and company."
Firm C: "We will enhance value for our stockholders, customers, employees, and public." "We will create an environment that fosters personal growth, and allows individuals to achieve their full potential."

The last policy statement does reinforce a generally self-affirming stance toward employees, which should support positive socialization outcomes, but other aspects of socialization of women and non-U.S. citizens may be undermining this positive message.

Gender and Nationality Issues

Several respondents commented on aspects of gender when discussing their careers. Numerous Asian women stated that they wanted to be employed in U.S. firms because they perceived U.S. firms to permit more career advancement for women, but that these hopes were only partially realized. Some women mentioned the extent to which women were not viewed as suitable for management positions. "It is easy for a woman to get a clerical position, but harder to become a manager" declared one Singaporean woman. A Japanese woman described ways in which her career plans did not fit cultural constraints that were only partially under control of the firm: "There are blocks to my career here. If I became a candidate for office manager, which is very likely because I am Japanese, being a business *woman* (her emphasis) may become a block because the Japanese insurance market is still very much male dominated." Gender differences in domestic role demands also influenced organizational commitment: "I don't want to work an extremely long day. I want to finish by 5:00 to 6:00 p.m. to be with my family" declared a Thai woman.

Because Japanese and Chinese nationality did not predict perceptions of fit or misfit on career goals but did predict lower behavioral and affective commitment, we must search for additional explanations of organizational commitment. Asian managers' responses and the literature on dimensions of fit suggest at least four possible explanations: personality misfits, normative misfits, values misfits, and discrimination. We did not collect personality data, and no respondents suggested this was a reason for difficulty with their organizations, but some evidence did appear for other dimensions of lack of fit that might contribute to lower commitment.

Evidence exists for some discrimination on the grounds of nationality, in addition to gender, although explanations may be complex. In every country, managers and HR executives declared that U.S. nationals had different career paths than Asian managers, and several mentioned more-limited opportunities for Asian managers. In a few cases it was due to Asian managers' reluctance to move out of their home country, which would be required for promotion above country manager. Also, limitations in English language accounted for some career differences. One Taiwanese man said, "There are fewer opportunities for me here (in this firm). They must use Americans or English-speaking nationals for higher positions." Several managers stated they would move anywhere and get any language training needed, but they were still pessimistic that they could be promoted into higher positions in home offices in the United States. These differences in career paths may be interpreted as indicators of lower group status of non-U.S. national groups. If the managers do perceive that their groups have a lower status than U.S. managers in the organization, this may contribute to lower individual identification with the organization, and support beliefs and actions that promote higher national group status (as predicted by social identity theory).

Differences in cultural values are widely acknowledged between most Asian countries and the United States, but culturally related value and norm differences more specific than the broad dimensions of individualism, power distance, uncertainty avoidance, and masculinity (Hofstede, 1980) were cited as reasons for thinking about leaving the firm. "I want my career here but there are blocks. I don't know how long I can bear the pressure. I am frank ([*sic,*] meaning I will be frank). This is not the Thai way. I don't like politics!" exclaimed one Thai manager. A revealing Japanese comment highlighted normative differences: "A big difference here is, in Japan we are more cooperative with our competitors." Comments such as these indicate that cultural pluralism may need to go beyond tolerance of culturally related behavioral differences in performing individual job tasks and extend to central ways of doing business. If these differences are too great, it may cause Asian employees to dislike working for U.S. firms.

Other Factors Influencing Commitment

Another possible explanation for lower commitment is unrelated to predictors of fit, but is related to other causes of organizational commitment not taken into account in this research. These include the nature of the job, lifespan changes, and different organizational attachment mechanisms. One employee in Bangkok might be echoing a U.S. manager when he said, "If my current job responsibilities are not cleared up by management, I certainly plan to leave this company and do [*sic*] my own business." His desire to leave the firm seemed less specifically related to his national culture and more strongly related to difficult job circumstances.

Older employees may disengage from the firm, or change their career goals, whether they are Asian or American. A Singaporean said: "For the last 20 years of my career, I have spent my time climbing the corporate ladder. In the next 10 years and beyond, climbing the corporate ladder will not be my major preoccupation. I am prepared to move down the corporate ladder in exchange for a well-balanced life."

This career plan may well be congruent with the firm's plans for his future, but would still reflect lower affective commitment to the firm.

Some scholars have proposed that affective connections between employees and the firm may involve different mechanisms for Asians, including role compliance, obligation bonding, and affiliation within groups (Redding, Norman, & Schlander, 1994). A striking example of a different attachment was given by a Japanese manager describing his career: "If I could change jobs, I would teach English to Japanese. . . When I selected this job, it was like fate for me. So I don't want to change my job here. It is my fate." The element of fate, and loyalty to organizational members, as differentiated from loyalty to the U.S. parent firm, were also mentioned by several Thai managers. The reliance on fate is somewhat different from explanations European American managers might give for why they would or would not continue to work for their employer, but it does describe behavioral commitment not linked to dimensions of I-O fit usually discussed in the U.S. literature. These and other alternative explanations will need extensive follow-up in future studies.

Limitations

In addition to omitting explanations of commitment other than career goal fit, this study has several features that limit its generalizability and usefulness. The sample size was small in each country, so specific country differences could not be determined, even though national differences exist between the Chinese countries included in this study. Because of the small sample size, it was not possible to study only those managers who had recently entered the organization, that is, those who were experiencing the most intense socialization pressures and who might quickly find out that they did not fit and leave. The sample was skewed by including more long-tenure employees who had already found their needs met by the organization and long ago had decided to stay, and by omitting those who left in their first year because they did not fit. Including organizational tenure in these analyses only partially corrected for this limitation.

All measures were collected in one instrument, and all aspects that might promote positive intergroup interaction were measured with only one item, which increased the probability that some of the effects found might be common measurement effects rather than construct relationship effects. In addition, shared networks, exact socialization strategies, relative status of different national groups, the exact ways that different cultures may support or conflict with organizational cultures, and knowledge of other cultures were not measured in this study. These aspects of socialization may be more important in understanding organizational cross-cultural fit phenomena than the results of this study can indicate.

Questionnaires were administered in English, which was a second language for the Asian managers. All managers were required to use English in their jobs in U.S. firms, and the interviews were used to clarify any obvious language problems; however, problems arising from different meanings of important study constructs undoubtedly remained.

In spite of these limitations, the fact that the findings were consistent and in the expected direction across multiple predictors and multiple outcome measures suggests that these relationships are substantive enough to justify further study. When combined with the findings cited in the literature, they also suggest a few tentative recommendations for MNCs.

Recommendations for Cross-National Socialization

The first and most obvious recommendation is for organizations to develop explicit socialization and operating policies that support additive multiculturalism and to examine how their organizational cultures can be strengthened to reinforce this acculturation strategy. In effect, this means creating a strong organizational culture based on multiculturalism. Findings from intraorganizational diversity and cross-national research sources and extraorganizational intergroup contact situations all confirm the importance of this policy for positive individual and organizational outcomes. In particular, the relative status of different national groups needs to be clarified such that each national group believes that it is of equal status to all others. This type of organization is sometimes called a global organization, in which any nation can be seen as a potential best contributor of any specific organizational function or employee.

The second recommendation is to expand formalized socialization practices, such as are currently used by many organizations in home offices, to sites in other nations. Although many other HRM programs have to be custom-fit to a particular country, use of common socialization programs that are related to effectiveness in multiple national settings may be one example of integration that particularly encourages a single strong organizational culture promoting organizational competitiveness. The content of the socialization needs to affirm important aspects of national and gender cultural identity, as well as emphasizing similarity on organizationally relevant dimensions of individual differences not related to national or cultural differences, such as job skills. The content of socialization, as well as other work design, needs to focus on rewarding cooperative, network-building work on tasks specifically related to meeting superordinate organizational goals.

In addition to socialization mechanisms, other aspects of positive intergroup interactions need to be addressed in the way the organization does its work—that is, the organizational culture that is supposed to bind employees to the organization. Cross-cultural contacts that are voluntary, between people of equal status, and between people who have some knowledge of each others' cultures promote positive interactions. Strong organizational cultures that promote these ways of getting the jobs done can be expected to lead to more effective organizations in which employees from multiple national origins can thrive.

References

Allaire, Y., & Firsirotu, M. E. (1983). Theories of organizational culture. *Organizational Studies, 11*(1), 47-74.

Allen, N. J., & Meyer, J. P. (1990a). Organizational socialization tactics: A longitudinal analysis of links to newcomers' commitment and role orientation. *Academy of Management Journal, 33*, 847-858.

Allen, N. J., & Meyer, J. P. (1990b). The measurement and antecedents of affective, continuance, and normative commitment to the organization. *Journal of Occupational Psychology, 63*(1), 1-18.

Arnold, J., & Nicholson, N. (1991). Construing self and others at work in the early years of corporate careers. *Journal of Organizational Behavior, 12*, 621-639.

Berry, J. W., & Kim, U. (1988). Acculturation and mental health. In P. Dasen, J. W. Berry, & N. Sartorius (Eds.), *Cross-cultural psychology and health* (pp. 207-236). London, UK: Sage.

Berry, J. W., Poortinga, Y., Segall, M., & Dasen, P. (1992). *Cross-cultural psychology.* New York: Cambridge University Press.

Blau, G. (1987). Using a person-environment fit model to predict job involvement and organizational commitment. *Journal of Vocational Behavior, 30,* 240-257.

Boyacigiller, N. A., Kleinberg, M. J., Phillips, M. E., & Sackmann, S. H. (1996). Conceptualizing culture. In B. J. Punnett & O. Shenkar (Eds.), *Handbook for international management research* (pp. 157-208). Cambridge, MA: Blackwell.

Brislin, R. U. (1981). *Cross-cultural encounters: Face to face interaction.* New York: Pergamon.

Brown, L. D. (1983). *Managing conflict at organizational interfaces.* Reading, MA: Addison-Wesley.

Buck, R. (1978). Boundary maintenance revisited: Tourist experience in old order Amish communities. *Rural Sociology, 43,* 221-234.

Caldwell, D. F., Chatman, J. A., & O'Reilly, C. A. (1990). Building organizational commitment: A multifirm study. *Journal of Occupational Psychology, 63,* 245-261.

Chatman, J. (1989). Improving interactional organizational research: A model of person-organization fit. *Academy of Management Review, 14,* 333-349.

Clark, R. D., & Maass, A. (1988). The role of social categorization and perceived social credibility in minority influence. *European Journal of Social Psychology, 18,* 381-394.

Cox, T. (1991). The multicultural organization. *Academy of Management Executive, 5*(2), 34-47.

Dawis, R. V., & Lofquist, L. H. (1984). *A psychological theory of work adjustment.* Minneapolis: University of Minnesota Press.

Dowling, P., & Schuler, R. (1990). *International dimensions of human resource management.* Boston: PWS-Kent.

Dulfer, E. (1995). Human resource management in multinational and internationally operating companies. In R. Peiper (Ed.), *Human resources management: An international comparison* (pp. 261-283). New York: DeGruyter.

Erez, M., & Earley, P. C. (1993). *Culture, self-identity, and work.* New York: Oxford University Press.

Feldman, D. C. (1988). *Managing careers in organizations.* Glenview, IL: Scott Foresman.

Ferdman, B. (1992). The dynamics of ethnic diversity in organizations: Toward integrative models. In K. Kelley (Ed.), *Issues, theory, and research in I-O psychology* (pp. 339-384). Amsterdam: North Holland.

Ferdman, B. (1995). Cultural identity and diversity in organizations: Bridging the gap between group differences and individual uniqueness. In M. M. Chemers, S. Oskamp, & M. A. Costanzo (Eds.), *Diversity in organizations* (pp. 37-60). Thousand Oaks, CA: Sage.

Gillespie, K. (1989). U.S. multinationals and the foreign MBA. *Columbia Journal of World Business, 24*(2), 15-51.

Granrose, C. S., & Portwood, J. (1987). Matching individual career plans and organizational career management. *Academy of Management Journal, 30,* 699-720.

Greenhaus, J. H., & Callanan, G. A. (1994). *Career management* (2nd ed.). Fort Worth, TX: Dryden.

Hackman, J. R. (1992). Group influences on individuals in organizations. In M. D. Dunnette & L. M. Hough (Eds.), *Handbook of industrial and organizational psychology* (2nd ed., Vol. 3, pp. 199-267). Palo Alto, CA: Consulting Psychologists Press.

Hebden, J. E. (1986). Adopting an organization's culture: The socialization of graduate trainees. *Organizational Dynamics, 15*(1), 54-72.

Hirschhorn, L., & Gilmore, T. (1992, May-June). The new boundaries of the "boundary-less" company. *Harvard Business Review,* pp. 104-115.

Hofstede, G. (1980). *Culture's consequences.* Beverly Hills, CA: Sage.

Holland, J. L. (1985). *Making vocational choices: A theory of personality and work environments* (2nd ed.). Englewood Cliffs, NJ: Prentice Hall.

Jones, G. R. (1986). Socialization tactics, self-efficacy, and newcomers' adjustments to organizations. *Academy of Management Journal, 29,* 262-279.

Judge, T. A., & Ferris, G. R. (1992). The elusive criterion of fit in human resource staffing decisions. *Human Resource Planning, 15*(4), 47-67.

Keefe, S. E. (1992). Ethnic identity: The domain of perceptions and attachment to ethnic groups and cultures. *Human Organizations, 51*(1), 35-43.

Keesing, R. M. (1974). Theories of culture. *Annual Review of Anthropology, 3*(1), 73-97.

London, M., & Stumpf, S. (1982). *Managing careers.* Reading, MA: Addison-Wesley.

Meindl, J. R., Hunt, R. G., & Lee, W. (1989). Individualism-collectivism and work values: Data from the U.S., China, Taiwan, Korea, & Hong Kong. *Research in Personnel and Human Resources Management, 7(Suppl. 1), 59-77.*

Moscovici, S. (1980). Toward a theory of conversion behavior. In L. Berkowitz (Ed.), *Advances in experimental social psychology* (Vol. 13, pp. 209-239). New York: Academic Press.

Muchinsky, P. M., & Monahan, C. J. (1987). What is person-environment congruence? Supplementary versus complementary models of fit. *Journal of Vocational Behavior, 31,* 268-277.

Murphy, H. B. M. (1965). Migration and the major mental disorders. In M. B. Kantor (Ed.), *Mobility and mental health* (pp. 221-249). Springfield, IL: Charles C Thomas.

Pascale, R. (1985). The paradox of corporate culture: Reconciling ourselves to socialization. *California Management Review, 27*(2), 6-41.

Redding, S. G., Norman, A., & Schlander, A. (1994). The nature of individual attachment to the organization: A review of East Asian variations. In M. D. Dunnette & L. M. Hough (Eds.), *Handbook of industrial and organizational psychology* (2nd ed., Vol. 4, pp. 647-688). Palo Alto, CA: Consulting Psychologists Press.

Rosenzweig, P., & Singh, J. (1991). Organizational environments and the multinational enterprise. *Academy of Management Review, 16,* 340-361.

Schein, E. H. (1978). *Career dynamics.* Reading, MA: Addison-Wesley.

Schein, E. H. (1990). Organizational cultures. *American Psychologist, 45*(2), 109-119.

Schneider, S. C. (1988). National versus corporate culture: Implications for human resource management. *Human Resource Management, 27,* 231-246.

Tajfel, H., & Turner, J. C. (1986). An integrative theory of intergroup conflict. In W. G. Austin & S. Worchel (Eds.), *The social psychology of intergroup relations* (pp. 33-47). Monterey, CA: Brooks/Cole.

Taylor, D. M., & Moghaddam, F. M. (1994). *Theories of intergroup relations* (2nd ed.). Westport, CT: Praeger.

Triandis, H. C. (1995). A theoretical framework for the study of diversity. In M. M. Chemers, S. Oskamp, & M. A. Costanzo (Eds.), *Diversity in organizations* (pp. 11-36). Thousand Oaks, CA: Sage.

Tung, R. L. (1987). Expatriate assignments: Enhancing success and minimizing failure. *Academy of Management Executive, 1*(2), 117-126.

Vancouver, J. B., & Schmitt, N. W. (1991). An exploratory examination of person-organization fit: Organizational goal congruence. *Personnel Psychology, 44,* 333-352.

Van Maanen, J., & Barley, S. R. (1985). Cultural organization: Fragments of a theory. In P. J. Frost, L. F. Moore, M. R. Lewis, C. C. Lundberg, & J. Martin (Eds.), *Organizational culture* (pp. 31-53). Beverly Hills, CA: Sage.

Van Mannen, J., & Schein, E. H. (1979). Toward a theory of organizational socialization. In B. M. Staw & L. L. Cummings (Eds.), *Research in organizational behavior* (Vol. 1, pp. 204-264). Greenwich, CT: JAI.

10

The Effects of Culture on Mentoring Relationships
A Developmental Model

SUSAN E. MURPHY
ELLEN A. ENSHER

The increasing diversity of the global workforce has been well documented by organizational scholars and practitioners (Fernandez, 1991; Jamieson & O'Mara, 1991; Loden & Rosenor, 1991). Today's employees and their customers represent greater ethnic and racial heterogeneity than ever before, both domestically and internationally (Federal Glass Ceiling Commission, 1995; Naisbitt, 1994). Innovations in technology, the economic advancement of previously underdeveloped nations, and a greater consumer demand for a wide array of products and services have contributed to the globalization of organizations (Fernandez, 1991; Naisbitt, 1994). These environmental forces present 21st-century employees and their managers with unique challenges. For managers, the impetus is to empower their employees (Byham & Cox, 1994) and facilitate their career development within a culturally diverse context (Morrison, 1996). One important factor that contributes to employees' career success is the development of a heterogeneous network of mentors who vary in organizational affiliation, experience, and ethnicity (Thomas, 1990).

Mentoring is particularly important for people who are ethnic or gender minorities in U.S. organizations and abroad, because it can reduce many of the barriers to upward mobility that they typically face (Cox, 1993; Ragins, 1994). Most diverse mentoring relationships involve a European American male mentor of higher organizational status paired with a female or minority employee of lower organizational rank (Thomas, 1990). Mentors help to socialize a protégé to an organization's norms, which can have positive effects on organizational commitment, job satisfaction, and retention (Fagenson, 1989; Zey, 1984). Mentors can also provide minority individuals with access to the informal networks and power structure that are critical for upward mobility and long-term career success (Kram & Hall, in press). Protégés, as compared to employees without mentors, receive more promotions, greater pay, and have more career mobility (Noe, 1988; Ragins, 1989). Therefore, diverse mentoring relationships could ultimately increase the representation of minorities in senior management.

One type of diverse mentoring relationship that has received little attention is that of cross-national mentoring. With the increase of multinational firms establishing operations in foreign countries, some employees find themselves working in foreign countries with managers and coworkers from the host country (De la Torre & Toyne, 1978; Rhinesmith, 1991). In addition, even U.S. workers who remain at home may encounter cross-national supervisory and mentoring relationships (De la Torre & Toyne, 1978; Rhinesmith, 1991). It seems likely that many of the same cultural issues that apply to diverse mentoring relationships among employees within the United States may apply to cross-national mentoring relationships as well. The purpose of this chapter is to outline the effects of culture on mentoring by introducing a model that integrates multiple social psychological perspectives on this process.

Incorporating Culture Into the Mentoring Process

Why should we expect that culture affects the nature of mentoring relationships? Social role enactment is one social process that is very much the product of the culture in which a person is brought up (Moghaddam, Taylor, & Wright, 1993). Furthermore, according to Triandis (1995), when people of different cultures work together, their ethnocentrism can result in misunderstanding, which in turn affects their attraction for one another. Therefore, mentoring as a social process may be experienced differently to the extent that culture affects the interaction process.

Triandis (1995) provides a useful definition of both physical and subjective culture, which can be used in the study of cross-national mentoring. *Physical culture* is less applicable because it refers to objects such as roads, buildings, and tools. For the mentoring process, *subjective culture* is most applicable. It includes the social norms, values, and beliefs inherent in a culture. Hofstede's (1980) work on differences in cultural values proposed a number of dimensions that could potentially affect the nature of the mentoring relationship: *individualism-collectivism,* the degree to which individual needs are given higher priority over those of the group; *power distance,* the degree of centralization in organizations; *uncertainty avoidance,* the degree to which individuals seek to avoid unpredictable situations, and *masculinity/femininity,* the degree to which an individual values assertiveness and competitiveness. Recently Hofstede and Bond (1988) also introduced the concept of *long-term* versus *short-term orientation,* the extent to which people value factors associated with the future, such as thrift and persistence, compared to values that focus on the past, such as social obligation and tradition. These five dimensions can form unique combinations of the typical values of members of various country clusters. For example, Asian and Latin cultures such as Mexico score higher on collectivism than the United States, which scores higher on individualism.

Hofstede's cultural values have implications for specific social processes like mentoring. For example, the degree to which members of various cultures comply with requests or conform in decision-making situations varies across cultures. For example, a country such as Singapore scores low on the individualism dimension, high on power distance, low to medium on uncertainty avoidance, medium on masculinity, and high on long-term orientation. In contrast, the United States is high on individualism, low on power distance, low on uncertainty avoidance, moderately high on masculinity, and low on long-term orientation. Research shows differences in conformity depend on whether the suggestion for conformity is expressed by a group of strangers, or by an authoritarian leader (Moghaddam et al., 1993).

Not only does the national culture affect an individual's interactions in general, and mentoring in particular, but corporate culture also influences social behavior. In relationships that are less well defined, such as those in informal mentoring relationships, corporate culture may have less of an effect, whereas cultural values may tend to play a larger role. Also, organizational demography, or the extent to which an organization is heterogeneous on certain demographic variables such as race, age, gender, or tenure, may affect how cross-national mentoring relationships develop (Pfeffer, 1983).

Acculturation levels also affect differences in social processes. Ferdman (1994) described acculturation as "the extent to which an individual manifests the group's typical cultural features" (p. 44). It is important to remember that cultural differences may not always apply uniformly to groups or to individual members of an observable race or ethnic group (Cox, 1990). Ayman (1993) explained one difficulty in research across cultural groups as arising because social groups either may appear different physically, or may hold different cultural values. Many people who look different may in fact hold similar values, however, as do many immigrant groups who have assimilated in the United States. Also, people who share ethnic similarity may hold different values (e.g., white Europeans from France and white Americans). Ayman explained that it is a person's values, which may or may not be known, that are "most likely to affect an actor's expectations, behavior, and reactions" (p. 155).

In summary, the discussion of cultural differences across various groups can be useful, but it is also important to remember that the degree of acculturation, corporate culture, organizational demography, and an individual's unique values can affect the degree to which culture influences cross-national mentoring.

A Developmental Model of Mentoring

In this chapter we propose a new developmental model that builds on Kram's (1983) four-stage mentoring model by incorporating principles from the comprehensive work on role making (Graen & Scandura, 1987; Graen & Uhl-Bien, 1991). In particular, we use two recent works that outlined the cross-cultural implications for leader-member exchange development (Graen & Wakabayashi, 1994) and how diversity affects developing leaders (Scandura & Lankau, in press). These comprehensive theoretical models provide a useful overview of the many psychological processes involved in role making that have implications for the development of effective mentoring relationships. We also incorporate earlier theory on leader-member exchange development that drew from attribution theory, role theory, and from leadership, social exchange, and upward influence processes (Dienesch & Liden, 1986).

Leader-member exchange (LMX) theory (Graen, 1976; Graen & Cashman, 1975) examines dyadic supervisor and subordinate relationships in depth. These dyadic relationships parallel some of the interactions between mentors and protégés. The theory is based on the conceptualization of leadership as a negotiated role between superiors and subordinates. This supervisor/subordinate relationship takes two contrasting forms. The first is characterized by the extent to which the leader treats a subordinate as an "in-group member." This type of relationship is characterized by the leader giving a high level of trust and support to the subordinate. The second type of relationship is one in which the leader treats a subordinate as an "out-group member." In this relationship, the leader's behavior toward the subordinate falls within the confines of the formal employment contract. Research has shown that subordinates who are treated as in-group members, or have what are known as "high-quality exchanges" with their leaders, exhibit a number of important benefits, such as better performance (Liden & Graen, 1980; Vecchio & Gobdel, 1984), lower turnover, (Dansereau, Cashman, & Graen, 1973), and greater satisfaction (Graen, Novak, & Sommerkamp, 1982).

Graen and Uhl-Bien's (1991) recent summary of the LMX developmental process begins with the "stranger" phase of the relationship. This phase is characterized by relationship building, or what they call "role finding," and low-quality leader-member exchanges. Within this phase both members of the leader-subordinate pair decide whether the relationship will remain at this phase or progress. The next phase is called "acquaintance" and is the role-making phase of the relationship. This phase is characterized by mixed reciprocity and medium levels of leader-member exchange. The last phase is called "mature"; during this phase role implementation occurs and leader-member exchange quality is high.

In summary, research on the development of quality leader-member exchanges provides a valuable basis for understanding the developmental process in mentoring. Similar to the relationship between a leader and subordinate, mentoring is a two-way influence process; therefore, the needs, motivations, and behavior of both the mentor and protégé must be considered. There are multiple stages of development of the relationship, and both effective leadership and mentoring relationships may lead to increased job and career satisfaction (Fagenson, 1989; Zey,

1984). Figure 10.1 describes a proposed model of mentoring development that incorporates existing mentoring research and the dyadic
role-making process.

The Effects of Culture on
Cross-National Mentoring Relationships

Within the model of cross-national mentoring developed in this
chapter, there are many points at which cultural differences may affect
the nature of a mentoring relationship between two individuals. For
example, as suggested by Triandis, Kurowski, and Gelfand's (1994)
model for studying cultural differences, low cultural distance (differences in religion, language, economics, and politics) and high knowledge
of the other's culture, are precursors to perceived similarity. Perceived
similarity provides the opportunity for positive contact, which in turn,
can lead to rewards, more positive intergroup attitudes, and further
interactions.

To support our model we include selected social psychological
studies of members of four major cultural groups: Asian, Spanish
speaking, African American, and European American cultures. We
chose to include these groups, first, because they represent four groups
with distinct subjective cultural differences, and second, because members of these groups are most likely to enter into U.S. cross-national
mentoring relationships, given the recent history of U.S. cross-national
business ventures. We have extended the mentoring development model
to include the manner in which cultural differences may affect each
phase of the mentoring process (see Figure 10.2).

Phase 1: Attraction

In the beginning of mentoring relationships, as in leader-member
dyads, there is the process of initial attraction that leads to positive
affect or liking between dyad members. This initial attraction plays an
even larger role in informal mentoring relationships than in super-
visor/subordinate pairs because the mentor and the protégé usually both
have a choice as to forming the relationship. In this initial attraction
phase, the mentor and the protégé will rely on basic observable

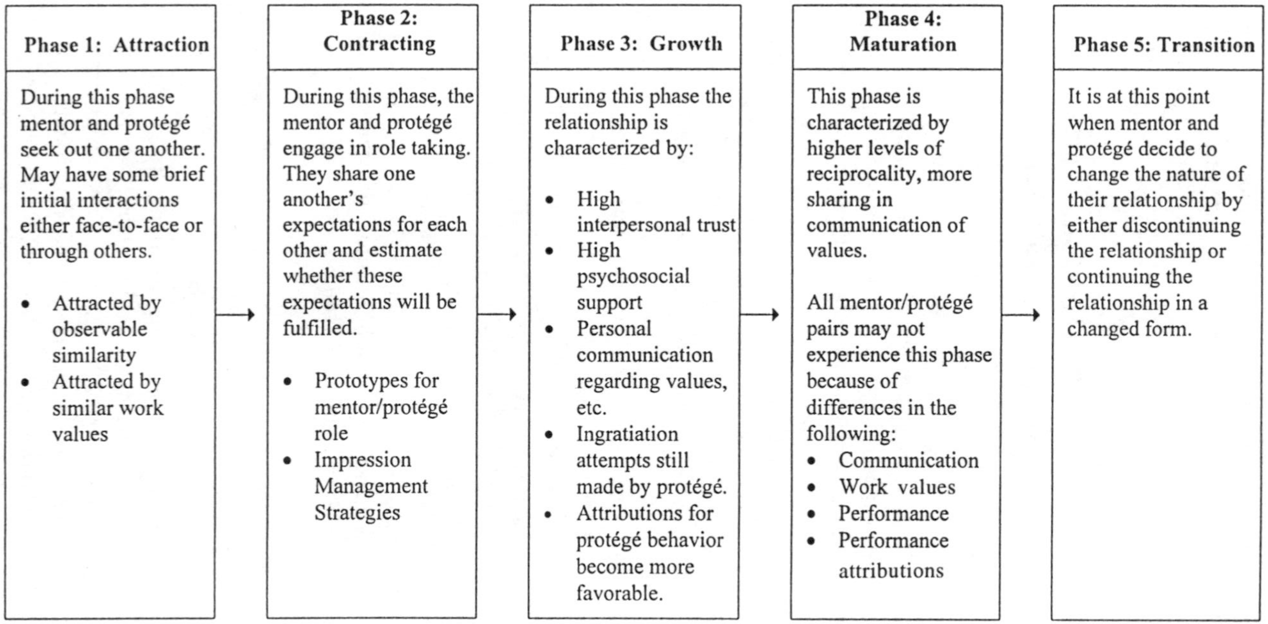

Figure 10.1. Overview of Proposed Model of Mentoring Relationship Development

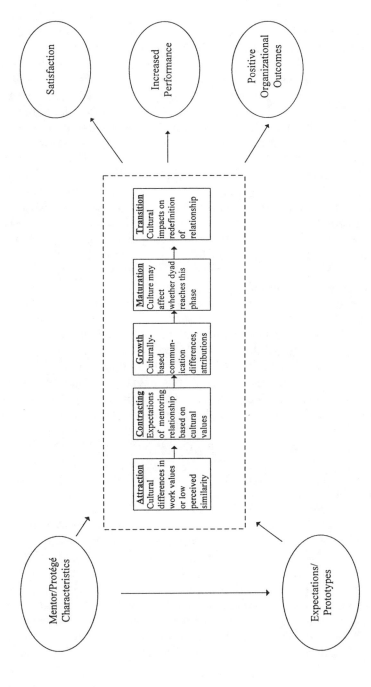

Figure 10.2. Cultural Influences on the Mentoring Relationship

similarities and differences to make determinations regarding how much they like one another (Ensher & Murphy, in press).

There is a large literature in the psychology of interpersonal attraction that describes how observable similarity leads to attraction (cf. Berscheid, 1985). In general, people tend to be attracted to, and are more likely to interact with, those that they perceive to be similar to themselves (Byrne, 1971). Similarity can refer to actual demographic similarity or perceived attitudinal similarity. Several studies have found that demographic similarity between supervisors and subordinates was positively related to supervisors' liking of their subordinates (Judge & Ferris, 1993; Tsui & O'Reilly, 1989; Wayne & Liden, 1995). Wayne and Liden (1995) found that demographic similarity worked through perceived similarity to affect supervisors' performance ratings of their subordinates. Similarity also predicts liking in mentoring relationships. Ensher and Murphy (in press) found that mentors paired with same-ethnicity protégés liked their protégés more than mentors paired with different-ethnicity protégés.

The mentoring literature has given little attention to other protégé or mentor characteristics such as ability, work values, or personality variables that may affect the amount of initial attraction and subsequent positive affect in a relationship. Value differences in cross-national mentoring relationships may influence the degree of initial attraction. For instance, the strong emphasis on familism among Latinos may result in hesitation regarding seeking assistance from those outside of one's family nucleus; therefore, a Latino protégé may initially be reluctant to seek counsel from an outside mentor (Rosado, 1995). Organizations with formal mentoring programs may want to include incentives that attract the entire family, involve the entire family, or both, such as initiation or recognition functions, when soliciting participation from Latino protégés.

In the same manner, Asians' belief in collectivism may deter them from wanting to stand out by seeking assistance. For example, Markus and Kitayama (1991) report that Filipinos feel it is important for people to maintain smooth interpersonal relations and try to be agreeable under difficult circumstances (Church, 1987). This includes being sensitive to what others are feeling and then adjusting one's behavior. Because of these values, an Asian protégé may be reluctant to indicate lack of understanding or to point out a mentor's mistakes "to save the mentor's face." Thus an Asian protégé may avoid overt conflict and engage in behaviors that seem passive to a non-Asian mentor.

Dickens and Dickens (1981) discussed how African Americans may exhibit "protective hesitation" and be reluctant to initiate relationship with European American mentors out of "cultural paranoia" because of their exposure to racism and discrimination in the past and fear of rejection in the future. Kram and Hall (in press) found validation for this concern. They observed that European American senior managers in one corporation had greater concerns about the competence of their non-European American colleagues than of their European American colleagues. Such concerns could translate into a decreased likelihood of European American mentors initiating mentoring relationships for non-European American protégés and vice versa.

Phase 2: Contracting

It is during this second phase that a mentor and protégé test their preexisting schemas and prototypes concerning the roles each will take in the relationship. They also assess the perceived costs and benefits of the relationship. This phase of the relationship is similar to medium-quality LMX (role making). Fairhurst (1991) found that in these LMX relationships, communication was dominated by cooperative patterns including role negotiation, polite disagreement, and coaching. As the mentor and protégé progress through the contracting phase, differences in expectations may affect the nature of the mentor/protégé relationship.

Social cognitive approaches to leadership proffered by Lord and his colleagues (Lord & Maher, 1991) have helped researchers understand the perceptual processes that affect the study of leadership. They find that subordinates hold prototypes about the behaviors and traits associated with effective leaders. These prototypes in turn affect judgments of leadership effectiveness. This process may also occur within the mentoring relationship during the contracting stage.

In the contracting phase of the mentoring relationship, culture is most likely to affect prototypes and role expectations. In addition, the actual desired behaviors associated with the prototypes of an effective mentor and protégé may vary across cultures. Ayman (1993) explored cultural differences in perceptions of leadership, with findings that have specific implications for cross-cultural mentoring. In studies of Iranian managers by Ayman and Chemers (1983) and Chemers (1969), implicit leadership theories were revealed. The earlier study (Chemers, 1969) asked Iranian subordinates to describe their American leaders, whereas the later study had asked Iranian subordinates to describe Iranian leaders. The factor structures for these ratings were very similar for both sets of leaders. The Iranian subordinates saw both their American and Iranian leaders as being "benevolently paternalistic." Therefore, rather than describing the behaviors of their American and Iranian leaders differently, the subordinates' implicit theories of effective leaders, unique to their culture, affected their leader behavior ratings and produced fairly identical ratings for the leaders from distinctively different cultures. Mentors and protégés with differing cultural background may hold different implicit theories of an effective mentor that will affect the contracting phase.

Smith, Misumi, Tayeb, Peterson, and Bond (1989) found that the meaning of specific leader behaviors varied within different cultures. Specifically, British and Japanese workers both agreed on the importance of supervisors giving feedback, but the preferred manner in which this feedback was given differed. Japanese workers did not like feedback given in a direct manner, whereas British workers preferred this style.

Social exchange theory (Homans, 1961), as applied to mentoring, explains that individuals will form and maintain relationships with others, insofar as they believe the benefits will outweigh the costs of being in the relationship (Ensher, 1996). Psychosocial (i.e., love/emotional) support and instrumental (i.e., status, information, and services) support are the most frequent currencies of exchange between mentors and protégés (Kram, 1983; Noe, 1988; Ragins & Cotton, 1991). A typical exchange between a mentor and protégé might be one in which a mentor provides a protégé with increased status via affiliation with the mentor, while in return, the protégé is a source of emotional satisfaction and support to the mentor.

Evidence for cultural differences in desired mentoring behaviors comes from a recent study on the role of mentoring for a sample of Hispanic managers (Murphy & Nguyen, 1996). The managers' type of acculturation was related to their perceptions of the types of relationships they had with their mentors. Those managers who adopted an acculturation style of assimilation reported receiving higher levels of career support from their mentors, compared to those who adopted an integration mode of acculturation. The causal direction in this relationship is unclear, and it is possible that managers adopting an assimilation mode sought out mentors who provided the type of support they preferred.

There is another large literature on impression management used by LMX researchers. Liden and Mitchell (1989) explored in depth how impression management techniques, such as ingratiation, work in the formation and continuation of leader and subordinate interactions. They outlined a number of tactics used by subordinates to increase the likelihood of a supervisor providing high-quality leader-member exchanges with a subordinate. These impression management techniques may vary by culture and can influence the nature of the mentor-protégé interaction as the relationship becomes more mature.

A recent review by Crittenden and Bae (1994) summarized a number of studies tying impression management to attributions in Asian cultures. For example a study conducted in Hong Kong (Bond, Leung, & Wan, 1982) revealed that individuals who used self-effacing strategies in making attributions for their performance were seen as having greater social responsibility and likability, whereas individuals who used self-enhancement strategies were seen as more productive. Research on impression management differences between Hispanics and non-Hispanics is nonconclusive. Booth-Kewley, Rosenfeld, and Edwards (1992) found that Hispanics were more likely to engage in self-enhancing strategies, although a more recent article (Rosenfeld, Booth-Kewley, Edwards, & Alderton, 1994) did not find support for this claim. If mentors and protypes are from different cultures, impression management efforts to enhance the relationship may fail.

Although specific mentoring behaviors may vary by culture, the preferred form of the mentoring relationship also may vary. Because Asians tend to have a collectivist rather than individualistic orientation, group mentoring may be effective. Blake and Davison (1995) cited the benefits of group mentoring in both academic and corporate settings. Some of the benefits include increased social support, opportunities for networking and training, and exposure. Kram and Hall (in press) described one example of this in the Nynex corporation, which uses mentoring circles. The purpose of these mentoring circles is to create interaction and opportunities for development between one or several senior managers and junior or mid-level professionals. Thus, cultural differences in the contracting phase could affect the different types of support and different forms of the mentoring relationship that may be selected by protégés with different cultural backgrounds.

Phase 3: Growth

After each member of the dyad explores and tentatively agrees on their respective roles in the relationship, the mentor and protégé move into the growth phase, which is similar to what Graen and Uhl-Bien (1991) called the acquaintance stage. This phase includes an increased number of exchanges, in which trust and greater sharing of information occur. During this phase of the mentoring relationship the mentor and protégé begin to understand one another better and are more cognizant of each other's needs. It is likely that there is more informal communication in which values and intimacies are shared.

As a mentor continues to develop a relationship with a protégé, the two will often discuss recent successes or failures that the protégé experienced on the job. The mentor will make attributions as to the causes of the protégé's good and bad performance. Some research indicates that people with an internal locus of control tend to make internal attributions for their success, but external attributions for their failures (Rotter, 1966). The role of attributions for subordinate behavior was introduced by Mitchell and Wood (1980). Their early studies found that the sanctions administered by managers varied based on the attributions they made for a subordinate's poor performance and that there were discrepancies in the types of attributions that subordinates made for their own behavior compared to those the managers made. What implications do attributions have for the mentoring relationship? Martinko and Gardner (1987), in their comprehensive model of the leader-member attribution process, proposed that attribution processes change over time. As a mentoring relationship increases in trust and mutual respect, the likelihood of negative attributions may decrease.

Fletcher and Ward (1988) have found differences in attributional style for Western as compared to non-Western cultures. In their review of studies on cross-cultural attributions, they found that members of non-Western cultures are less likely to engage in the "fundamental attribution error" than are individuals from Western cultures. The fundamental attribution error is the pattern of explaining other people's behavior in terms of something about the person, rather than something about the situation, because situational factors are less salient to observers than are behaviors. When making attributions about individuals from other cultures, cultural differences may appear quite salient, and they may lead a person to make more dispositional than situational attributions as to causes for the other's behavior.

Other research also suggests that attributional differences exist between Asian and Western cultures. Some of this research has paid particular attention to variations in locus of control among Asian countries. A number of studies have revealed that Japanese individuals have a higher external locus of control than Americans (cf. Chandler, Shama, & Wolfe, 1983), whereas Koreans have a high internal locus of control (Kim, 1980). In attributions of responsibility, Japanese paid more attention to the role obligations of the offender, rather than to the person's behavior (Hamilton & Sanders, 1983). Asian students (Japanese, Korean, and Southeast Asian) attributed academic achievement to ability significantly less often than did American students, and also gave equal importance to effort attributions for both success and failure (Yan & Gaier, 1994).

Within the growth phase of mentoring, many types of interpersonal communication differences based on culture can affect the relationship. For example, Triandis, Marin, Lisansky, and Betancourt (1984) found that Hispanic workers expect to receive more positive social behavior and less negative social behavior. The cultural script of *simpatia* emphasizes the importance of behaviors that promote smooth and pleasant social relationships. Rosado (1995) outlined a number of implications for interpersonal communication based on the concept of *simpatia,* including a tendency to use small talk to build affective bonds, and the tendency to avoid confrontation and interpersonal conflict.

Kochman (1981) found that African American individuals are more likely than European Americans to draw attention to their positive qualities. Regardless of the cause of this behavior, it draws attention to those who exhibit it, and requires that they meet the standard they set for themselves. Forthrightness is another key characteristic, which often influences the manner in which conflict is addressed. Dickens and Dickens (1981) found that African American managers were more likely to confront an individual immediately in conflict situations, whereas European American managers were more conflict avoidant and tended to do nothing. A study by Waters (1992) looked specifically at the role of interaction styles in race-based conflict. He found that conversational norms regarding eye contact, speaking styles, and nodding the head, among others, are often interpreted differently in the African American culture than in the European American culture. For example, African Americans listeners use less eye contact than European Americans, which may lead to misunderstandings in interpersonal interactions (Weber, 1994). A European American speaker may feel that an African

American is not listening carefully. Alternatively, an African American speaker may see excessive eye contact from a European American listener as being too aggressive and not showing appropriate deference.

Rosado (1995) identified several implications of differing perceptions of power distance between mentors and protégés. Mentors should be aware that there may be a tendency for Latino protégés to conform to the mentor's wishes out of respect for the mentor's position. This can be a detriment to both mentors and protégés if protégés conform out of deference, not out of agreement. In addition, Rosado (1995) suggested that the Latino need for positive communication makes it is important for a mentor to engage in positive communication in the growth phase of the relationship, to build trust.

Thomas (1993) examined how diverse mentor-protégé pairs managed their differences in values and work styles. Partners in mixed dyads used two major strategies to deal with their racial differences: (a) denial and suppression, and (b) direct engagement. Denial and suppression is a strategy in which one or both parties treat racial issues as taboo, or as a nonissue. Direct engagement is an approach in which both parties discuss racial differences honestly and openly. Thomas found that the most satisfied and long-lasting mentor-protégé dyads could rely on either one of these approaches. It was important that the mentor and protégé used the same approach, however, regardless of which one they relied on. Thomas recommended that protégés develop a system of dual support that includes both same-race and cross-race relationships to provide different kinds of support.

Culture contributes to various aspects of the growth phase of the mentoring relationship. To the extent that communication incompatibilities arise, the length of this stage may be more prolonged for cross-cultural mentoring relationships than for same-culture dyads. The effectiveness in this phase in cross-cultural mentoring relationships also may be affected by discrepancies in attributional style.

Phase 4: Maturation

Many of the same processes that occur in Phase 3 determine the nature of the relationship in Phase 4. As the mentor and protégé's relationship continues to develop during the maturation phase, the relationship increases in stability. Within the LMX model, this is the point at which the relationship becomes routinized. Also at this point within LMX, communication is usually dominated by value congruence and true reciprocal support. Common communication and attributions cause the pair to feel that they think alike; they also back each other up when threatened, and they may talk in a code that is known exclusively by the pair (Fairhurst, 1991). Analysis of specific communication practices and changes in levels of different types of communication can provide a valuable understanding of the mentoring relationship in this stage.

Another important contribution of LMX research is the observation that some leader-subordinate dyads never make it past the growth phase. There is evidence that, even after long periods of time, some subordinates never experience high-quality interactions with their leader, and remain in relationships characterized by low-quality exchanges (Graen & Uhl-Bien, 1995). In mentoring relationships, interpersonal incompatibilities or unmet role expectations are two possible reasons that may prevent the mentor-protégé pair from entering a mature relationship. Furthermore, many of the same social psychological processes that explain the mentoring relationship's development in Phase 3 also contribute to the maturation level the mentoring relationship does or does not attain in Phase 4. For instance, continued differences in attributions for protégé performance may prevent the pair from experiencing a mature relationship. In addition, poorly performing protégés may receive decreasing levels of support from their mentors more than do protégés who perform well in their jobs. Cultural differences may underlie these problems; more specifically, cross-national mentoring pairs may be less likely to enter this phase of the mentoring relationship without the benefit of training to increase understanding of cultural differences.

Phase 5: Transition

At an advanced point in the mentoring relationship the mentor and protégé will determine whether the mentoring relationship will end or will transition into another type of relationship, such as that of friends or acquaintances (Kram, 1983). This transition phase may occur earlier in the developmental process, for example after the growth phase, if the mentoring relationship is not providing an exchange of mutual benefits. Research shows that mentors and protégés are more likely to separate rather than to redefine their relationships if they experience unmet expectations, loss of trust, jealousy, or shifting priorities and allegiances (Kizilios, 1990; Knackstedt, 1995; Myers & Humphreys, 1985). In earlier stages, mentors and protégés are concerned with the expected exchange of benefits, but in later phases they are in a position to evaluate the actual exchange of benefits (Ensher, 1996). The cost/benefit ratio, along with their perceptions of reciprocity, enables mentors and protégés to determine the future status of the relationship. If a desirable cost/benefit ratio cannot be reached, it is likely the relationship will end.

Cultural differences may have little effect on the mentor-protégé relationship if the pair has progressed through Phase 4 into this final phase of transition. In other words, any potential negative effects of cultural differences on the relationship will probably have been resolved by this phase. If the mentoring pair does not experience the Phase 4 stage of a mature relationship, however, culture may differentially affect the manner in which the relationship is either ended or redefined in Phase 5. Wilson (1994) has recommended that European American mentors employ specific strategies designed to decrease premature separation between mentors and protégés. These recommended strategies include (a) acknowledge that minorities face special hurdles, (b) recognize that lack of initiation is not the same as lack of desire, and (c) focus on similarities and learn about the cultural background of the protégé. Dickens and Dickens (1991) point out, however, that initiating a mentoring relationship is the responsibility of the protégé as well as the mentor.

Summary and Implications

This chapter offers an expanded model of the role-making process that occurs between a mentor and protégé throughout the life of their relationship. We have incorporated many social psychological principles not previously included in mentoring models to explain mentor and protégé interactions. Social exchange theory, attribution theory, person perception, impression management, and communication practices provide mechanisms that influence the effectiveness of mentoring relationships. We also outlined some likely effects of culture on cross-national mentoring relationships.

There are a number of practical implications of research in this area. Some of the major implications involve the type of training that organizations should provide to support cross-cultural or cross-national mentoring. The training content should focus on four areas: (a) understanding cultural differences that may affect the perceptions of another person's behavior; (b) increasing mentor and protégé communication skills, and their ability to understand how culture may contribute to ineffective communication; (c) encouraging mentors and protégés to set ground rules relevant to open communication; and (d) providing opportunities for the mentor to actively solicit feedback from the protégé.

It would also be helpful for organizations to support various configurations of mentoring through formal programs and reward systems. For example, organizations could sponsor dyadic mentoring, team mentoring, or mentoring circles, and special interest groups. Organizational members could be evaluated on their effectiveness as mentors for others, and helping employees to develop could be emphasized as a core competency by organizations. For example, given the prevalence of many professional user groups on the Internet, employees can find support from others in the form of peer mentors, or more traditional mentoring relationships.

Today many workers are separated from one another geographically in "virtual organizations" created when a centralized unit deploys a cadre of contractors to meet flexible project needs. In such situations, organizations need to provide technology such as electronic mail to all their members and encourage the use of it to communicate in a variety of ways. Mentoring by electronic communication can be an excellent tool to enable organizational members to create and maintain networks across professional and national borders.

One of the most important ways that organizations can ensure that cross-national mentoring relationships thrive is to provide an environment that values and rewards these relationships. Mentoring can be a mechanism for an organization to encourage full structural integration. This includes not only having equal representation of individuals at various levels of the organizations, but also having minority individuals included in informal networks. With its emphasis on inclusivity, mentoring is a process in which all organizational members can participate, either as a mentor or protégé. Organizations that provide a supportive environment for all permutations of mentoring relationships can maximize their diverse human potential, without alienating a majority or showing preference to a minority.

References

Ayman, R. (1993). Leadership perception: The role of culture and gender. In M. M. Chemers & R. Ayman (Eds.), *Leadership theory and research: Perspectives and directions* (pp. 137-166). San Diego, CA: Academic Press.

Ayman, R., & Chemers, M. M. (1983). Relationship of supervisory behavior ratings to work group effectiveness and subordinate satisfaction. *Journal of Applied Psychology, 68,* 338-341.

Berscheid, E. (1985). Interpersonal attraction. In G. Lindzey & E. Aronson (Eds.), *Handbook of social psychology* (3rd ed., Vol. 2, pp. 413-484). New York: Random House.

Blake, S., & Davison, A. (1995). Diversity as a catalyst for a new paradigm of mentoring: Organizational groups as a provider of mentoring functions in the academic and corporate sectors. In *Proceedings of the Diversity in Mentoring Conference* (pp. 84-93). Kalamazoo: Western Michigan University.

Bond, M., Leung, K., & Wan, K. C. (1982). The social impact of self-effacing attributions: The Chinese case. *Journal of Social Psychology, 118,* 157-166.

Booth-Kewley, S., Rosenfeld, P., & Edwards, J. E. (1992). Impression management and self-deceptive enhancement among Hispanic and non-Hispanic white Navy recruits. *Journal of Social Psychology, 132,* 323-329.

Byham, W. C., & Cox, J. (1994). *Heroes: Empower yourself, your coworkers, and your company.* New York: Harmony.

Byrne, D. (1971). *The attraction paradigm.* New York: Academic Press.

Chandler, T. A., Shama, D. D., & Wolfe, F. M. (1983). Gender differences in achievement and affiliation attributions: A five nation study. *Journal of Cross-Cultural Psychology, 14,* 241-256.

Chemers, M. M. (1969). Cross-cultural training as a means for improving situational favorableness. *Human Relations, 22,* 531-546.

Church, A. T. (1987). Personality research in a non-Western culture: The Philippines. *Psychological Bulletin, 102,* 272-292.

Cox, T. (1990). Problems with research by organizational scholars on issues of race and ethnicity. *Journal of Applied Behavioral Science, 26*(1), 5-23.

Cox, T., Jr. (1993). *Cultural diversity in organizations.* San Francisco: Berret-Kohler.

Crittenden, K. S., & Bae, H. (1994). Self-effacement and social responsibility. *American Behavioral Scientist, 37,* 653-671.

Dansereau, F., Cashman, J., & Graen, G. (1973). Instrumentality theory and equity theory as complementary approaches in predicting the relationship of leadership and turnover among managers. *Organizational Behavior and Human Performance, 10,* 184-200.

De La Torre, J., & Toyne, B. (1978). Cross-national managerial interaction: A conceptual model. *Academy of Management Review, 3,* 467-474.

Dickens, D., & Dickens, J. (1981). Problems of black managers can't be solved by them alone. *Management Review, 70,* 29.

Dickens, F., & Dickens, J. B. (1991). *The black manager: Making it in the corporate world.* New York: AMACOM.

Dienesch, R. M., & Liden, R. C. (1986). Leader-member exchange model of leadership: A critique and further development. *Academy of Management Review, 11,* 618-634.

Ensher, E. A. (1996). *Mentoring from a female and minority perspective.* Unpublished manuscript, Claremont Graduate School, Claremont, CA.

Ensher, E. A., & Murphy, S. E. (in press). The effect of race, gender, perceived similarity, and contact on mentor relationships. *Journal of Vocational Behavior.*

Fagenson, E. A. (1989). The mentor advantage: Perceived career/job experiences of protégés vs. nonprotégés. *Journal of Organizational Behavior, 10,* 309-320.

Fairhurst, G. T. (1991). *Leadership making and dyadic communications patterns among women leaders in industry: An anthropological linguistics approach.* Paper presented at the annual meeting of the Society of Organizational Behavior, Albany, NY.

Federal Glass Ceiling Commission. (1995). *Good for business: Making full use of the nation's human capital* (DHHS Publication No. ADM 164-569). Washington, DC: Government Printing Office.

Ferdman, B. M. (1994). Cultural identity and diversity in organizations. In M. Chemers, S. Oskamp, & M. Costanzo (Eds.), *Diversity in organizations: New perspectives for a changing workplace* (pp. 37-61). Thousand Oaks, CA: Sage.

Fernandez, J. P. (1991). *Managing a diverse workforce: Regaining the competitive edge.* Lexington, MA: Lexington Books.

Fletcher, G. J. O., & Ward, C. (1988). Attribution theory and processes: A cross-cultural perspective. In M. Bond (Ed.), *The cross-cultural challenge to social psychology* (pp. 230-244). Newbury Park, CA: Sage.

Graen, G. (1976). Role making processes in complex organizations. In M. D. Dunnette (Ed.), *Handbook of industrial and organizational psychology* (pp. 1201-1245). Chicago: Rand McNally.

Graen, G., & Cashman, J. (1975). A role-making model of leadership in formal organizations: A developmental approach. In J. G. Hunt & L. L. Larson (Eds.), *Leadership frontiers* (pp. 143-165). Kent, OH: Kent State University Press.

Graen, G., Novak, M., & Sommerkamp, P. (1982). The effects of leader-member exchange and job design on productivity and satisfaction: Testing a dual attachment model. *Organizational Behavior and Human Performance, 30*(1), 109-131.

Graen, G., & Scandura, T. (1987). Toward a psychology of dyadic organizing. In B. Staw & L. L. Cumming (Eds.), *Research in organizational behavior* (Vol. 9, pp. 175-208). Greenwich, CT: JAI.

Graen, G., & Uhl-Bien, M. (1991). The transformation of professionals into self-managing and partially self-designing contributors: Toward a theory of leadership making. *Journal of Management Systems, 3*(3), 33-48.

Graen, G., & Uhl-Bien, M. (1995). Relationship-based approach to leadership: Development of leader-member exchange (LMX) theory of leadership over 25 years: Applying a multilevel multidomain perspective. *Leadership Quarterly, 6,* 219-247.

Graen, G. B., & Wakabayashi, M. (1994). Cross-cultural leadership making: Bridging American and Japanese diversity for team advantage. In H. C. Triandis, M. D. Dunnette, & L. M. Hough (Eds.), *Handbook of industrial-organizational psychology* (2nd. ed., Vol. 4, pp. 415-446). Palo Alto, CA: Consulting Psychologists Press.

Hamilton, V. L., & Sanders, J. (1983). Universals in judging wrongdoing: Japanese and Americans compared. *American Sociological Review, 48,* 199-211.

Hofstede, G. (1980). *Culture's consequences: International differences in work-related values.* Beverly Hills, CA: Sage.

Hofstede, G., & Bond, M. (1988). The Confucius connection: From cultural roots to economic growth. *Organizational Dynamics, 16*(4), 4-21.

Homans, G. C. (1961). *Social behavior: Its elementary forms.* New York: Harcourt, Brace, Jovanovich.

Jamieson, D., & O'Mara, J. (1991). *Managing workforce 2000: Gaining the diversity advantage.* San Francisco: Jossey-Bass.

Judge, T. A., & Ferris, G. R. (1993). Social context of performance evaluation decisions. *Academy of Management Journal, 36*(1), 80-105.

Kim, B. K. (1980). Attitudes, parental identification, and locus of control of Korean, new Korean-Canadian, and Canadian adolescents. In V. Ujimoto & G. Hirabayashi (Eds.),

Visible minorities and multiculturalism: Asians in Canada (pp. 219-241). Toronto: Butterworth.

Kizilios, P. (1990, April). Take my mentor, please. *Training,* 49-55.

Knackstedt, J. (1995). Cross-gender mentoring: Barriers encountered by the female protégé. In *Proceedings of the Diversity in Mentoring Conference* (pp. 203-214). Kalamazoo: Western Michigan University.

Kochman, T. (1981). *Black and white styles in conflict.* Chicago: University of Chicago Press.

Kram, K. E. (1983). Phases of the mentor relationship. *Academy of Management Journal, 26,* 608-625.

Kram, K. E., & Hall, D. T. (in press). Mentoring in a context of diversity and turbulence. In S. Lobel & E. E. Kossek (Eds.), *Human resource strategies for managing diversity.* London, UK: Blackwell.

Liden, R. C., & Graen, G. (1980). Generalizability of the vertical dyad linkage model of leadership. *Academy of Management Journal, 25,* 598-606.

Liden, R. C., & Mitchell, T. R. (1989). Ingratiation in the development of leader-member exchanges. In R. A. Giacalone & P. Rosenfeld (Eds.), *Impression management in the organization* (pp. 343-361). Hillsdale, NJ: Lawrence Erlbaum.

Loden, M., & Rosenor, J. (1991). *Workforce America!: Managing employee diversity as a vital resource.* New York: Irwin.

Lord, R. G., & Maher, K. J. (1991). *Leadership and information processing: Linking perceptions and performance.* Boston: Harper Collins.

Markus, H. R., & Kitayama, S. (1991). Culture and the self: Implications for cognition, emotion, and motivation. *Psychological Review, 98,* 224-253.

Martinko, M. J., & Gardner, W. L. (1987). The leader/member attribution process. *Academy of Management Review, 12,* 235-241.

Mitchell, T. R., & Wood, R. E. (1980). Supervisor's responses to subordinate poor performance: A test of an attributional model. *Organizational Behavior and Human Performance, 25*(3), 123-138.

Moghaddam, F. M., Taylor, D. M., & Wright, S. C. (1993). *Social psychology in cross-cultural perspective.* New York: Freeman.

Morrison, A. (1996). *The new leaders: Guidelines on leadership diversity in America.* San Francisco: Jossey-Bass.

Murphy, S. E., & Nguyen, M. (1996). *The role of acculturation in work-related values, management style, and mentoring experiences of Hispanic leaders.* Unpublished manuscript, Claremont McKenna College, Claremont, CA.

Myers, D. W., & Humphreys, N. J. (1985). The caveats in mentorship. *Business Horizons, 38*(4), 9-14.

Naisbitt, J. (1994). *Global paradox: The bigger the world economy, the more powerful its smallest players.* New York: Morrow.

Noe, R. A. (1988). An investigation of the determinants of successful assigned mentoring relationships. *Personnel Psychology, 41,* 457-479.

Pfeffer, J. (1983). Organizational demography. In L. L. Cummings & B. M. Staw (Eds.), *Research in organizational behavior* (Vol. 5, pp. 299-357). Greenwich, CT: JAI.

Ragins, B. R. (1989). Barriers to mentoring: The female manager's dilemma. *Human Relations, 42,* 1-22.

Ragins, B. R. (1994). Diversity, power, and mentorship in organizations: A cultural, structural, and behavioral perspective. In M. M. Chemers, S. Oskamp, & M. Costanzo (Eds.), *Diversity in organizations: New perspectives for a changing workplace* (pp. 91-132). Thousand Oaks, CA: Sage.

Ragins, B. R., & Cotton, J. L. (1991). Easier said than done: Gender differences in perceived barriers to gaining a mentor. *Academy of Management Journal, 34,* 939-951.

Rhinesmith, S. H. (1991, February). Globalization. *Training and Development Journal,* pp. 23-29.

Rosado, J. (1995). Values and conditions in mentoring Latinos. In *Proceedings of the Diversity in Mentoring Conference* (pp. 262-270). Kalamazoo: Western Michigan University.

Rosenfeld, P., Booth-Kewley, S., Edwards, J. E., & Alderton, D. (1994). Linking diversity and impression management. *American Behavioral Scientist, 37,* 672-681.

Rotter, J. B. (1966). Generalized expectancies for internal versus external control of reinforcement. *Psychological Monographs, 80*(Whole No. 609), 1-28.

Scandura, T. A., & Lankau, M. J. (in press). Developing diverse leaders: A leader-member exchange approach. *Leadership Quarterly.*

Smith, P. B., Misumi, J., Tayeb, M., Peterson, M., & Bond, M. (1989). On the generality of leadership style measures across cultures. *Journal of Occupational Psychology, 62*(2), 97-109.

Thomas, D. A. (1990). The impact of race on manager's experiences of developmental relationships (mentoring and sponsorship): An intraorganizational study. *Journal of Organizational Behavior, 11,* 479-492.

Thomas, D. A. (1993). Racial dynamics in cross-race developmental relationships. *Administrative Science Quarterly, 38,* 169-194.

Triandis, H. C. (1995). A theoretical framework for the study of diversity. In M. Chemers, S. Oskamp, & M. Costanzo (Eds.), *Diversity in organizations: New perspectives for a changing workplace* (pp. 11-36). Thousand Oaks, CA: Sage.

Triandis, H. C., Kurowski, L. L., & Gelfand, M. J. (1994). Workplace diversity. In H. C. Triandis, M. Dunnette, & L. Hough (Eds.), *Handbook of industrial and organizational psychology* (2nd ed., Vol. 4, pp. 769-827). Palo Alto, CA: Consulting Psychologists Press.

Triandis, H. C., Marin, G., Lisansky, J., & Betancourt, H. (1984). *Simpatia* as a cultural script of Hispanics. *Journal of Personality and Social Psychology, 47,* 1363-1375.

Tsui, A. S., & O'Reilly, C. A. (1989). Beyond simple demographic effects: The importance of relational demography in superior-subordinate dyads. *Academy of Management Journal, 32,* 402-423.

Vecchio, R., & Gobdel, B. (1984). The vertical dyad linkage model of leadership: Problems and prospects. *Organizational Behavior and Human Performance, 34*(1), 5-20.

Waters, H. (1982). Race, culture, and interpersonal conflict. *International Journal of Intercultural Relations, 16,* 437-454.

Wayne, S. J., & Liden, R. (1995). Effects of impression management on performance ratings: A longitudinal study. *Academy of Management Journal, 38,* 232-260.

Weber, S. N. (1994). The need to be: The sociocultural significance of black language. In L. A. Samovar & R. E. Porter (Eds.), *Intercultural communication: A reader* (7th ed., pp. 220-225). Belmont, CA: Wadsworth.

Wilson, S. A. (1994). Mentoring minority female professionals: Strategies for successful relationships. In *Proceedings of the Diversity in Mentoring Conference* (pp. 357-368). Kalamazoo: Western Michigan University.

Yan, W., & Gaier, E. L. (1994). Causal attributions for college success and failure: An Asian-American comparison. *Journal of Cross-Cultural Psychology, 25,* 146-158.

Zey, M. G. (1984). *The mentor connection.* Homewood, IL: Dow Jones-Irwin.

11

Managerial Leadership in the United States and Mexico

*Distant Neighbors
or Close Cousins?*

PETER W. DORFMAN

JON P. HOWELL

In his seminal book *Distant Neighbors,* Alan Riding (1985) describes and explains numerous cultural differences between the United States and Mexico. Although much has been learned and written about the Mexican culture, Riding's observation still rings true that nowhere in the world do two neighbors understand each other so little. Increasing reciprocal trade and business interaction requires better cultural understanding between the countries. Many U.S. and foreign multinational corporations engage in joint ventures and large scale cooperative manufacturing endeavors in the form of Mexican *maquiladoras* (so called twin-plants). The success or failure of international operations often hinges on a company's ability to manage cross-cultural and cross-national differences (Shenkar, 1995). Consider the complexity and potential chaos of managing a Mexican maquiladora. Managers from Asia, Europe, and North America supervise a diverse workforce composed of Mexican nationals, parent-country nationals, and third-country nationals. Although language problems complicate the communication process between expatriate managers and subordinates, far greater difficulties seem to occur because of cultural misunderstandings and unmet expectations (Stephens & Greer, 1995).

What do we know about managerial processes in Mexico? Clearly, our knowledge about business and management processes has increased, as witnessed by the publication of several recent articles discussing cultural distinctions between the countries and their effects on management processes (e.g., Gowan, Ibarreche, & Lackey, 1996; Stephens & Greer, 1995). With rare exceptions, however (e.g., Morris & Pavett, 1992), the management literature is largely anecdotal, descriptive, and not empirically based. We know even less about *leadership* processes in Mexico, and how these processes differ from those of the United States. The study of cross-cultural leadership is important because many multinationals receive a large percentage of their profits from abroad and credit their success to effective leadership in these operations (Hodgetts & Luthans, 1994).

In this chapter we describe our programmatic qualitative and quantitative research program conducted to understand and contrast Mexican and U.S. leadership processes. We begin with a brief introduction to the process of leadership and discuss the impact of culture on both leadership and management processes in general. The next section ties together the cultural values and beliefs of Mexico and the United States with what is currently known about leadership processes in each country. Last, we present the results of five leadership research projects designed to further understand cross-cultural leadership.

Leadership Defined

The word "leadership" first appeared approximately 200 years ago in writings about political influence in the British Parliament. From Egyptian hieroglyphics, however, we know that symbols for "leader" existed as early as 5,000 years ago. Leaders have existed in all cultures throughout history. Although the subject of leadership has generated more than 7,500 academic papers, articles, and books, there is no consensually agreed on definition of leadership (Bass, 1990). Yet, most definitions of leadership include several core concepts, which are contained in the following definition: *Leadership is an influence process whereby usually one person influences a group toward achievement of group goals.* Leaders may influence the organization's objectives, organization of work activities, motivation of followers, facilitation of cooperative relationships and teamwork, and enlistment of support from people outside the group or organization (Yukl, 1994).

It may be hard to overstate the perceived importance of leadership to the American psyche—Americans put a premium on leadership. Even the few academic researchers who devalue the "real" impact of leadership (e.g., Meindl, Ehrlich, & Dukerich, 1985; Pfeffer, 1977), acknowledge that the belief in, or attribution of, leadership as a cause of organizational success is endemic to the U.S. culture. Organizational success is often attributed solely (but probably mistakenly) to the chief executive. Is leadership defined and conceptualized differently across cultures? No definitive answer to this question presently exists. But evidence indicates that evaluative interpretations of leadership vary across cultures and positive semantic evaluations of leadership are not universal (Hofstede, 1993). For example, Europeans seem less enthusiastic about the concept of leadership than Americans. Leadership has even been thought of as a "perverse effect" and an undesirable consequence of democracy (Graumann & Moscovici, 1986). It seems likely that the meaning and importance of leadership will vary across cultures, but a more precise understanding of the subtle cultural differences in how leadership is viewed must await further research.

The Impact of Culture on Management and Leadership

Although scholars agree that the concept of management and leadership are conceptually intertwined, they are not identical (Bass, 1985). Pointed debate among academicians has not resolved the precise nature of this relationship, but there seems to be general consensus that managing involves all of the functions of planning, organizing, staffing, and directing, whereby leadership may be exhibited in any one of these functions. Managers may or may not be viewed as good leaders, and leaders may or may not be good managers (Lord & Maher, 1991), but most managers and leaders do some of both.

Managers with intercultural responsibilities clearly understand the difficulty of working across national borders often required for joint ventures, strategic alliances, and mergers. In addition to obvious language problems that face managers in intercultural contexts, many management practices seem to be inexorably intertwined with cultural forces and seem strange to members of other cultures. For instance, the individualistic performance appraisal, reward and compensation practices characteristic of the United States are not the norm in more collectivistic Asian cultures (Erez, 1994). Hofstede (1993) argues that there are no such things as universal management theories and that theories as well as practices stop at national borders.

Our personal experiences in the Mexican maquiladoras reflect a difference in management styles between the U.S. and Mexican managers. For instance, to appear in complete control of situations and to maintain harmony, Mexican managers frequently give an overly optimistic *no problema* response to obviously difficult issues. Managers from the United States prefer to know about potential problems and likely delays rather than hearing unbridled optimism.

Cross-Cultural and International Leadership Research

Relatively few of the thousands of empirical leadership studies have been concerned with the impact of cultural influences on leadership (Bass, 1990). Consequently, we have no generally accepted theory of cross-cultural leadership. The ultimate leadership question from a cross-cultural perspective might look like the following: If the phenomenon of leadership is universal and found in all societies, to what extent is leadership culturally contingent? At first glance, it might seem obvious that leadership processes should reflect the vast differences found among cultures. Ample evidence points to cultural differences in values, beliefs, traits, and decision styles that are consistent with different management practices (Arvey, Bhagat, & Salas, 1991). It is therefore reasonable to argue that cultural differences should not only influence the kind of leadership that will be attempted, but will also influence the *effectiveness* of specific leadership actions, behaviors, or styles.

Nevertheless, what do we actually know about the impact of culture on leadership processes beyond a relatively simple point that leadership processes will reflect the culture in which they are embedded? Whereas speculation abounds, the *empirical* cross-cultural leadership research literature is sparse, often nontheoretical, fraught with methodological problems, and fragmented across a wide variety of publication outlets

(Dorfman, 1996). Far more questions than answers exist regarding the culturally contingent aspects of leadership. Through cross-cultural research, we may determine which aspects of a leadership theory are culturally universal and which aspects are culturally unique. From a practical viewpoint the cultural diversity found in worldwide multinational organizations creates a real management challenge. The following pages briefly describe several cultural generalizations and management practices in the United States as compared to Mexico.

U.S. Values and Culture

The United States is culturally unique in comparison to most other countries in the world. Hofstede (1980a) described the United States as highly individualistic, low on power distance and uncertainty avoidance, and medium on masculinity. Trompenaars' (1993) survey data from more than 15,000 respondents in 47 countries reinforces the characterization of the United States as being highly individualistic. In addition, U.S. organizational policies are "rule oriented" rather than "relationship oriented." Formally prescribed procedures "should" be applied equally to all employees. Personal relationships through friendships or family ties are not considered legitimate factors for making personnel decisions. Respect and status are accorded for achievements rather than being bestowed because of the "right" family background. In conformity with these cultural characteristics, U.S. human resource management practices emphasize merit as the idealized operating force in employment decisions (Arvey et al., 1991). This idealized model for personnel decisions is often violated, but remains a cultural norm and goal for U.S. organizations.

Managerial Leadership
in the United States

Leadership researchers have learned a good deal about leadership in the United States and much of this research has recently focused on charismatic leadership. This leadership behavior involves inspiring followers, managing meaning through creating symbols, myth making, using ceremonies, and defining the organization's culture (Bass, 1990). Additionally, leadership research in the United States has focused on contingency theories. These theories specify the organizational circumstances under which particular leader behavior patterns are most effective (cf. Indvik, 1986; Vroom & Jago, 1988). House's Path-Goal Theory of Leadership and Yukl's Multiple Linkage Model are examples of contingency theories. Each includes distinct leader behaviors, follower reactions, and situational moderators designed to predict individual or group outcomes such as follower commitment or performance. The contingency model presented in Figure 11.1 shows the leadership process as a set of causal leader behavior variables that influence the mediators-followers' job satisfaction and role ambiguity. These follower reactions are the most immediate results of a leader's behavior. Organizational commitment and job performance are outcome variables in the model. Job satisfaction affects organizational commitment, and possibly job performance, although the satisfaction-performance relationship is generally minimal in the United States. Satisfaction, commitment, and performance are affected by leader behaviors and role ambiguity. Job performance is also influenced by organizational commitment. Leadership behaviors are shown as having a direct and indirect effect on both follower outcomes. Leadership substitutes moderate leadership effects and have direct effects on mediators and outcome variables. For example, worker experience, education, and professionalism are leadership substitutes that result in high performance among employees who have little need for certain types of leadership. Culture is also an overall moderator of leadership effects and has a direct effect on the behaviors exhibited by leaders.

Six leadership behaviors important to our research have been extensively studied in the United States. *Supportive leadership* (showing respect, warmth, and concern for subordinates) has shown consistently strong positive relationships with followers' satisfaction and organizational commitment, as well as moderate to strong relationships with followers' role ambiguity and performance in the United States (Fisher & Edwards, 1988; Indvik, 1986). These findings may reflect the moderate masculinity and low power distance scores for the U.S. culture. Meta-analyses for *Directive leadership* (clarifying tasks, procedures, and expectations) in the United States have reported strong positive relationships with measures of follower satisfaction and role ambiguity and moderate positive relationships with follower performance (Podsakoff, Todor, & Skov, 1982). Yet, these effects are heavily

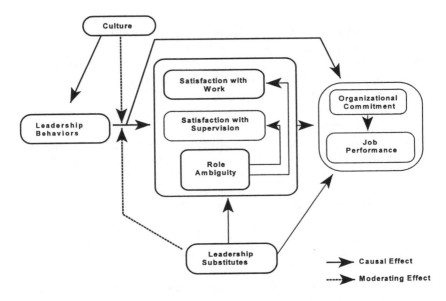

Figure 11.1. Theoretical Model of Leadership Processes

moderated by many organizational and individual follower characteristics (House & Mitchell, 1974; Yukl, 1994). *Participative leadership* (consulting with and obtaining suggestions and information from subordinates) is very popular in the United States and seems appropriate for the highly educated and increasingly professional workforce found in many U.S. organizations (Smith & Peterson, 1988).

Leader reward and *leader punishment* behaviors (providing positive or negative feedback contingent on individual performance) also reflect the high individualism and high-achievement motivation of U.S. workers. Researchers consistently have demonstrated significant effects for these leader behaviors in the United States. Numerous books and empirical studies have demonstrated the importance of *Charismatic leadership* (providing inspiration, challenging goals, and encouragement) at all levels in U.S. organizations (Bass, 1985; Conger & Kanungo, 1987). The high-achievement orientation of U.S. workers, especially managers and professionals, and a history of charismatic leaders may cause followers to respond well to charismatic leader behaviors in the United States.

Mexican Values and Culture

The Mexican culture is unique in Latin America. Although many countries in Latin America were conquered and colonized, Mexico alone is truly *Mestizo*—mixed-blood heritage (Riding, 1985). As a consequence of the conquest by Cortes in 1521, the Mexican people are neither Spanish nor Indian. Their culture is complex, and scholars have maintained a long tradition of inquiry searching for the true identity of the archetypical Mexican self (cf. Octavio Paz, 1961; *El Laberinto de la Soledad*). The following list of cultural characteristics has been collected from these sources and provides a basis to develop hypotheses about effective management and leadership processes in Mexico. Nevertheless, we must be careful about stereotyping an entire culture. Some scholars of Mexican culture, such as Alberto Ruy-Sánchez (1995), implore us to understand that the Mexican society, like that of the United States, is complex and heterogeneous.

1. The Mexican society is characterized by a powerful religiosity, adherence to traditions, a ceremonial mode of behavior, use of a formal language, and a strong sense of status and power relationships (Riding, 1985).

2. Mexico is a patriarchal society. The father is the head of the family and it is his role to protect and provide for the family. His authority is unquestioned.

3. Mexican values are rooted in cultural traditions of authoritarianism, dependence, patriotism, emotional behavior, and hard work.

4. The family is extremely important in Mexican culture. Because of the importance of the extended family, staying close to roots and home is highly valued.

5. "Time" is a flexible construct. The imprecise nature of time and lack of concern for punctuality appears in many work and nonwork endeavors. Rather than indicating laziness, however, a lack of punctuality may result from completing other activities involving personal relationships (e.g., finishing conversations), which take precedence over time constraints.

6. Respect is very important, and children learn early to respect authority and status. There is a strong sense of where one belongs on the social strata (Mendonsa, 1988).

7. Behavior between individuals is dictated by socioeconomic status, age, and gender. Certain rules must be followed in specific situations to avoid offending others.

8. The concept of *machismo* is promulgated in modern society through the paternalistic focus of the culture. The concept is complex, and in the workplace may involve behavior characterized by pride, resistance to doing what is considered "women's work," and failure to admit mistakes or ignorance. (Teagarden, Butler, & Von Glinow, 1992).

9. In a culture where courtesy is of prime importance and excessive frankness and curiosity are considered in bad taste, degrees of accuracy in communication may be variable to avoid confrontation, embarrassment, or hurt feelings.

10. Interpersonal relationships are extremely important for effective transactions and negotiations. Personal relationships must be nurtured carefully through courtesy and regard for others to gain commitment (Kras, 1994).

Managerial Leadership in Mexico

From this description of Mexican culture, we should not be surprised to find that leadership in Mexico differs from leadership in the United States. Mexican history is filled with revolutionary charismatic leaders whose names are continuously honored and celebrated. Current political leaders often adopt key Mexican charismatics from the past as "spiritual" advisors (Riding, 1985). These historical figures are strongly masculine and possess a high degree of power. The authoritarian tradition in Mexico still resists incursions of western liberalism, such as seeking input from all levels for decision making. Participative leadership, as practiced in Western Europe and North America, requires individualistic followers, trusting relationships between managers and followers, and a structure for participation (Dorfman et al., in press). None of these conditions are present in Mexican culture, which is highly collectivist, nontrusting, and elitist, without a history or framework for wide participation in organizational processes.

Managers and supervisors in Mexico typically maintain a sizeable social distance from followers, and command respect and loyalty in the image of a *patron* or father figure (Teagarden et al., 1992). These traditions generally imply a status-oriented authoritarian style when dealing with followers (Gutierrez, 1993; Stephens & Greer, 1995).

Workers in Mexico also expect to be taken care of by their employers, and interpersonal relationships are characterized by courtesy and friendliness. Mexicans expect rewards and recognition for their roles in the hierarchy (de Forest, 1991). They also often avoid confrontations and withhold bad news from others to preserve individual dignity and face (Gutierrez, 1993).

Although these cultural tendencies incorporate much that typifies the Mexican national character, managerial practices are changing due to international trade, international investment, and cooperation between Mexico and other countries. Nevertheless, these cultural norms are particularly relevant to leadership in Mexico and many of them are likely accurate today.

Research on Leadership in Mexico and the United States

Project 1: Understanding Managerial Leadership in Mexico

Our initial effort to understand management and leadership processes in Mexico began in the 1980s by thoroughly reviewing published material about managerial leadership in Mexican organizations and maquiladoras. Maquiladoras usually take the form of manufacturing operations that use large numbers of skilled and unskilled machine operators. Semifinished materials enter Mexico from the United States and are then assembled into final products (e.g., televisions, automobile engines). Although multinational companies pay a "value added tax" on the assembled product, they profit by paying relatively low wages to Mexican workers compared to the wage scales in the parent company's country. Mexican people gain from the program because (a) the maquiladoras aid in Mexico's progress toward becoming a highly industrialized nation, (b) they help reduce the high levels of unemployment and underemployment in Mexico, and (c) they provide an important source of export income. Wages for the maquiladora workers are low by American standards, but are set by the Mexican government and are higher than other Mexican wages for equivalent work (Grunwald, 1985). Nevertheless, the maquiladora industry has always been controversial and will likely remain so subsequent to the passage of the North American Free Trade Agreement (NAFTA).

Our initial goal was to learn as much as possible about the human resource management practices, organizational functioning, and leadership styles in these operations. We tried to obtain an intuitive understanding of the overt and subtle aspects of leadership in each culture by interviewing U.S. and Mexican managers employed in maquiladoras. These interviews took place over 2 years. We discussed management, personnel, and leadership issues with three levels of employees (plant managers, mid-level professionals, and lower-level workers) in more than 20 maquiladora plants. Our goal within the leadership domain was to determine if leadership is perceived as playing a vital role in the management of maquiladoras, and if so, which leadership styles seem to be most effective. From the numerous comments about the importance of leadership, we were convinced that leadership mattered.

The overall findings seemed to support the importance of several leadership behaviors that are popular in the United States but there were additional insights. Authoritarian management styles have been easily accepted by Mexican workers and managers. Nevertheless, a heavily autocratic approach that emphasizes threats and punishment (the "big stick") is also likely to fail. Mexican workers do not approve of and do not respond to rudeness, profanity, or public reprimands by their managers.

Respecting the pride and customs of Mexican workers is also essential. There appears to be a social Darwinist belief that superiors are more competent and deserving. Request for subordinate input on management decisions may erode the subordinate's faith in the manager and be viewed as a sign of weakness. Thus, Mexican managers perceive less need to share information and objectives with subordinates and have less belief in the efficacy of participative management styles than do United States managers.

Managers often resist "lowering" their status by talking directly to operators, which then leads to communication barriers between organizational levels. Workers frequently are intimidated by status differences. They are reluctant to discuss problems with supervisors because conflict between individuals is to be avoided at almost any cost. Mexican middle managers also often delegate mundane work to others beneath them in the hierarchy, show little interest or willingness to follow up on its completion, and disregard the importance of obvious time delays for critical projects. The insights provided by these interviews provided groundwork for our first large-scale comparative empirical research on leadership in Mexico and the United States.

Project 2: Leadership Field Study

We initiated the Mexican portion of this project in the late 1980s and it continued with several iterations throughout the early 1990s. We employed standard survey methodology. The results presented here represent data from 427 Mexican managers and professionals sampled from 4 maquiladoras, and 140 U.S. managers and professionals in similar organizations. We chose middle- and low-level managers and professionals instead of top-level leaders because these positions are prevalent and influential in virtually all large business organizations. From our previous interviews, we already knew that managers in the maquiladoras were conceptually familiar with and often discussed the importance of leadership for company success. The general leadership model in Figure 11.1 was operationalized for this study as shown in Figure 11.2.

It is hypothesized that leadership is a significant causal variable that affects follower reactions such as followers' role ambiguity and job satisfaction, which in turn affect outcome variables such as organizational commitment and job performance. Direct effects of leader behaviors on outcomes were also hypothesized and tested whenever possible. Culture is presumed to effect the amount of each specific type of leadership provided, and more important, the effectiveness of that leadership. Leadership substitutes were not a focus of this study.

Leadership behaviors. The actual leader behaviors studied were *directive, supportive, participative, contingent reward* and *contingent punishment,* and *charismatic* behaviors. Each of these has shown potential importance in cross-cultural research. These leader behaviors have also been claimed by researchers to be universally important across cultures, are used by U.S. managers and management trainers abroad, or both (Bass, 1991; Dorfman, 1996; Dorfman & Howell, 1988; Dorfman & Ronen, 1991; Farh, Podsakoff & Cheng, 1987; House, 1991; Misumi & Peterson, 1985). The following six patterns of leadership behavior were measured:

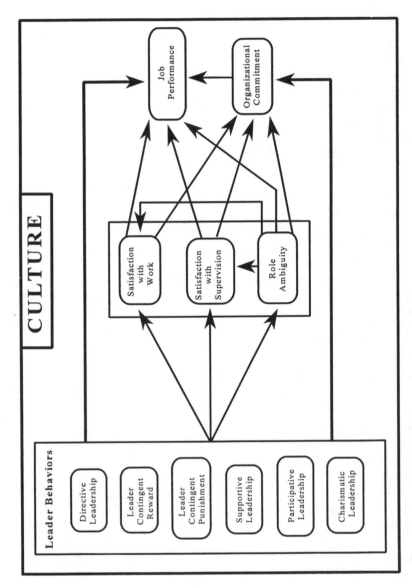

Figure 11.2. Operationalized Model of Leadership Processes

1. Directive—clarifying performance expectations, assigning tasks and specifying procedures.

2. Supportive—indicating a concern for the welfare of subordinates; showing warmth, respect, and trust.

3. Contingent reward—providing social rewards (praise, positive feedback, and recognition) contingent on high performance.

4. Contingent punishment—voicing displeasure and providing negative feedback contingent on poor performance.

5. Charismatic—inspiring and developing confidence among followers, setting challenging goals, and encouraging high expectations.

6. Participative—consulting with, asking for suggestions, and obtaining information from subordinates for important decisions.

Follower reactions and outcome variables. Follower reactions in this study were self-report measures including satisfaction with supervision and satisfaction with work measured by the Job Descriptive Index (Smith, Kendall, & Hulin, 1969). Role ambiguity, an important employee perception that is influenced by leader behaviors, also served as a follower reaction (Rizzo, House, & Lirtzman, 1970). Organizational commitment, assessed through the scale developed by Porter and Smith (1970), served as one outcome variable. This scale clearly corresponds to affective commitment (Meyer & Allen, 1991). As a second outcome variable, we were able to obtain job performance data for the U.S. and Mexico samples through company records.

Questionnaire translation and administration. Several techniques were used to maximize functional and conceptual equivalence of the translated questionnaires. The original questionnaire was translated into Spanish by two bilingual researchers intimately familiar with the work environment in that country. Back translation by a different translator helped identify potential misunderstandings. Finally, pretests clarified most remaining problems and misunderstandings. Respondents were assured anonymity and confidentiality.

Analysis strategy. A strong test of leadership effectiveness was possible by analyzing the data separately for both countries using structural equation modeling (LISREL VII). This technique is designed to explore

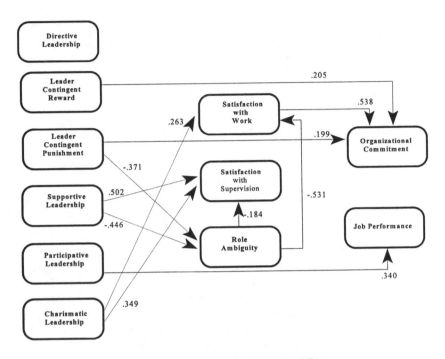

Figure 11.3. LISREL Leadership Model for the United States

causal relationships between exogenously determined constructs (e.g., leader behaviors) and endogenously determined follower reactions and outcome variables (e.g., role ambiguity and job performance).

U.S. hypotheses. For the United States, we predicted supportive and participative leadership would have a high degree of positive impact, but directive leadership would not have a significant impact on the managers and professionals being studied. In addition, leader contingent reward and punishment behaviors were expected to have strong positive impacts in the U.S. sample. We also expected that charismatic leader behavior would have significant effects in the U.S. sample.

Mexico hypotheses. We predicted that both directive and supportive leadership would have positive effects in Mexico. We expected that leaders' contingent reward would have a positive impact, but contingent punishment behaviors would have a negative impact on followers in

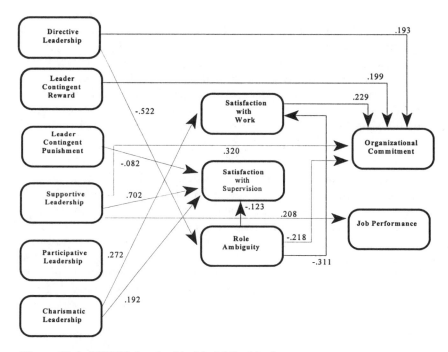

Figure 11.4. LISREL Leadership Model for Mexico

Mexico. We also predicted charismatic leadership would have a strong positive impact on Mexican followers, but participative leadership would not.

Predicted differences. We expect that Mexico will differ from the United States on the effectiveness of directive leadership (more effective in Mexico), participative leadership (more effective in United States), and leader contingent punishment behavior (positive impact in the United States, negative in Mexico).

The final accepted LISREL models for the United States and Mexico are shown in Figures 11.3 and 11.4. Tests of hypotheses regarding the effectiveness of specific leadership behaviors are discussed separately for each sample.

Results in the United States. All leadership behaviors, with the exception of directive leadership, had significant effects in the United

States (see Figure 11.3). Contingent reward behavior increased organizational commitment; contingent punishment behavior increased organizational commitment and decreased role ambiguity; supportive leadership increased satisfaction with supervision and decreased role ambiguity; participative leadership increased follower performance; and charismatic leadership increased satisfaction with work and supervision. Supportive, participative, charismatic, and leaders' contingent punishment behaviors all had strong effects. Directive leadership had no impact.

Results in Mexico. Four of the predicted leader behaviors had significant positive effects (see Figure 11.4). Directive leadership increased organizational commitment and decreased role ambiguity; contingent reward behavior increased organizational commitment; supportive leadership increased satisfaction with supervision and follower performance; and charismatic leadership increased satisfaction with work and supervision. Directive, supportive, and charismatic leadership all produced strong effects. The effect of participative leadership was nonsignificant as predicted, and contingent punishment had a negative effect also as predicted.

Discussion. The positive effects of leader supportiveness and contingent reward behavior in both countries are not surprising. Supportive leaders show concern for followers and are considerate and available to listen to followers' problems. Contingent rewarding leaders show appreciation for followers' good performance and provide recognition and compliments. The correlation between these two leader behaviors was >.65 for both the United States and Mexico (leaders who are concerned and considerate are also often seen as appreciative and complimentary). Although reward systems in collectivist cultures are usually described as group oriented (Bond, 1986; Hofstede, 1980b), individualized performance-contingent social rewards by the leader seem to be important even in collectivist cultures such as Mexico.

Charismatic leadership also had a positive effect in both countries; it affected both satisfaction with work and satisfaction with supervision. The results for directive leadership differed between the countries. We expected the extremely high individualism and low power distance of the U.S. culture, combined with the participative climate common among professionals and managers in U.S. organizations, to at least partially neutralize the effects of leaders' directiveness. The results are consistent with this expectation. It is significant that a directive leader who clarifies goals, expectations, and task assignments for individual followers is helpful, even in collectivist cultures.

The effects of participative leadership and contingent punishment behavior were also specific to each country. Our participation scale included items such as asking followers for suggestions, giving consideration to followers' inputs, and modifying proposals in light of follower objections. Participation was predicted to be ineffective in Mexico, due to its military history and religiosity. Strong central leadership and low individualism (high collectivism) discourages individual desires to affect organizational processes. This prediction was supported. In contrast, participative leadership in the U.S. sample was the strongest predictor of follower performance and the level of participation displayed by supervisors in the United States was higher than in Mexico. For Mexico, supportive leadership was the strongest predictor of performance.

The significant impact of leaders' contingent punishment behavior was predicted in the United States where giving feedback to individual followers (positive and negative) is emphasized in management training. As predicted, this leader behavior had a negative impact in Mexico. This finding may support the notion that *simpatico,* or an attitude of respect to others in Mexico, can lead to difficulties when criticizing poor job performance.

Project 3: Focus Groups

In the next phase of our research efforts, we were interested in verifying the conceptual equivalence of leadership constructs from the U.S. and Mexican perspective. That is, for leadership constructs to be completely equivalent, they should be conceptually equivalent (similar meanings), functionally equivalent (similar purpose), and metrically equivalent (similar measurement properties) across cultures. Our goal for the focus group project primarily addressed conceptual equivalence—clarifying the meaning and subsequent enactment of specific leadership behaviors. Recall that in the comparative study (Project 2) we studied the functional equivalence of leadership constructs as indicated by the influence or impact of leadership on attitudes and perceptions of followers. In Project 4, to be discussed below, we address metric equivalence through additional questionnaire research. By using a qualitative methodology in the focus group project we expected to tease out possible subtle meanings of leadership that may have been missed through the quantitative comparative project previously discussed. To this end, we wanted a free-flowing discussion of leadership from Mexican nationals whereby "leadership" could be defined from an "emic" perspective.

The techniques used in the focus group discussions were straightforward. Each focus group session began by asking participants to think of particular situations or incidents in which outstanding leadership was exhibited. In cases where prompting was needed to get the discussion started, participants were asked to think of outstanding business or political leaders and describe what they were like, why they were effective, and what they did to make them extraordinary. We were interested in establishing whether specific behaviors that define (or enact) a leadership function in the United States vary from those in Mexico. Previous cross-cultural research has shown that a supervisor discussing a subordinate's personal problems without the subordinate present may be seen as supportive in some cultures but not others (Peng, Peterson, & Shyi, 1991). We expected that similar distinctions about the enactment of leadership might emerge from our focus groups in Mexico.

Our first focus group was a pilot of our procedure using Hispanic, Anglo, and Mexican National students at New Mexico State University. In this first focus group, we used Hispanic and Anglo students enrolled in an advanced management class. Following this pilot test, we used two sets of Mexican Nationals enrolled in the "English as a Second Language Program" at New Mexico State University to explore our research issues. These students were either managers or professionals who worked in Mexico. Our final focus group session was conducted in Mexico. This focus group session was held at the Juarez campus of Monterrey Technology Institute with faculty and managers who were obtaining advanced graduate education at the Institute. Each person had substantial technical work experience, managerial work experience within their employing companies, or both. Participants were prepared for the focus group by being given the following instructions in advance: Think about an effective/outstanding leader and describe the characteristics and behaviors that made this person effective.

Two leadership constructs dominated these discussions—supportive leadership enacted through carefully crafted interpersonal relations, and participative leadership enacted in a manner not entirely consistent with American norms. The following discussion of supportive and participative leadership summarizes findings with the manager, professional, and educator focus groups.

Supportive leadership and interpersonal relations. The most salient impact of Mexican culture on leadership is the importance of maintaining good interpersonal relations. The common thread running throughout the various descriptions of what constitutes outstanding Mexican leadership is captured with terms such as trust, respect, sensitivity, interest, and humaneness. The "bond" between the leader and the follower is critical. Gaining trust, dealing with people as "human beings" and not just as workers, and maintaining courtesy and respect for individuals pervaded most discussions (e.g., "As soon as the level of trust is broken, everything will start to disintegrate").

The ability to be *simpatico* reflects the emic expression of the phrase "interpersonal relationships" for U.S. respondents. *Simpatico* is the ability to treat people with a special sensitivity to their dignity and worth as individuals, to demonstrate respect and empathy, and to bring out the uniqueness and special characteristics in each person. It would be hard to develop this ability without paying close attention to the origins of the Mexican people and their cultural roots. As one participant stated,

> The American culture is very different from ours. Ours revolves around the family. We are very family oriented. We are very protected throughout our lives. We grow up, we reproduce ourselves, and we continue to depend on our parents. . . . There is a feeling of unity, of love that exists until you cease to exist. . . . And this is what will be involved in the shaping of a Mexican leader. We tend more toward the protection of the people.

Leaders know their subordinates by name and they know something about their personal lives and inquire often with sincere interest about their families. The example of a manager who went to his subordinate's home to pay a visit to the subordinate's wife and new baby was discussed as a typical occurrence in Mexico; one that would be expected of a leader who is *simpatico*. This demonstrates the respect given to the importance of family in the life of every Mexican.

In addition, physical demonstration indicating caring and warmth was frequently mentioned as an important trait of outstanding leadership. One participant stated: "In general I think our Latin culture, our Mexican culture is much more physical in terms of shaking hands, patting them on the back, and so on. . . . We are more physical by virtue of our cultural roots. And so an outstanding leader cannot be very distant all the time. He must be physical within certain limits and maintain that balance."

Participative leadership. Our focus group participants often mentioned the importance of participative leadership in Mexico. Although similarities exist, the exact meaning and the enactment of participative leadership did not seem to be identical in the two countries. For instance, consider the definition of participation from one of the participants: "The elite [managers] may be expected to offer suggestions, design strategies, and develop proposals, which are then discussed by individuals [subordinates] who are expected to carry out the ideas." We might speculate that acting on suggestions by subordinates may not be as critical to participative leadership in Mexico as it is in the United States.

In addition, the manner of involving subordinates in decisions is clearly different in at least one respect. When interacting with subordinates to solve problems, a common Mexican managerial technique is for managers to deal with more than one person at the same time and in the same room, even though the problems may be very different. This indicates a polycronic orientation toward time, where a manager may be engaged in several activities simultaneously and be highly involved in multiple personal interactions (Hall & Hall, 1990). Many North Americans complain about such meetings. As one participant noted, the uninformed North American will perceive the situation as chaotic, but leadership is exhibited, in that the "leader has to maintain control over everything and make sure that each person who came to him with a problem is attended to." Communication of ideas, requests, problems, and solutions can be very subtle and indirect, yet the manager pays attention to each individual's concerns and addresses them, focusing on the person as the most important component within the interaction.

Obviously, the collective social atmosphere in Mexico is different than what one would expect to find in the United States. The important point is that all individuals must believe they can participate in problem solving (even commenting on issues brought up by others in the room). One participant gave the following explanation regarding participative behavior. "The leader needs to know his subordinates very well and that's why this behavior [collective problem solving], on the surface [appears] very disorganized, [but] really makes sense in managing people more effectively."

Additional observations. The importance of maintaining contact with one's roots is critical and is consistent with the concept of *simpatico*. A leader's desire to stay close to his birthplace within the country was seen as a very natural and important consideration in his emotional well-being, just as his extended family is important in his life for love, warmth, and support. Therefore, a leader's reluctance to relocate was not seen as a form of inflexibility or noncommitment, as it might be considered in the United States.

One surprising outcome from our focus groups concerned the almost complete absence in the discussion of the importance of power or status in Mexican leadership. As Riding (1985) suggests, Mexican society as a whole functions through relationships of power. The sense of hierarchy and use of titles such as *licenciado* (literally defined as the licensed ones, indicating a university education) is pervasive. An examination of Mexican companies shows high levels of power stratification across organizational levels. Yet this aspect of Mexican culture generally was not mentioned in our discussion groups. An exception to this lack of reference to an obvious cultural characteristic occurred in one discussion in which all participants seemed to agree that high-level leaders will use their "persona" to command allegiance. This construct of persona clearly overlaps current U.S. conceptions of charismatic leadership. In this particular case, the manager being referred to was quite powerful within the organization.

Project 4: Cross-Cultural
Measurement Equivalence Issues

The fourth project addressed the issue of construct equivalence from a measurement perspective. Whereas the focus groups concerned conceptual equivalence (similar meanings) of leadership constructs, and the survey data concerned functional equivalence (similar purpose), this part of the research effort was most concerned with metric equivalence (similar measurement properties) of leadership scales designed to measure leadership behaviors across cultures. In addition to meeting the functional/conceptual equivalence criterion, direct comparisons among cultures using inferential statistics requires metric equivalence— similar operationalization of constructs with items that mean the same thing across cultures. Thus, even for situations in which similar items signify a specific leader function, metric equivalence requires that numerical values on a scale must indicate precisely the same magnitude of the construct, regardless of the population under consideration (Hui & Triandis, 1985).

Metric equivalence issues also relate to the issue of conceptual equivalence in the following way. Serious questions should be raised about the conceptual equivalence of a leadership function in cases where specific items designed to measure a specific leadership function (e.g., participation) are not found to be metrically equivalent across cultures. For example, Smith, Peterson, Misumi, and Tayeb (1989) found that a question relating to a supervisor discussing a subordinate's personal problems without the subordinate present was seen as being consistent with a Maintenance leadership function in Japan, but not so for America. Obviously, if a lack of metric equivalence indicates that leadership scales are composed of different items in various cultures, issues of conceptual equivalence are also brought to the forefront.

We were fortunate to work with a colleague, Jim Weber (1996), who for his dissertation tackled the extremely difficult task of contrasting the effectiveness of various statistical techniques that have been used to investigate equivalence issues. The essence of the measurement problem involves a basic, yet critical issue. If we assume that there are a core set of basic leadership behavior patterns or styles, to what extent will cultures vary in the specific leadership behaviors that constitute these patterns? This issue revisits the often-discussed "emic/etic" cultural distinction: Universal aspects of cultures are etic, and unique aspects of a culture are emic (Triandis, Kurowski, & Gelfand, 1994). Conventional wisdom, primarily based on previous research by Smith and colleagues (Smith et al., 1989; Bond & Smith, 1996), attests to the validity of general leadership patterns that are enacted in culturally specific ways. Although the Smith et al. (1989) research was groundbreaking, the issue of leadership enactment is far from being resolved. Jim Weber's (1996) dissertation addressed the following conceptual and methodological issues: To what extent do commonly used leadership scales contain both etic and emic components? Can a thorough understanding of a specific culture lead to designing leadership items that are indeed specific to that culture, and to no other culture? To what extent are available statistical techniques designed to answer the previous two questions?

In his research, Weber used items from previous leadership scales that should be etic. In addition, he developed a set of items that should be specific or emic to a particular country. For instance, the leadership item "considers my feelings before acting" has been used in cross-cultural leadership studies as part of supportive leadership (Dorfman & Howell, 1988). In contrast, the item "carefully considers a person's level of status when handing out job assignments" was developed specifically to portray directive leadership in Mexico. Questionnaire surveys were administered to government workers in the United States, Japan, Korea, and Mexico.

The initial question was whether general leader behavior patterns are operationalized differently across cultures (essentially replicating the Smith et al. study). Weber's results indicated that almost without exception, items believed to be generalizable across national cultures, in fact met our expectation of universality (including the United States and Mexico). Results for items designed to be emic were even more interesting from a cross-cultural perspective, in that very few items turned out to be emic as predicted. Most items designed to be emic, actually resulted in being assessed as etic. Nevertheless, there were a few items culturally unique for Mexico. "Wields great personal power and influence within the organization" was an emic item in Mexico indicating charismatic leadership. In addition, some items seemed to characterize leadership in countries with similar cultural dimensions. For example, the item regarding status when making job assignments was common to both Mexico and Korea—countries generally supporting power distinctions in the workforce but medium on risk taking and reducing uncertainty.

The results show the clear superiority of structural equation techniques (i.e., LISREL for simultaneous factor analysis in several populations) over the correlational and factor analytic techniques, for identifying emic and etic items. Additional techniques such as item response theory (IRT) for multigroup analysis of polytomous scales (e.g., PARSCALE), hold promise to investigate equivalence issues, but this technique has not been fully developed nor tested at the time of this chapter's publication.

Project 5: Global Leadership and
Organizational Behavior
(GLOBE)

Our last project, which is currently underway, also involves Mexico and the United States. This project is part of a much larger project labeled GLOBE. House, Hanges, and Agar (1994), and colleagues from more than 60 nations are engaged in a long-term programmatic series of cross-cultural leadership studies. The projects' scope is immense, and managerial samples will represent all country clusters (Ronen & Shenkar, 1985). Also joining us in this project is Dr. Carmen Santana Melgoza. She has been instrumental in analyzing all of the interview data, obtaining research samples in Mexico, and interpreting subtle aspects of the Mexican culture.

An initial aspect of the GLOBE project involves an investigation of leadership prototypes across cultures. The social information process-ing literature (Croker, Fiske, & Taylor, 1984; Rosch, 1975) provides a nice conceptual framework to explain the development of leadership prototypes, and mechanisms by which cultural values impact leadership prototypes. For instance, Shaw (1990) suggests that much of the cross-national literature indicating differences in managerial beliefs, values, and styles can be interpreted as showing culturally influenced differen-ces in leader prototypes.

A central question is: To what extent are specific traits and attributes universally endorsed as contributing to effective leadership, and to what extent are attributes linked to cultural characteristics? The senior inves-tigators of the GLOBE project predict that leadership attributes such as hard work and achievement orientation will be universally applicable, whereas attributes such as leader spirituality, leader subtlety, and har-mony will be more strongly endorsed by Asian cultures than Western cultures. Because we are responsible for the project in Mexico, we are hypothesizing that leadership attributes that emphasize human relations skills (e.g., patience and empathy) and cultural expectations (e.g., familial respect and collective responsibility) will be particularly im-portant. We expect that leader behaviors that exemplify important prototypes will be more effective than behaviors that are irrelevant, or are antithetical to these prototypes.

Conclusion and Summary:
Leadership in Mexican and U.S. Cultures

The results of our empirical research studies (Projects 2 & 4) support Bass's (1990) contention regarding the validity of both the "universal" and the "culture specific" perspectives in the study of leadership across cultures. We found cultural differences and similarities in the effectiveness of leadership behaviors in Mexico and the United States. Three leadership behaviors—support, contingent reward, and charisma—showed positive impacts in both countries. The remaining three leadership behaviors had very differing impacts between the two countries. Whereas directive leadership had a positive impact in Mexico but not the United States, participative leadership had its positive impact in the United States but not Mexico. Leader contingent punishment had a positive influence in the United States but a negative influence in Mexico! Each culture has an additional impact on the amount of each leadership behavior shown by leaders when interacting with subordinates. For example, U.S. supervisors are more participative than Mexican supervisors. The dissertation project (Project 4) also indicated that leadership functions are probably enacted in universal as well as culturally specific ways. Nonetheless, more universal behaviors were found than culturally specific behaviors. As a general summary of the empirical research, we feel confident that some leader behaviors are transferable across the two cultures (in addition to being translatable), but might require "fine tuning" when applied to each culture group. Other leader behaviors are probably not transferable and obviously should be avoided, minimized, or substituted (e.g., criticizing less than stellar job performance).

From our qualitative research (Projects 1 & 3) we offer the following observations. The Mexican and U.S. perspectives on what constitutes outstanding leadership appear to have unique as well as similar aspects. A commitment to a clear vision of what needs to be accomplished, consideration of others when making decisions, good communication skills, and personality characteristics that include trustworthiness, honesty, and sincerity are common to both cultures. In contrast, effective leadership in Mexico requires a sensitivity and commitment to the Mexican culture. In this patriarchal society, the "bond" between the leader and follower is of utmost importance. For instance, although leaders from both countries are expected to have good human relations skills, the Mexican leader must engage subordinates in a manner that indicates respect, and personal caring for the individual. The importance of emphasizing the individual, over that of being a slave to time constraints, rules, or procedures, was seen as a vital part of practicing interpersonal skills in Mexico.

Focus group participants felt that rules were the guiding force in dealing with people in the U.S. style of leadership, whereas the individual was the primary component with the Mexican style. Cultural roots emphasizing protection, love, warmth, caring, and sensitivity are brought out in leadership behaviors with followers. The protectionist aspects of the culture are very much ingrained in how the concept of outstanding leadership is defined. It is also a prime requisite in the characteristic of being *simpatico.*

Where do we go from here? Three additional avenues of research are being pursued. First, recall that our overall model (Figure 11.1) incorporates leadership substitutes. These variables represent a systematic way of incorporating individual, task, and organizational moderator variables in the contingency view of the leadership process (Howell, Bowen, Dorfman, Kerr, & Podsakoff, 1990). Substitutes theory posits the existence of three types of leadership moderators. *Enhancers* increase the impact of a leader behavior, *neutralizers* decrease the effect of a leader behavior, and *true substitutes* replace the impact of the leader behavior with a positive effect of their own. The transferability of leadership substitutes across cultures is disputed, although relatively untested (Fahr et al., 1987; Misumi & Peterson, 1985), but leadership substitutes do reflect the popular notion of self-management (Smith & Peterson, 1988) as an alternate source of motivation, performance, and positive follower attitudes. We intend to test the applicability of leadership substitutes in Mexico.

As a second research avenue, also recall that our overall model shows culture as a causal variable affecting the level of leader behaviors. The role of culture as a moderator of leadership effectiveness in Figure 11.1 is also explicit. The research reported in this chapter did not, however, specifically incorporate a *measure of culture* within our analyses. Fortunately, we have measures of several cultural dimensions that can be used in an analysis strategy with data from Projects 2, 4, and 5. Using quantitative measures of cultural dimensions should enable us to more precisely determine the exact moderating influence of "culture" as opposed to "nationality" in our analyses so far.

Third, the current GLOBE project may result in adding important concepts of perceived power and leadership image to complement the often-studied leadership behaviors in cross-cultural leadership research. We suggest that all three of these concepts will play an important role in the management of cross-cultural organizations and groups of all types.

References

Arvey, R. D., Bhagat, R. S., & Salas, E. (1991). Cross-cultural and cross-national issues in personnel and human resource management: Where do we go from here. In G. R. Ferris & K. M. Rowland (Eds.), *Research in personnel and human resources management* (Vol. 9, pp. 367-407). Greenwich, CT: JAI.

Bass, B. M. (1985). *Leadership and performance beyond expectations.* New York: Free Press.

Bass, B. M. (1990). *Bass and Stogdill's handbook of leadership,* (3rd ed.). New York: Free Press.

Bass, B. M. (1991, August). *Is there universality in the full range model of leadership?* Paper presented at the annual meeting of the National Academy of Management, Miami, FL.

Bond, M. (1986). *The psychology of the Chinese people.* Hong Kong: Oxford University Press.

Bond, M. H., & Smith, P. B. (1996). Cross-cultural social and organizational psychology. *Annual Review of Psychology, 47,* 205-235.

Conger, J. A., & Kanungo, R. (1987). Toward a behavioral theory of charismatic leadership in organizational settings. *Academy of Management Review, 12,* 637-647.

Croker, J., Fiske, S. T., & Taylor, S. E. (1984). Schematic bases of belief change. In J. R. Eisen (Ed.), *Attitudinal judgment* (pp. 197-226). New York: Springer-Verlag.

de Forest, M. E. (1991). When in Mexico . . . *Business Mexico, 1,* 38-40.

Dorfman, P. W. (1996). International and cross-cultural leadership. In B. J. Punnett & O. Shenkar (Eds.), *Handbook for international management research* (pp. 267-348). Cambridge, MA: Blackwell.

Dorfman, P. W., & Howell, J. P. (1988). Dimensions of national culture and effective leadership patterns: Hofstede revisited. *Advances in International Comparative Management, 3,* 127-150.

Dorfman, P. W., Howell, J. P., Hibino, S., Lee, J. K., Tate, U., & Bautista, A. (in press). Leadership in Western and Asian countries: Commonalities and differences in effective leadership processes across cultures. *Leadership Quarterly.*

Dorfman, P. W., & Ronen, S. (1991, August). *The universality of leadership theories: Challenges and paradoxes.* Paper presented at the annual meeting of the National Academy of Management, Miami, FL.

Erez, M. (1994). Toward a model of cross-cultural industrial and organizational psychology. In H. C. Triandis, M. D. Dunette, & L. M. Hough (Eds.), *Handbook of industrial and organizational psychology* (2nd ed., Vol. 4, pp. 559-607). Palo Alto, CA: Consulting Psychologists Press.

Farh, J. L., Podsakoff, P. M., & Cheng, B. S. (1987). Culture-free leadership effectiveness versus moderators of leadership behavior: An extension and test of Kerr and Jermier's "substitutes for leadership" model in Taiwan. *Journal of International Business Studies, 18,* 43-60.

Fisher, B. M., & Edwards, J. E. (1988). Consideration and initiating structure and their relationships with leader effectiveness: A meta-analysis. *Proceedings of the Academy of Management Annual Meeting,* 201-205.

Gowan, M., Ibarreche, S., & Lackey, C. (1996). Doing the right things in Mexico. *Academy of Management Executive, 10,* 74-81.

Graumann, C. F., & Moscovici, S. (1986). *Changing conceptions of leadership.* New York: Springer-Verlag.

Grunwald, J. (1985). The assembly industry in Mexico. In J. Grunwalk & K. Flamm (Eds.), *The global factory: Foreign assembly in international trade* (pp. 137-179). Washington, DC: Brookings Institution.

Gutierrez, S. (1993, March/April). Can you make it in Mexico? *Financial Executive, 9*(2), 20-23.

Hall, E., & Hall, M. (1990). *Understanding cultural differences.* Yarmouth, ME: Intercultural Press.

Hodgetts, R. M., & Luthans, F. (1994). *International management* (2nd ed). New York: McGraw-Hill.

Hofstede, G. (1980a). *Culture's consequences: International differences in work-related values.* London: Sage.

Hofstede, G. (1980b, Summer). Motivation, leadership, and organization: Do American theories apply abroad? *Organizational Dynamics,* pp. 42-63.

Hofstede, G. (1993). Cultural constraints in management theories. *Academy of Management Executive, 7*(1), 81-94.

House, R. J. (1991, August). *The universality of charismatic leadership.* Paper presented at the annual meeting of the National Academy of Management, Miami, FL.

House, R. J., Hanges, P., & Agar, M. (1994). *Global leadership and organizational behavior effectiveness (GLOBE).* Calgary, Canada.

House, R. J., & Mitchell, T. R. (1974). Path-goal theory of leadership. *Contemporary Business, 3,* 81-98.

Howell, J. P., Bowen, D. E., Dorfman, P. W., Kerr, S., & Podsakoff, P. M. (1990, Summer). Substitutes for leadership: Effective alternatives to ineffective leadership. *Organizational Dynamics,* pp. 21-38.

Hui, C. H., & Triandis, H. C. (1985). Measurement in cross-cultural psychology: A review and comparison of strategies. *Journal of Cross-Cultural Psychology, 16*(2), 131-152.

Indvik, J. (1986). Path-goal theory of leadership: A meta-analysis. *Proceedings of the Academy of Management Annual Meeting,* 189-192.

Kras, E. S. (1994). *Modernizing Mexican management style.* Las Cruces, NM: Editts.

Lord, R., & Maher, K. J. (1991). *Leadership and information processing: Linking perceptions and performance.* Boston: Unwin-Everyman.

Meindl, J. R., Ehrlich, S. B., & Dukerich, J. M. (1985). The romance of leadership. *Administrative Science Quarterly, 30,* 78-102.

Mendonsa, E. L. (1988). How to do business in Latin America. *Purchasing World, 32*(7), 58-59.

Meyer, J. P., & Allen, N. J. (1991). A three component conceptualization of organizational commitment. *Human Resource Management Review, 1,* 61-89.

Misumi, J., & Peterson, M. F. (1985). The performance-maintenance (PM) theory of leadership: Review of a Japanese research program. *Administrative Science Quarterly, 30,* 196-223.

Morris, T., & Pavett, C. M. (1992). Management style and productivity in two cultures. *Journal of International Business Studies, 23,* 169-179.

Paz, O. (1961). *The labyrinth of solitude: Life and thought in Mexico.* New York: Grove.

Peng, T. K., Peterson, M. F., & Shyi, Y. (1991). Quantitative methods in cross-national management research: Trends and equivalence issues. *Journal of Organizational Behavior, 12,* 87-107.

Pfeffer, J. (1977). The ambiguity of leadership. *Academy of Management Review, 2,* 104-112.

Podsakoff, P. M., Todor, W. D., & Skov, R. (1982). Effects of leader contingent and noncontingent reward and punishment behavior in subordinate performance and satisfaction. *Academy of Management Journal, 25,* 810-821.

Porter, L. W., & Smith, F. J. (1970). *The etiology of organizational commitment: A progress report.* Unpublished manuscript, University of California-Irvine.

Riding, A. (1985). *Distant neighbors.* New York: Vintage.

Rizzo, J. R., House, R. J., & Lirtzman, S. I. (1970). Role conflict and ambiguity in complex organizations. *Administrative Science Quarterly, 15,* 435-454.

Ronen, S., & Shenkar, O. (1985). Clustering countries on attitudinal dimensions: A review and hypothesis. *Academy of Management Review, 10,* 435-454.

Rosch, E. (1975). Universals and cultural specifics in human categorization. In R. Brislin, S. Bochner, & W. Lonner (Eds.), *Cross-cultural perspectives in learning* (pp. 177-201). New York: Russell Sage.

Ruy-Sánchez, A. (1995). Approaches to the problem of Mexican identity. In R. L. Earle & J. D. Wirth (Eds.), *Identities in North America: The search for community* (pp. 40-55). Stanford, CA: Stanford University Press.

Shaw, J. B. (1990). A cognitive categorization model for the study of intercultural management. *Academy of Management Review, 15,* 626-645.

Shenkar, O. (1995). *Global perspectives of human resource management.* Englewood Cliffs, NJ: Prentice Hall.

Smith, P. B., Kendall, L. M., & Hulin, C. L. (1969). *The measurement of satisfaction in work and retirement.* Chicago: Rand-McNally.

Smith, P. B., & Peterson, M. F. (1988). *Leadership, organizations, and culture.* London: Sage.

Smith, P. B., Peterson, M. F., Misumi, J., & Tayeb, M. (1989). Testing leadership theory cross culturally. In J. P. Forgas & J. M. Innes (Eds.), *Recent advances in social psychology: An international perspective* (pp. 383-391). Amsterdam, The Netherlands: North-Holland.

Stephens, G. K., & Greer, C. R. (1995). Doing business in Mexico: Understanding cultural differences. *Organizational Dynamics, 24,* 39-55.

Teagarden, M. B., Butler, M. C., & Von Glinow, M. A. (1992). Mexico's *maquiladora* industry: Where strategic human resource management makes a difference. *Organizational Dynamics, 20*(3), 34-47.

Triandis, H. C., Kurowski, L. L., & Gelfand, M. J. (1994). In H. C. Triandis, M. D. Dunette, & L. M. Hough (Eds.), *Handbook of industrial and organizational psychology* (Vol. 4, 2nd ed., pp. 769-827). Palo Alto, CA: Consulting Psychologists Press.

Trompenaars, F. (1993). *Riding the waves of culture: Understanding cultural diversity in business.* London: Economist Books.

Vroom, V. H., & Jago, A. G. (1988). *The new leadership: Managing participation in organizations.* Englewood Cliffs, NJ: Prentice Hall.

Weber, J. (1996). *Equivalence of leadership scales.* Unpublished doctoral dissertation, New Mexico State University, Las Cruces.

Yukl, G. A. (1994). *Leadership in organizations* (3rd ed.). Englewood Cliffs, NJ: Prentice Hall.

Author Index

Subject Index

challenging, 240, 247
cultural, 80-81, 84
group or team, 63, 124-126, 129-
130, 142, 177, 193, 236
individual, 187-188, 191, 198-
199, 205, 206
organizational, 48, 170, 175, 187-
188, 190-199, 238
superordinate, 193-195, 198, 208
Group dynamics, 1-4, 88, 113, 172
Group process, 2, 125, 203, 224-227
Growth, 12, 125, 203, 224-227

Harassment, 32, 50-51, 167
Harmony, 67, 72-73, 79, 114-131,
147, 155, 237, 258
Health, 24, 29-32, 81
Hegemony, 44
Heritage, 11, 24, 197, 241
Heterogeneity, 212
Hierarchy, 28, 46, 55, 78-79, 120,
128-129, 243-244, 255. *See
also* Status
High school, 96-98, 107
Hispanics, 97, 222-223, 225, 251.
See also Latino
History, 17, 43, 99-100, 135, 194,
217, 235, 240-242, 251
Home country, 61, 86, 173, 191, 204
Homogeneity, 23, 182
Hong Kong, 11, 165, 183, 187, 196-
197, 223
Hong Kong Bank, 163, 168, 178, 180
Host country national, 163, 169-170,
174, 213
Human nature, 9, 76-77, 80

IBM, 164, 169
ICAO, 140, 153, 156
Identity, 28, 127, 187-188, 190, 192,
199, 241. *See also* Self

centrality, 198, 201-202
cultural, 11, 21-22, 24, 208
ethnic, 17, 187-188, 192
self, 10, 26, 116, 128, 195
social, 5, 116, 128, 130, 205
Ideology, 19, 24, 28
Illusionary understanding, 146
Inclusiveness, 19
Indigenous peoples, 20, 40
Indirect request, 176
Individual-organizational fit, 11-12,
187-207
Individualism, 38, 115, 118, 147,
172, 205, 214, 240, 250-251
Indonesia, 105
Industrial Relations
Association, 167
Inefficiency, 48
Influence, 18, 37, 39, 45, 105-106,
114, 116, 125, 189, 235, 257
cultural, 4-5, 9, 13, 39, 51-65, 67,
82-83
process, 84, 216, 235
Information:
ambiguous/incomplete, 145-146,
153
cultural, 188, 194
missed, 140
party line, 140, 142, 154
processing, 64, 258
sources, 72, 74, 77, 80
transmission, 144, 146, 152-153
Ingroup, 3, 4, 216
Immigrant, 20, 42, 168, 215
Impression management, 117, 223,
228
Integration, 62, 69, 182, 187
global, 110, 169, 172, 182
mode of acculturation, 5, 7-8, 22-
32, 192, 203, 222
structural, 166, 187, 208, 229
Interaction, 5, 90-110, 114-128, 174-
176, 180, 183, 191, 202

About the Contributors

John W. Berry is Professor of Psychology at Queen's University, Kingston, Ontario. He received his B.A. from Sir George Williams University (Montreal) and his Ph.D. from the University of Edinburgh in 1966. He has been a lecturer at the University of Sydney, a Fellow of the Netherlands Institute for Advanced Study, and a visiting Professor at the Université de Nice and the Université de Genève. He is a past Secretary-General and past President of the International Association for Cross-Cultural Psychology, has been an associate editor of the *Journal of Cross-Cultural Psychology,* and is senior editor of the just-published *Handbook of Cross-Cultural Psychology.* The author or editor of over 20 books in the areas of cross-cultural, social, and cognitive psychology, he is particularly interested in the application of cross-cultural psychology to public policy and programs in the areas of acculturation, multiculturalism, immigration, health, and education.

Jeannie Davison is a research assistant with the San Jose State University Foundation, working in the Crew Factors Group at NASA-Ames Research Center. She is pursuing an M.A. degree in experimental psychology at San Jose State University. She received her B.S. in aviation safety and psychology from Metropolitan State College of Denver in 1995 and holds a private pilot's license.

Peter W. Dorfman is Professor of Human Resources Management at New Mexico State University, Las Cruces. He received his M.A. and Ph.D. degrees from the University of Maryland and formerly taught at Rice University and Montana State University. His research interests span the fields of human resources management and organizational behavior. He is currently investigating the impact of cultural influences on managerial behavior and leadership styles, as well as serving as an expert witness in employment discrimination court cases.

P. Christopher Earley is Professor of Management in the Graduate School of Management at the University of California, Irvine. He received his Ph.D. in industrial and organizational psychology from the University of Illinois, Urbana-Champaign. His research interests include intercultural and international aspects of organizational behavior, such as the relationship of cultural values to work group dynamics, the role of face and social structure in organizations, and motivation across cultures.

Ellen A. Ensher is an external organizational consultant with both domestic and international clients, holds a master's degree in public administration from the University of Southern California, and is currently completing her Ph.D. in organizational psychology at Claremont Graduate School. Her research focuses on the effect of social exchanges on diverse mentoring relationships and organizational outcomes.

Ute Fischer is a research scientist with the Georgia Institute of Technology. She earned a Ph.D. in 1990 from Princeton University in cognitive psychology with a specialization in psycholinguistics. She has conducted research on second language acquisition, repair strategies in discourse, dynamic decision making, and cultural differences in discourse strategies.

Sharon G. Goto is Assistant Professor of Psychology at Pomona College. She received her B.A. from the University of California, Los Angeles, and her A.M. and Ph.D. in social/organizational psychology from the University of Illinois, Urbana-Champaign. Her research focuses on cultural diversity issues, largely with Asian American populations. She is particularly interested in cross-cultural interpersonal interactions in the workplace, and strategies that foster success for ethnic minorities in the workplace.

Cherlyn Skromme Granrose is Professor of Organizational Behavior at Claremont Graduate School. She received her Ph.D. from Rutgers University in 1981 and taught organizational behavior and human resources at Temple University School of Business and Management for 12 years. She has had a Fulbright summer seminar award to South Korea and Taiwan, a Fulbright research award to Singapore, and a Fulbright teaching award to the People's Republic of China. Her research interests include Asian managers' careers, women's work-family choices, and participative decision making.

Jon P. Howell is Professor of Management and Organizational Behavior at New Mexico State University, Las Cruces, and also president of two corporations. He earned an M.B.A. from the University of Chicago and a Ph.D. from the University of California, Irvine. His primary research interests are leadership, substitutes for leadership, and international management.

Martha Maznevski is Assistant Professor in the management and international areas at the McIntire School of Commerce, University of Virginia. Her research, teaching, and practice focus on understanding cultural differences, specifically how they influence business interactions, and how to bridge and integrate those differences for high performance in multinational settings.

Fathali M. Moghaddam has taught and done research in a number of Third World, European, and North American countries. He came to his present professorial position at Georgetown University after employment at McGill University and the United Nations. His most recent books are *The Specialized Society: The Plight of the Individual in an Age of Individualism* and *Social Psychology: The Search for Universals in Human Social Behavior* (in press). His main scholarly interest is to help develop a science of normative behavior, a project whimsically titled *"instead of* traditional social sciences."

Susan E. Murphy is Assistant Professor of Psychology and Associate Director of the Kravis Leadership Institute at Claremont McKenna College. She earned an M.B.A. and a Ph.D. from the University of Washington, and has been associated with the University of Washington and a management consulting firm. Her current research focuses on the role of mentors in leadership development and the importance of early leadership experiences, and she has consulted with government and private businesses in the United States and Japan.

Judith Orasanu is a principal investigator in the Flight Management and Human Factors Division at NASA-Ames Research Center. She has a Ph.D. in experimental psychology from Adelphi University. For years she has been conducting research on distributed decision making in aviation, involving flight crews, dispatchers, and controllers. She has coedited a book on naturalistic decision making and works extensively with airline crew training programs.

Stuart Oskamp is Professor of Psychology at Claremont Graduate School. He received his Ph.D. from Stanford University and has had visiting appointments at the University of Michigan, University of Bristol, London School of Economics and Political Science, University of New South Wales, and University of Hawaii. His main research interests are in the areas of attitudes and attitude change, environmentally responsible behavior such as recycling and energy conservation, and social issues and public policy. His books include *Attitudes and Opinions* and *Applied Social Psychology,* both in their second editions. He has served as president of the American Psychological Association Division of Population and Environmental Psychology and the Society for the Psychological Study of Social Issues (SPSSI) and as editor of the *Journal of Social Issues.*

Mark F. Peterson is Professor of Management at Texas Tech University and Visiting Professor of Management at Florida Atlantic University. His Ph.D. is from the University of Michigan. He has published over 60 articles and chapters, many of them analyzing culture and intercultural relations from the perspectives of organization behavior and organization theory. In collaboration with Peter B. Smith of the University of Sussex and others, he has been developing an "event management" view of sense making in organizations through research papers and a book titled, *Leadership, Organizations, and Culture: An Event Management Perspective.*

Amy E. Randel is a doctoral candidate at the University of California, Irvine. She earned a bachelor's degree in psychology from Brown University. Her research interests include cross-cultural organizational behavior, group behavior, self-efficacy, and ethics/values in management.

Rosalie L. Tung holds a Chair in International Business at Simon Fraser University (Canada). She is an authority on international management and the author of eight books and many articles on international business in academic and professional journals. According to a recent issue of the *Journal of International Business Studies,* she is the fifth most-cited author in international business. She is involved in management development and consulting around the world.

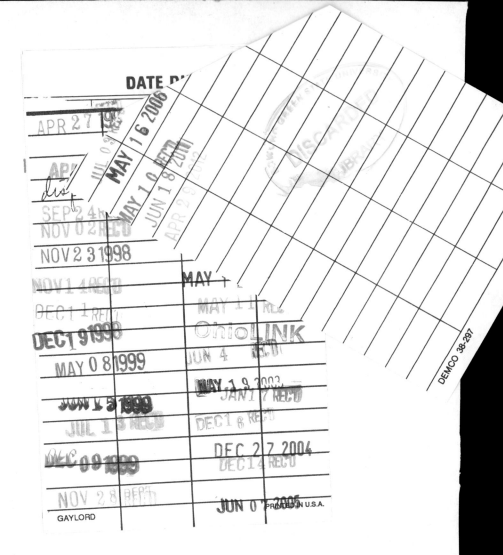